OCCUPATIONAL COSTUME IN ENGLAND

"The Postman's Knock"
(Song Cover 1852–6)

OCCUPATIONAL COSTUME IN ENGLAND

FROM THE ELEVENTH CENTURY TO 1914

PHILLIS CUNNINGTON
& CATHERINE LUCAS

WITH CHAPTERS BY
ALAN MANSFIELD

COLOUR FRONTISPIECE
64 PLATES AND OVER 300 DRAWINGS

ADAM & CHARLES BLACK
LONDON

FIRST PUBLISHED 1967
REPRINTED WITH CORRECTIONS 1968
BY A. AND C. BLACK LIMITED
4, 5 AND 6 SOHO SQUARE LONDON W.1

SBN 7136 0372 0

Printed in Great Britain by
W. & J. Mackay & Co Ltd, Chatham

CONTENTS

		PAGE
	INTRODUCTION	11
I.	WORKERS ON THE LAND	13
*II.	SEAMEN AND FISHERFOLK	52
III.	MINERS, COAL CARRIERS, NAVVIES	67
IV.	TRADESMEN AND CRAFTSMEN PART 1	80

Carpenters, 80
Paper Caps, 86
Builders, 91
Smiths, 100
Textile Workers, 105
Tailors, 111

V.	TRADESMEN AND CRAFTSMEN PART 2	114

Butchers, 114
Millers, Bakers and Cooks, 122
Liquor Trade, 134
Street Vendors, 143

VI.	HOUSEHOLD SERVANTS—MEN	156
VII.	HOUSEHOLD SERVANTS—WOMEN	195
*VIII.	TRANSPORT	215

Railways, 215
Cabbies and Cads, Bus and Tram Crews, 222

IX.	POSTAL SERVICES AND STAGE COACHES	232
*X.	POLICE	251

*XI.   FIREMEN   261

XII.   MISCELLANEOUS SERVANTS OF THE PUBLIC   277
       Dustmen, 277
       Chimney-sweeps, 279
       Linkboys, 282
       Lamplighters, 285
       District Messengers, 287
       Barbers, 288

XIII. MEDICAL PROFESSION   295
       Barber-surgeons, 295
       Physicians, 299
       Surgeons and Hygiene, 309
       Quacks, 314
       Apothecaries, 317
       Nurses, 318

XIV.   EVOLUTION OF PROTECTIVE CLOTHING   328

XV.   SOME SPECIAL RELATIONS OF CLOTHING TO
       WORK   353
       Clothing in Relations to Carrying, 353
       Sartorial Symbols, 370
       Costume for Advertisement, 380
       The Rationale of Irrational Clothes, 386

       BIBLIOGRAPHY AND LIST OF MUSEUMS   395

       SOURCES OF FIGURES   404

       INDEX   415

*CHAPTERS BY ALAN MANSFIELD

THE PLATES

"The Postman's Knock" 1852–6   *frontispiece*

PLATE		FACING PAGE
1a	Men mowing in the month of June. 1100–50	
1b	Shepherds in winter. 1150–60	16
2a	Shepherd. *c.* 1330	
2b	Gardener. *c.* 1350	17
3a	Shepherd. *c.* 1360	
3b	Men reaping, woman gleaning. 1377–99	20
4a	Men with scythes. 1397	
4b	Shepherds wearing long gowns. Early fifteenth century	21
5	John Tradescant the elder, later gardener to Charles I. *c.* 1611	28
6a	Carter in "Frock". Second half of seventeenth century	
6b	Hedger in smock-shaped garment. 1890s	29
7a	"Ye gen'rous Britons, Venerate the Plough". 1801	
7b	Farm lad in smock. *c.* 1870	32
8a	Thomas Coke, attendant and shepherds at Holkham Hall. 1808	
8b	Reaper. *c.* 1890s	33
9a	Woman milking. *c.* 1200	
9b	George III with a haymaker. *c.* 1790–1810	48
10a	Haymakers. 1785	
10b	Milk woman with yoke. 1805	49
11a	Sailor. 1788	
11b	Fisherman. 1840	64
12a	Victorian fisherfolk.	
12b	Boatman wearing embroidered jersey. *c.* 1900	65
13a	Fisher girls. 1890	
13b	Yorkshire fisherfolk. 1814	80
14a	Miner in costume of *c.* 1570.	
14b	"The Collier". 1814	81
15a	Surface workers at a coal mine. *c.* 1830–50	
15b	Stone breakers on the road in Yorkshire. 1814	96
16a	Masons building Hunstanton. *c.* 1433	
16b	Brick makers. 1901–10	97
17a	Smiths at work. 1840s	
17b	Wensley Dale knitters. 1814	112

PLATE   FACING PAGE

18a Women factory workers dressed in protective aprons. 1842
18b Cross-legged tailor of twentieth century.   113
19a Butcher wearing apron over fashionable suit. 1397
19b Butcher in straw boater hat as worn from 1890s.   128
20a Cook. *c.* 1340
20b Turnspit. *c.* 1340   129
21a Baker's delivery man. 1805
21b Chefs wearing the "cauliflower" or "French" hat in its extreme form.
     1965   144
22   Drayman and trouncer. 1792   145
23a Milk girl. 1820
23b Milk roundsman. Late nineteenth century   160
24a Marshall and assistant serving at marriage feast. 1377–99
24b Petticoat breeches and shoulder knot. *c.* 1670   161
25   Negro page-boy. 1732–4   188
26a Page and "Tiger". 1848
26b Chauffeur. *c.* 1920   189
27a Doorman to the British Museum at Montague House. 1840
27b Groom in smock-like overall. 1846   196
28a Pharaoh's daughter and her maid. 1377–99
28b Lady and her maid. *c.* 1630s   197
29a Lady's maid lacing up her mistress. *c.* 1829
29b Birth of St Edmund. Midwife and maid. 1433   208
30a Domestic servant. 1686
30b An English family at tea. *c.* 1720   209
31   Parlourmaid serving at tea party. 1893   224
32a Engine driver. 1852
32b L.N.W. Guard. 1852   225
33   Coach-stand waterman, or cad. 1805   226
34   Bus conductor. *c.* 1862   227
35a Metropolitan Omnibus. 1888
35b Horse-tram crew. 1897   238
36a Mail coach driver. 1832
36b Mail coach. 1838   239
37a Country letter carrier. 1843
37b Country postman on "Penny-farthing". *c.* 1900   242
38a Telegraph messenger boy. 1904–26
38b Stage coach postilions. 1846   243
39   Watchman. Sixteenth century   254

PLATE   FACING PAGE

40a Watchman. 1828
40b A provincial policeman. 1855   255
41a Metropolitan Police constables. *c.* 1864–5
41b Manchester City Police sergeant of the 1860s.   260
42a Manchester City constable. *c.* 1910
42b Sergeant and constables of Manchester. *c.* 1910   261
43a Silver arm badge of Sun Fire Office Fireman.
43b "Sun" fireman of 1805.   268
44a Edinburgh Fire Engines Establishment. 1850
44b Fireman of the Royal Exchange Insurance Brigade. *c.* 1830   269
45a Two firemen on Merryweather tricycle fire apparatus. *c.* 1890
45b Fireman's uniform. Early twentieth century   276
46   Chelmsford Fire Brigade. Early twentieth century   277
47a Dustman. 1808
47b Dustman. 1834   284
48a "Flying dustman." 1878
48b Linkboy. 1738   285
49a Lamplighter on his round. 1780s
49b Lamplighter up a ladder. 1805   308
50a "The Benevolent Physician". *c.* 1792
50b Students and staff of St Bartholomew's Hospital, London. 1901   309
51a Royal Free Hospital, staff and students. 1913
51b Surgeons operating in frock coats. 1882   316
52   Operation. *c.* 1892–6   317
53a "The Rapacious Quack". *c.* 1792
53b "Street Doctor". 1877   320
54a "The Apothecary". *c.* 1750
54b A Nightingale nurse. *c.* 1860   321
55   Milk-seller. *c.* 1810   336
56a Manx herring-gutters washing down their oilskin "brats".
56b Butcher boys in aprons and oversleeves. 1805   337
57a Thigh pads of wood, used in turfing. Early twentieth century
57b Thatcher, with leather knee pad. Twentieth century   340
58a Tubal Cain, the smith. *c.* 1360
58b Post-boy's boot. Seventeenth century
58c "Mersea pattens" (backsters). Twentieth century   341
59   Leech-gatherers. 1814   348
60   Grave-digger in Shakespeare's time.   349
61a Straw boater as butcher's sign, Glastonbury.   370

PLATE   FACING PAGE

61b   Shoeblack in red uniform jacket. Nineteenth century   370
62   A Jack-of-all-Trades on the stage. 1797   371
63   Wally Jones, shoeblack. Twentieth century   382
64   Well-diggers. *c.* 1360   383

The sources of the halftone illustrations are given with their captions. The sources of the line illustrations in the text can be found on pages 404–14.

ACKNOWLEDGEMENTS

We should like to thank the following for expert help: Mr E. Atkinson, Miss P. M. Baker, Mr T. W. Bagshawe, the late Canon Boston and Mrs Boston, Dr François Boucher, Miss M. Canney, Mr James Cramer, Mr A. B. Doncaster, Mr F. G. Emmison, Professor John Fuller, Mr G. E. Fussell, Mr Miles Hadfield, Miss Z. Halls, Rev. C. W. Lawrence, Commander W. E. May, Miss J. Powrie, Dr M. Rowbotham, Mr J. W. Scholes, Mr H. A. Smith of Chartered Insurance Institute, Mr H. J. Smith of Messrs Merryweather & Sons, Mr A. A. Whife of the *Tailor & Cutter* and Mr B. L. Wolpe; also the Chief Constables of Birmingham, Liverpool and Manchester, the Chief Fire Officer of Sheffield and the Commissioner of Metropolitan Police.

We also thank the staffs of the following institutions: British Museum (Departments of Printed Books, of MSS. and of Prints and Drawings), Strangers' Hall Museum, Norwich, Manx Museum, Museum of English Rural Life, Reading, Courtauld Institute of Art, Fire Protection Association, Post Office Records Office, Grocers' Company of London, Guildhall Library and the Pharmaceutical Society of Great Britain.

We are specially grateful to Mr J. F. Botham, photographer, West Mersea, for skilful services, to Mrs R. Luckham for invaluable help throughout, and finally to Dr E. J. Dingwall for his expert advice and encouragement.

INTRODUCTION

Nothing to do but work,
Nothing to eat but food,
Nothing to wear but clothes,
To keep one from going nude.

B. Franklin King, 1894

Little has been written up to the present on the costume worn by people at work, since compared with high fashion its documentation has always been scanty. This book, covering a period of English history from the eleventh century to 1914, is an attempt to fill the gap.

In medieval times, particularly, verbal description of working clothes is rare and reliance has sometimes had to rest on contemporary pictures. These, of course, cannot always be taken quite literally owing to the use of colour for decoration and symbolism, and because of stylization and the artist's idiosyncrasies. But fortunately even medieval illuminated MSS. are rich and varied enough to give a reliable general picture when this is closely looked for. The illustrations given throughout the book are all taken from contemporary English sources.

Obviously in a single volume the treatment of such a wide subject cannot be fully comprehensive or detailed. The ground covered is shown by the Table of Contents. Some repetition of basic facts may be noticed in the book; this is because the aim has been to make each section, so far as possible, complete in itself. A gradual evolution is described from the comparative uniformity of medieval costume to the later rich variety related to particular occupations. Accounts are given of adaptive garments that have lasted for centuries, such as the smith's or moulder's boot, the hedger's mitt and the carter's smock. Many traditional accessories like the carpenter's paper cap, the butcher's boater and the barber's chequered apron are described, and the origin is traced of historic relics such as the footman's shoulder-knot and the stripe on a postman's trousers.

In two final chapters on some special relations of clothing to work, attention is drawn to the factors that have promoted or hindered the development of truly functional occupational costume in England.

CHAPTER I

WORKERS ON THE LAND

. . . Stoode one of the hindmost of the route[1],
For soft, and no whit forth putting was hee;
Full sunbrunt was his forehead and his snoute . . .
Of Kendall very course his coate was made . . .
Upon his gyrdle hong a rustye blade. . . .
He had a shyrt of canvas hard and tough . . .
This was a husbandman, a simple hinde.

c. 1568. F. Thynn (?), *Debate between Pride and Lowliness.*

Mute as he may have been himself, the husbandman of the past has neither been unsung nor unportrayed. His poverty and humility were favourite subjects in early literature. In the role of his Biblical prototypes he was an ever-recurring subject of medieval art and his setting and his seasonal activities made him a source of inspiration to painters of every time. Thus even the early Middle Ages have left us a record of his life and dress.

At any particular period the clothing of medieval people in all walks of life would be cut on comparatively uniform lines. Working people were distinguished from the more leisured classes in that they wore more wool—generally russet or Kersey—and no silk;[2] their materials were of coarser weave, ornament scanty and styles often some decades behind the fashion. Diversity of design increased slowly with time, first marking out the classes more sharply (in about the sixteenth century onwards) and then the individual occupations. Near the end of our period there was an outburst of special adaptations of costume, in all directions, accompanied by a reduction again in the gaps between the classes.

[1] Group on horseback.
[2] "Taffeta phrases, *silken* terms precise
Three-piled hyperboles, spruce affectation . . .
I do foreswear them; and I here protest . . .
Henceforth my wooing mind shall be express'd
In *russet* yeas, and honest *kersey* noes"!
Shakespeare, *Love's Labour's Lost* V, ii.

Within the agricultural community we shall confine ourselves to those who spent most of their time actually at work on the land, omitting the farmer himself when he was mainly a supervisor. Among the workers there was some slight distinction even in very early times between shepherds and the rest; later, gardeners begin to stand out and carters assume rather a character of their own; otherwise all are much alike and in medieval days also resemble the servants, carpenters, even fishermen or any other workers of their time.

MEN

Medieval Times

Judging by illuminated calendars of the months, the average eleventh-century labourer wore little at work all the year round but a woollen tunic or kirtle, belted and bloused to make it knee length, with or without a loose-sleeved supertunic put on over the head. If he had anything on his feet, it would be leather shoes and wrinkled cloth hose (knitting was unknown in England till much later); the latter he might reinforce with leg bandages, which were cloth strips wound like puttees over the stockings, such as are used to this day by shepherds in some parts of the country (see Plate 1b). He went barelegged more often than at any time later (Fig. 1). It was the shepherds, when they watched their flocks by night or in winter, who most often used a cloak (Fig. 2).

1. Labourers carrying a soe. Belted tunics. 11th century.

2. Shepherds, one with cloak, both with tunics and shoes. 11th century.

Throughout the Middle Ages, for underwear there would be a shirt and braies (underpants) typically reaching to the knee, with the material tucked between the legs so as to resemble an infant's pilch (Fig. 3). These were supported by being rolled over a cord near waist-level. After the twelfth century they were made so that the cord emerged at intervals, the exposed portions serving as points of attachment by strings for the long stockings. Scarcity of needles and scissors probably account for the comparative shapelessness of all the garments.

In the twelfth century a sharp contrast did exist between the labourer's appearance and that of his master. The rustic is often seen in long garments to the ankle, rather like trousers, which are really glorified braies. For hot work this is all he wore (see Plate 1a). Otherwise there would be a tunic, now a little closer fitting than before, and this had sleeves which, unlike those of the gentry, were still loose enough to roll up. The cloak was commonly a sort of hooded cape (see Plate 1b, the shepherd on the left). But a separate hood was

3. Thrashing with flails. Tunics exceptionally short. In (*b*) the braies are cut very
simply and a corner of the lower edge looped up to the waist string. *c.* 1340.

now normal headgear and shepherds, especially, had these made of sheepskin
with the wool showing. In Plate 1b the man on the right turns his face into
his hood away from a dazzling vision.

Short boots were worn and at harvesting a wide-brimmed hat, or, failing
that, a fillet of twisted straw (Fig. 23, p. 40).

Strangely enough, trouserlike garments, which became rare again in the
thirteenth century, vanished during the fourteenth and scarcely reappeared
for six hundred years. Braies were again short enough not to show below the
tunic (now called cote) unless it was hitched up into the belt (Fig. 4). The
thirteenth century saw the supertunic (surcote) developing new kinds of
sleeves, but peasants clung to the loose short-sleeved styles, if they wore one
at all. Upper classes began to wear a sort of tabard, of which more below.

The first half of the fourteenth century is specially well documented.
As well as many less publicly known but invaluable manuscripts, the Queen
Mary and Luttrell Psalters and the *Holkham Bible Picture Book*, with their
hundreds of miniatures showing everyday life, were all produced between
about 1320 and 1340. At this time, while gentlemen began to favour tight

PLATE I

PLATE I

(*a*) Men mowing in month of June, wearing only long braies. 1100–1150.

British Museum. MS. Landsdowne 383 (Shaftesbury Psalter).

(*b*) Shepherds in winter. One in hooded cape, tunic, hose and short boots; the other in sheepskin hood, tunic and leg bandages over hose (his face hidden in the hood). 1150–1160.

British Museum. MS. Cot. Nero C IV (St Swithin's Psalter).

PLATE 2

PLATE 2

(*a*) Shepherd. Tabard style supertunic over long-sleeved tunic; mitts; wrinkled cloth "soled hose"; hat with strings, worn over a hood. *c*. 1330.

British Museum. MS. Add. 47682 (Holkham Bible Picture Book).

(*b*) Gardener. Tabard-shaped sur-cote with lappets; exceptionally long cote (possibly because the figure represents the risen Christ), hat over hood; bare feet; iron-shod wooden spade in the hand. *c*. 1350.

Misericord carving, Lincoln Cathedral.

4. Digging and tree-felling. (*a*) Tunic with front vent. (*b*) Tunic hitched into its belt; coif and cap. 1320–59. (After Mathew Paris.)

doublets and fitting overgarments, the normal wear for workmen was still a belted tunic (cote), with or without an overgarment. Their tunics might be very short, otherwise they hitched them up, and there would be a front or side vent for easier walking. The overgarment, not often worn at work, was sometimes more or less fitting and had a side slash so that a man could get at the dagger hanging on his belt underneath. A popular shape, however, was that shown in Plate 2a. This is the "tabard" which Chaucer's plowman wore on his pilgrimage and is perhaps the prototype of the garment called "smock" today. Put on over the head, the tabard type was made essentially of two rectangles partly joined together. In one variety[1] it was wide enough to fall over the upper arm as a cape sleeve (Fig. 5 and Plate 2b). In ornamental form the tabard came to characterize heralds and has done so down to this day. For extra warmth peasants still wore the now quite unfashionable hooded cloak.

There was an assortment of leg- and footwear. The most elaborate was a

[1] A "garnache".

5. Ploughman in side-vented tunic with contrasting lining; hood (with liripipe) under hat; parti-coloured mitts. Driver in tabard-shaped supertunic (with lappets) over front-vented tunic. *c.* 1340.

pair of coloured hose worn with shoes or with well-fitting small boots. Alternatively there were soled hose. These were cloth stockings with thin leather soles, worn without shoes even on rough ground (see Plate 3b).

Sometimes, abandoning all attempts at footwear, men used stockings that had no feet. These either had an instep-strap (stirrup-hose, as in Fig. 6), or else ended at the ankle with or without a little fringe (footless hose, as in Fig. 7 and Plate 3a).

In the fourteenth century there was a passion for wearing gloves—for weeding, ploughing and all sorts of jobs. These were more often of cloth than leather and were usually mitts with thumb and one or two compartments for fingers. They were gauntleted and could be parti-coloured (Fig. 5 and Plate 3a).

Indoors and out, except in hot weather, it was customary to wear a white coif tied under the chin like a baby's cap. Out of doors the hood, often with contrasting lining, could be worn over it. There was quite a spate of different styles in hats (see Plate 2a and Fig. 5), and these might be perched on top of the hood. Neatly made straw hats are shown in Plate 3b. Piers Plowman in summer weather would have been dressed more or less like the men in this Plate (3b). We are given a vivid description of his normal winter wear—all in deplorable condition:

6. Adam in a sheepskin cloak with two side vents for the arms;
stirrup-hose (instep strap but no feet), turned down at the top over a
garter. Cain in long tunic hitched up by belt; bare feet. *c.* 1330.

His ho(o)d was ful of holes
And his heare [hair] out.

His cote was of a specially coarse cloth called cary. The strings tying up his
stockings, as so often happened with active workers, were all broken:

His hosen over-hongen his hok-shynes [crooked shins]
On everich syde
Al beslomered in fen
As he the plow folwede.

His two mittens were made all of rags, the fingers quite outworn. Likewise
his "knoppede shon" (hobnailed shoes) were full of patches and his toes
peeping out.[1]

[1] W. Langland, *The Creed of Piers Plowman*. Edited by G. Thomas Wright. Written probably in the reign of Richard II.

7. Poor man receiving cloak from St. Martin. Hooded cape over shirt; footless hose (with garters) pulled up over braies; no tunic or supertunic. *c.* 1280.

A very different vision of the labourer was that of John Gower, writing, just at the time of peasant uprisings.

> Labourers of old were not wont to eat of wheaten bread. Their dress was of hodden grey[1]. . . . Ah, age of ours, whither turnest thou? for the poor and small folk who should cleave to their labour . . . demand to be better fed than their masters . . . moreover bedeck themselves in fine colours and fine attire whereas (were it not for their pride and their conspiracies) they would be clad in sackcloth as of old.
>
> 1375. J. Gower, *Mirour de l'omme.* [*Speculum Meditantis*] Translated by G. G. Coulton, 1938.

In corroboration of Gower, Plate 4a suggests that at least some workers might be quite fashionable—pointed shoes, ornamental buttons on their tight doublets and hair like that of a contemporary smart and "merry" young man, described by Chaucer, which "strouted as a fanne, large and brode" (*Canterbury Tales, c.* 1387).

---

[1] Natural, unbleached.

PLATE 3

PLATE 3

(*a*) Shepherd. Hooded cape; footless hose fringed at the ankle, gauntleted gloves. *c.* 1360.

British Museum. MS. Egerton 1894.

(*b*) Men reaping, woman gleaning. Men in loose doublets and hats of straw or willow; one wears shoes, one ankle-boots and one soled hose rolled below knee. Woman in ground-length kirtle trimmed with buttons. 1377–1399.

British Museum. MS. Roy. 1 E IX.

PLATE 4

PLATE 4

(*a*) Men with scythes. Tight fitting doublets, large caps, pointed shoes. 1397.

Misericord carving, Worcester Cathedral. (Photograph by courtesy of S. Whiteley, Hatch End, Pinner).

(*b*) Shepherds wearing, for warmth, long gowns, with the "bagpipe" sleeves of the period. One wears hat on top of hood. Early 15th century.

Carving, Exeter Cathedral. By kind permission of the Dean and Chapter.

In the fifteenth century, when the tight doublet was still in fashion and the standard overgarment was some form of elaborately designed "gown" with belt, working people's clothes were apt to be looser and more uniform in shape. Their gowns might be parti-coloured and trimmed, but were generally shorter than was fashionable (Fig. 8). However, a carving in Exeter Cathedral shows a shepherd in a calf-length gown sporting the huge bagpipe sleeves that were so much in vogue in Henry IV's reign (Plate 4b).

8. (*a*) labourer with iron-shod wooden spade. Short gown, hood with very long liripipe wound round the head. (*b*) Man pruning. Parti-coloured gown with the "bagpipe" sleeves of the period; side fastened ankle-boots. 1400–10.

The hose now fitted more closely and were joined at the top to form "tights" supported by strings to the doublet. Hoods had the apex drawn out into a long pendulous tippet or liripipe. Wide-brimmed hats seem to have been preferred to the elaborate turbanlike "chaperon" and other headgear of the upper classes.

Shepherds clung to the old-fashioned cloak right through to the seventeenth century; a short one called a courtepye or curstbye is mentioned in the following passage. Here a poor shepherd dresses up to accept an invitation from the King:

> In russet clothing he tyret hym tho,
>   In kyrtil[1] and in curstbye
> And a blak furred hode
> That wel past to his cheke stode
>   [So that] the typet might not [go] wrye.
> The mytans clutt for gate he nozt.
> [The mittens patched forgot he not.]
>   Fifteenth century. *Tale of King Edward and the Shepherd*[2]

Fifteenth-century misericords from King's Lynn show clothing reduced to a minimum in hot weather—harvesting is done in shirts (which barely reach the hip) and nothing else is visible but soled hose. Even these were discarded at times.

Tudor and Jacobean Times

In Tudor days, while the gentry wore shapely waisted jerkins over their doublets, labourers were generally in a loose belted garment buttoned across the chest, having an open knee-length skirt. Some variants were called jackets or jerkins, and others, looser and full skirted, were cotes; either could be sleeveless. The doublet would be of canvas, fustian[3] or leather and the jerkin either of cloth or, like a soldier's, of buff (oiled ox-hide). "Tights", still called hose, remained the usual legwear.

The ploughman in Fig. 9 has an extra pair of overstockings and a pair of serviceable thick-soled boots fastened by tabs in front. These are very unlike the footwear of the upper classes but imply prosperity; one of the herdsmen in Spenser's *Shepheardes Calendar* (1579), wears nothing but "tights" and a shirt. Others have a jacket and cloak as well, but still no shoes, and the lads' hose are naturally very ragged about the feet (Fig. 10).

The wardrobe of a small farmer living in a cottage at Bletchingly in 1561 included "3 cotes, 1 chamblet[4] jerkin, freas growne (frieze gown), lether doblet, 2 pr. of hose".

During Elizabeth I's reign trunk hose (tights with bulbous tops) came into fashion. Many peasants, like the above-mentioned shepherds, avoided these

---

1 Perhaps an old-fashioned tunic taking the place of the doublet.
2 In Charles Hartshorne's *Ancient Metrical Tales*, 1829.
3 Something like corduroy, but twilled rather than corded.
4 A cloth. The quotation is from G. E. Fussell's *English Rural Labourer*, 1949.

9. Ploughman. Loose belted jerkin, over-stockings to the knee, boots
with front tab fastening. *c.* 1525.

10. Shepherds. (*a*) Old style loose
doublet and cloak. (*b*) Ragged
breeches. Both have ragged hose
and carry shoulder bags. 1579.

rather awkward garments, but they were certainly worn in moderate form by some. The distended upper part was called "breech" or "upper stock" and the remainder "nether stock". The peasant and the rich man are symbolized by the poet in his *Debate between Pride and Lowliness* (1568) as "cloth breeches" and "velvet breeches"—in fact, as two contrasted pairs of trunk hose described as follows:

Cloth breeches:—

>   These last were but of cloth withouten pride
>   And stitche, ne gard [trimming] upon them was seene
>   Of cloth I say both upper stock and neather,
>   Paned [slashed] and single lyned next to the thie;
>   Light for the were, meete for al sort of weather.

Velvet breeches:—

>   . . . goodly velvet breech . . .
>   For it was all of velvet very fine,
>   The neather stocks of pure Granada silke
>   Such as came never upon legges of mine . . .
>   This breech was payned in fayrest wyse
>   And with satten very costly lined
>   Embrodered according to the guise
>   With golden lace full craftely engined.

The poet's account of two peasants is also worth quoting. A grazier wore

>   . . . a jerkin made of buffe . . .
>   A faire cloake upon his backe
>   and on his head a felt.

His description of the husbandman with which we opened this chapter goes on

>   A strawen hatte he had upon his head
>   The which his chinne was fastened underneath . . .
>   A payre of startuppes had he on his feete
>   That lased were up to the small of the legge.
>   Homelie they were and easier than meet [more easy than tidy].

The startuppes (short boots) had wooden pegs in their soles. Ruff and collar were conspicuous by their absence. Nevertheless he was skilled "in his harrow and his plowe" and "earned well his bread".

The more practical alternative to trunk hose, namely separate breeches and stockings, came in during the 1570s and was soon adopted by labourers. With some exceptions this remained the legwear of country working men right on into the nineteenth century. The man pruning (Fig. 11) shows breeches typical of the time, but in his case left loose below the knee.

Gardeners were beginning in Elizabeth's reign to acquire a skill and assume a prestige which from now on was often expressed in their rather smarter clothes. In *A Perfite Platform of a Hop Garden*, by R. Scott (1576), we see men

Spit in thy hand, and annoint the sprouts therewith, and no Hare will hurt them.'

11. Man pruning. Long-skirted jacket, breeches undone at the knee. 1594.

tending the plants who wear ruffs, feathered hats and very full breeches in the fashionable style called "Venetians".

The carving shown in Plate 5 portrays, in about 1611, a man who later became gardener to Charles I. There can be no doubt about the elegance here; but he was evidently not above doing a job of work. He wears his jerkin open (the doublet can be seen underneath).

Seventeenth and Eighteenth Centuries

During the first half of the seventeenth century the major change in upper-class fashion was towards the abandonment of the jerkin altogether, so as to reveal the doublet itself, and a modification to a more natural shape in the breeches. There was a vogue for fastening doublet sleeves by numerous smart buttons, but this was too much for the working man.

12. Shepherds. Old style jacket and flat-crowned hat, buttoned boots, large pouch carried on waist band. 1642.

A countrey fellow plaine in russet clad
His doublet mutton-taffety sheep-skins
His sleeve at hand button'd with two good pins.

1616. S. Rowlands, *Doctor Merry-Man.*

Among workers there was little change throughout the century, for
although the fitting jerkin disappeared gradually, surviving only in the
occasional buff jerkin, the alternative loose jacket persisted (Fig. 12). The
breeches tended to be baggy for a long time, but there was a fondness for
sugar-loaf hats, which were in the fashion (Fig. 27). For hot work or hot
weather a man wore breeches and shirt only, with perhaps a cap (Fig. 13).
About now, for the first time, agriculturists sometimes wore aprons (Fig. 14).

13. Labourer in shirt, breeches, start-ups and
cap. 17th century.

It remained customary (and was not unknown even in the twentieth
century) for labourers to receive clothing as part of their contract. In 1601,
we read,

Chargeable servantes or labourers will not serve or work under five pounds
and a fustian doublet,[1]

[1] E. Maxey, *A New Instuction [sic] of Plowing and Setting.*

14. (*a*) and (*b*) Men planting; both in aprons, (*a*) bearded, wearing old-fashioned hose. (*c*) Ploughman in breeches without apron. 1601.

and in 1641:

> Some labourers condition to have an olde suite, a payre of breeches, an olde hatte, or a payre of shoes.[1]

Details of a swineherd's wardrobe are given in a contemporary account-book. Note that his leather garments were going to be made to measure:

> 1632 Martynmas. Layd out for the swynerd for a pair of shoes, 16d, 2 skinnes for his breeches, and thred 1d, lyninge 11d, for mendinge his clothes 3d, and heel hobbs [hobnails] 2d.[2]

As a variation on the typical breeches there was a fleeting reappearance of "trousers", seen only occasionally and on very humble yokels and serving-men (Fig. 15).

In *Academy of Armory*, by Randle Holme, published in 1688, people of every conceivable calling are depicted, and the figures represent (real or imaginary) armorial bearings. The book being what it is—something between a compendium of heraldry and a general encyclopedia—and having,

[1] *Rural Economy in Yorkshire in 1641.* Edited by C. B. Robinson, 1857.
[2] Ibid.

PLATE 5

PLATE 5

John Tradescant I (later gardener to Charles I). Jerkin open,
showing doublet; ruff, fashionable hat. *c.* 1611.

Carving on newel post, Hatfield House. (By kind permission of Lord Salisbury).

PLATE 6

PLATE 6

(*a*) Carter in "Frock", a smock-shaped over-garment. 2nd half of 17th century. (Cf. Pl. 6*b*)

Engraving in Academy of Armory *by R. Holme, 1688.*

(*b*) Hedger in smock-shaped garment probably made from a sack; mitts; "yarks" hitching up trousers. 1890s.

Photograph by courtesy of Hereford City Library.

15. Rustic, in trouser-like garments worn at his time only by very humble folk; he has apparently a short jerkin over a long doublet. 17th century.

moreover, taken many years to write, it is impossible to assign most of the costumes to any precise period. Safest to say simply that they belong somewhere between *c.* 1650 and 1688.

Five rustics are figured in doublets and more or less bulging breeches of mid-century style. In addition an interesting step in the evolution of the smock is recorded. While the day labourer simply has an apron, and the shepherd a long unbelted "loose coat" almost like a smock open in front (Figs. 16 and 17), the carter has a really typical closed smocklike garment

16. "Labouring Man". Apron, baggy breeches. Second half of 17th century.

17. Shepherd in "Loose Coat" and "round Breeches". Second half of 17th century.

which Holme calls "A Linnen or canvas Coat" (see Plate 6a). It is fascinating to compare this with the primitive investment worn by a hedger in the 1890s (Plate 6b)—the lines are almost identical. The hedger's smock is clearly made of two conjoined rectangular pieces and may indeed be simply a sack with a hole for his head. Compare Thomas Hardy's description, in *Under the Greenwood Tree*, of Thomas Leaf's "long white smock of pillow-case cut".

In about 1670 there was a revolution in gentlemen's dress: the doublet was at last replaced by the much more modern-looking coat and waistcoat. Workers followed suit near the end of the century.

The farmworker of the early eighteenth century has a decidedly urban appearance. In 1726 Hogarth shows him carrying a hayrake, but wearing the long coat of the day, with the fashionable deep, button-trimmed, cuffs and pockets. Aprons were largely given up for farmwork. A concession to comfort was leaving the buckskin breeches undone at the knees.

Of footwear we have an account by the observant traveller Kalm in his *Visit to England . . . in 1748*.[1]

> The shoes which the labouring man commonly used were strongly armed with iron, which followed the shape of the heel and somewhat resembled a horse-shoe. [The soles had nails all round and also in the centre.] They sometimes had gaiters which were not fastened to the shoes . . . these are strapped together on the outer side of the leg.

[1] P. Kalm, *Account of His Visit to England . . . in 1748*. Translated by J. Lucas, 1892.

Short boots called "highlows" (see Plate 7a), like startups, were a favourite alternative with working men and, in some areas, wooden clogs.

Kalm was much impressed by the prevalence of perukes or periwigs:

> Men all wore them, farm servants, clod-hoppers, day labourers ... in a word all labouring folk go thro' their every day duties all with peruques on their heads.

In the second half of the century a picturesque wide-brimmed "bully-cock" hat was characteristic, like that in Plate 7a, and typical summer wear is shown in Plate 10a.

18. Youth in smock (unembroidered); milkmaid in cap, long dress and long apron. 1802.

Smocks (*Eighteenth and Nineteenth Century*)

In some settings, true "smocks" as we understand the term, made of white or holland linen drill, became popular by the middle of the eighteenth century and they remained so for over two hundred years. These were like the earlier garment except for having acquired full-length sleeves (Fig. 18). They were called "frocks"[1] or "slop-frocks", later "smock-frocks". Their earliest

---

[1] Not to be confused with the gentleman's undress coat of the late eighteenth century which, because of its looseness, took the name of frock from the working man's garment.

blossoming and longest duration seem to have been in Sussex, but their use varied with the job and the district, even the occasion. That it was far from universal is clear from indirect contemporary evidence quoted by G. E. Fussell (1949)[1] and by Margaret Jones (1957),[2]. The illustrator of W. Howitt's *Book of the Seasons* (1831) gives a smock only to the shepherd out of twelve countrymen figured. Nevertheless Howitt describes, as though typical, the rustic who starts as a farm boy running errands and then learns to plough, and grows up into

> A tall long *smock-frocked*, straw-hatted ancle-booted fellow and is metamorphosed into a labourer.
>
> 1838. *The Rural Life of England.*

All in all it seems that the average labourer avoided the smock during very active work or when using machinery, because it would get in the way. If, as our "ancle-booted fellow" may have done, he wore it ploughing, he sometimes screwed up the end as in Plate 7a.

On the other hand, hanging straight down, and full enough to stand away from the body (it would be made of some 8 yards of material), it was an excellent shedder of rain, especially when supplied with a large or even multiple cape-like collar (see Plate 7b). When, in the common form, it was closed all round, it was also windproof. The smock was therefore ideal for shepherds, with their exposure to all weathers (see Plate 8a). Others who favoured it for the same reason were carters—as was interestingly fore-shadowed in the seventeenth century (Plate 6a). They would wear it even when on horseback beside the wagon (Fig. 19). Fanny Burney, in 1789, refers to "carters' loose gowns" at Romsey,[3] and indeed there was a fashion at that time among ladies for a very wide dress hanging straight from yoke to hem called the "Waggoner's Frock".

Cobbett's *Rural Rides* (1830) and Thomas Hardy's novels both suggest that other country workers wore a smock when off duty, and perhaps, for many, this was its chief use.

> I can remember that [in late 18th century] parson could not attempt to begin his sermon till the rattling of their hob-nailed shoes ceased. I have seen, I am sure, as many as five hundred men and boys in smock frocks coming out of

[1] *The English Rural Labourer.*
[2] "The Vanished Smock", in *Country Life*, 11th April 1957.
[3] *Diary and Letters of Madame D'Arblay.* Edited by C. Barrett, 1905.

PLATE 7

PLATE 7

(a) "Ye gen'rous Britons, Venerate the Plough." Smock (unembroidered, buff coloured) swathed round the waist; red waistcoat; bullycock hat; highlows. 1801.

Drawn, engraved and published by Valentine Green.

(b) Lad in a smock of c. 1870 date and of open shape, with extra cape-collar and deep smocking on breast and cuffs.

Photograph by courtesy of Museum of English Rural Life, Reading.

PLATE 8

PLATE 8

(a) Thomas Coke, attendant and shepherds at Holkham Hall. Shepherds have long smocks, bullycock hats and gaiters. 1808.

Painting by Thomas Weaver at Rothamsted Experimental Station, Harpenden. (Detail.)

(b) Reaper. Waistcoat, trousers hitched up by "yarks"; felt hat. *c.* 1890s.

Photograph by courtesy of Hereford City Library.

19. Waggoner (with eight-horse stage-waggon) riding in a smock. 1820.

church . . . At the Holly Bush at Headley [in 1822] there was a room full of fellows in white smock frocks.

Again Hardy, picturing in a mid-century setting some countrymen assembling for choir practice, writes:

Stalwart ruddy men and boys . . . mainly in snowy white smock frocks embroidered upon their shoulders and breasts in ornamental forms of hearts, daggers, zigzags.

1872. *Under the Greenwood Tree.*

The smock has a variety of forms which have been described from surviving specimens by Anne Buck.[1] In colour it was usually white or fawn, but a

[1] "The Countryman's Smock", in *Folk Life*, I, 16, 1963.

brown one made in about 1840 still exists in St Albans Museum and Mary Mitford in *Our Village* (Berkshire) mentions that a carter

> sometimes in cold weather throws over all a smock-frock and last winter . . . [assumed] . . . one of that light blue Waterloo such as butchers wear.
>
> 1824–32.

Actually blue was very popular in the Midlands.

As regards the embroidery, which controls the folds as well as decorating, this developed only at the very end of the eighteenth century and gradually became more elaborate in the nineteenth. This "smocking" was generally done in white or buff thread. There seems no evidence that there was any correspondence between the various designs and the wearers' jobs.

By 1883, according to Thomas Hardy once more, in "Wessex":

> The genuine white smock frock . . . and the whitey brown one . . . are rarely seen now afield.
>
> *Longman's Magazine.*

In Surrey, Sussex and Suffolk, especially, it survived tenuously into the twentieth century, but with somewhat degenerate embroidery, and was soon a thing of the past.

The outdoor apron retained its place chiefly with milkers, e.g. in the form of the "pinner" in "Wessex", and frequently with gardeners (see below).

Nineteenth and Twentieth Centuries—general wear

At the opening of the nineteenth century gentlemen, at long last, went into trousers. Working men, as we have seen, had adopted these occasionally in the past, but they were slow to be converted now. Although by the 1820s one would occasionally see artisans in trousers (often rolled up), they almost universally wore breeches, with leggings or gaiters, till after the middle of the century. Hardy, looking back to about the 1850s, writes of the leather leggings of a dairyman milking[1] and again:

> A thin fleece of snow having fallen . . . those [villagers] who had no *leggings* went to the stable and wound wisps of hay round their ankles to keep the insidious flakes from the interior of their boots.
>
> 1872. *Under the Greenwood Tree.*

---

[1] *Tess of the D'Urbervilles*, 1891.

Leather breeches were liked because they were immensely durable. Alfred Williams, in *Round About the Thames* (1922), says that an old man of his acquaintance called "Leather Breeches" wore a pair of buckskins in the late nineteenth century which were traditionally believed to have been worn in his family for a hundred years, "wrinkled and withered with age and filthy", but existing.

Trousers, however, were in fairly general use even at the time Hardy was recalling above, for he says of reapers that they wore

> . . . print shirts and *trousers*, supported round their waists by leather straps rendering useless the two buttons behind.
>
> 1891. *Tess of the D'Urbervilles.*

The conventional dress by the 1880s, for example in an Oxfordshire hamlet, was

> a suit of stiff brown corduroy, or in summer corduroy trousers and an un-bleached drill jacket known as a sloppy.[1]

For the labourer's trousers, fustian or "moleskin" cloth were also used. The men very often—as it were nostalgically—made them more like breeches by hitching them up with a buckled strap under the knee (failing that by string, bootlace or straw) as in Plate 8b. The strap is variously called yark, york, bo-yank, liger, pitsea, etc., in different parts of the country. This gave freedom to the knees and was said also to prevent field mice from running up the leg. But they were just as much worn by city labourers.

In the nineteenth century the fashionable tall-crowned hat replaced the bullycock until the latter was revived under the name of "billycock". The story was told in 1872 as follows. When visiting the country estate of Areley in about 1842

> one of the eminent firm of Christie [hatters] remarked that the chimney pot hats of the peasants were not at all suitable for working men and that he would try to invent something better. . . . A few weeks after this a packet of "billycocks" arrived . . . were distributed among the labourers and became so popular that . . . they spread all over the country.
>
> *Notes and Queries*, Ser. IV, IX.

Only at about the turn of the century was the billycock entirely superseded by smaller felts, straws or caps.

[1] Flora Thompson, *Lark Rise to Candleford*, 1954.

The twentieth century was characterized by a considerable shedding of clothing and by the time we part with him the labourer was wearing much less on his body and often nothing at all on his head.

Gardeners remained, as before, somewhat of an aristocracy among land-workers, but they clung to the traditional apron. Painted Chelsea and Worcester figures of the second half of the eighteenth century suggest that already blue had become the conventional colour for this, and so it remained, right down to the present century. In 1960 a gardener, looking back at his youth, wrote:

> Aprons I have worn and those of most gardeners in this district, [Sussex] were made of navy blue serge.
>
> E. Catt, in Country Life, 8th September 1960.

Even a twentieth-century girl gardener at Kew would sport a blue apron—and incidentally the incongruity of this with her very short shorts ran pretty close that presented by her prototype a hundred years before—the tailcoat and topper with a spade (see below).

On the whole, gardeners kept more closely than other outdoor workers to

20. Gardener. Fashionable square-cut tail-coat; apron; cocked hat. 1807.

21. Gardeners in aprons, breeches and "highlows". 1836–7.

the fashions of the day. Country individuals were conservative as to their legwear (Figs. 20 and 21), but in the neighbourhood of London even a journeyman gardener was already in trousers in 1826 (cotton ones in summer). A later example is shown in Fig. 22. Between the 1811 and 1824 editions of *Book of Trades* . . . the gardener depicted in a tailcoat (Fig. 299, p. 391) changed the shape of his hat to an up-to-the-minute full-blown topper.

In the days of cheap labour the lives of journeymen gardeners as well as of day labourers were bedevilled by bad weather; but even in penury there was a difference in dress between the two classes of sufferers.

Unemployed agriculturists and frozen-out gardeners are seen during a frost in gangs of from 6 to 20 [in London, to beg.] The gardeners differ from the agriculturists and 'navvies' in their costume. They affect *aprons* and old straw hats . . . their tones [of voice] less rusty and unmelodious. The navvies roar, the gardeners squeak.

1862. H. Mayhew, *London's Underworld.*

22. Gardener. Trousers, waistcoat and apron.
1870.

We might end on a more cheerful note, with a Sketch of Boz in 1834–5. Dickens's imagination, fired by the sight of a second-hand pair of boots, conjures up a delightful picture of the gardener they would suit:

> a ... hearty looking pair of tops ... and we had got a jovial market gardener into them—just the very thing for him. There were his huge fat legs, bulging over the tops and fitting them too tight to admit of his tucking in the loops he had pulled them on by; and his blue apron tucked up round his waist; and his red handkerchief and blue coat and a white hat stuck on one side of his head.

WOMEN

Throughout the whole of our period working women's skirts were long and full. It was hardly before the eighteenth century that even the ankles showed. The attempted emancipation of women in the matter of dress at the end of the nineteenth century allowed a few ladies to wear bloomers for cycling and some eccentrics to go in for "rational clothes". But this made no impression on country workers (who might have really benefited) until the days of the "land girl" in 1914. Again, from earliest times till near the end of the Victorian era women, apart from unmarried girls, always wore a headdress of some kind or other, both indoors and out. As with the men, the clothing of women in the Middle Ages was at first loose and flowing; it then gradually conformed to the shape of the body from the waist up.

Until the middle of the sixteenth century women of all classes wore a long garment known as a kirtle. On top of this, indoors or out, an overgarment of some kind was usual, but the long tight sleeves of the kirtle always showed until the middle of the fifteenth century. Then they were hidden by the sleeves of the overgarment, now called "gown", if this was worn. Whatever she was doing—milking, ferreting, weeding, minding the sheep or washing a churn in the river, the countrywoman's kirtle and/or gown touched, or even trailed on the ground and her silhouette differed little from that of a lady of rank.

In the eleventh to thirteenth centuries, over the kirtle everyone wore the type of overgarment called at first "supertunic", later "surcote", like the men's. It had either wide sleeves or none at all. Figure 23 is from a miniature unique in that it shows how a woman coped with a stooping job, like gleaning, while wearing a supertunic with sleeves as long and wide as those of a kimono or a surplice. She got the two sleeves tied together in a knot behind her shoulders.

Out of doors for extra warmth a ground-length cloak was used, which in the thirteenth century might be hooded.

The hair was often controlled by a coarse net, and working women, but never ladies, in the thirteenth century sometimes wore nothing over this. Usually, regardless of convenience, their heads were further covered and their hair largely concealed. Three of the ladies' styles of headdress are seen on peasants—first a shoulder-length white veil alone (eleventh to fourteenth centuries inclusive), secondly a barbette and fillet, thirdly a wimple and veil (late twelfth to mid-fourteenth centuries mainly.) The barbette and fillet, shown in Plate 9a were specially typical of the thirteenth century. Head dresses were usually of white linen (see opp. p. 48).

For underwear the sole garment was a coarse linen shift, confusingly known as a "smock". This continued right up to the end of the eighteenth century, when it became a "chemise".

In the fourteenth century, while ladies usually appeared in an ornamental surcote, women often worked just in their kirtles. But the prevailing open-sided sleeveless type of surcote is seen on the girl with a pail of goats' milk in Fig. 24.

The wimple, a sort of bandage over the chin and neck, fastened above the head and covered by a veil, is shown on the fourteenth-century shepherdess in Fig. 25. She wears a hooded cloak over all. The woman in Fig. 281, p. 367, shows the wimple better.

Separate hoods were now worn, for warmth, but unlike those of the men were sometimes quite open in front. In Fig. 24 the girl has an open hood and the weary woman who has been breaking up sods has a closed one.

Sometimes, as before, only the hairnet was worn and the hair would be arranged under it in plaits or bunches over the ears. Countrywomen did not attempt to keep a fillet in place over a net alone. Ladies, who always did, needed "more than half a basin full of pins" to secure it.

23. Harvesting. Men in tunics and cloth hose; one wears a fillet of straw. Woman gleaner gathering grain into her supertunic; its long wide sleeves are tied together behind her neck; skirt and tight sleeves of kirtle show underneath supertunic; blue veil on head. *c.* 1150.

24. (*a*) Girl carrying pail of goat's milk. Open-sided surcote ornamented on the breast; apron embroidered at waist; kirtle sleeves
showing; open hood. (*b*) Woman with mallet for breaking sods.
Kirtle, hood, apron. *c.* 1340.

Long bibless aprons (barm cloths) were now common.

> A barmclooth eek as whyt as morne milk
> Up-on her lendes, ful of many a gore [folds][1]

Aprons were often gathered at the top, with a band of geometric embroidery
rather like smocking (Fig. 24).

> And by hir girdl hung a purs of leather.[2]

Purses were common, but gloves are seen far less than on men. In the
Luttrell Psalter, where a man and a woman are shown together weeding, it is
significant that he, but not she, indulges in gloves.

Poverty, which must have often hindered the development of suitable

---

[1] Chaucer, *Canterbury Tales,* c. 1387.
[2] W. Langland, *Creed of Piers Plowman.* Late fourteenth century.

25. Shepherdess in cloak, wimple and veil.
c. 1320.

clothing, did, at least in extreme cases, tend to shorten the skirt a little. Piers Plowman's wife, in penury, had a "cote" (kirtle) "cutted ful hyeyhe".[1] For the rest she was wrapped in a winnowing sheet to protect her from the weather and went "barefoot on the ice".

The gay miniatures in manuscripts, if taken alone, would indeed give us a false idea of the actual appearance of many contemporary working folk. For example, women are hardly ever depicted barefoot. It was not for several centuries that a shabby exterior was seen as paintably picturesque; and it is generally for decorative reasons that people are shown wearing bright colours rather than the russet (reddish brown or grey) of their normal everyday wear.

In the fifteenth century farm women usually adhered to the sideless surcote, being slow to adopt the new high-waisted "gown", with its funnel-shaped or "bagpipe" sleeves which would cover the more convenient sleeves of the kirtle.

A prominent characteristic of fifteenth-century fashion, the elaborate headdresses, could not be displayed by working women. They continued to wear nets or veils.

Stockings, if any, were still coarse "blanket hose" held up by garters. Shoes of normal shape or heel-less slippers, like our mules of today, were the usual footwear.

[1] Ibid.

During Elizabeth I's reign the kirtle became a skirt, worn with separate bodice. Although called "petticoat", the kirtle was meant to show, even when an (open-fronted) gown was worn as well. The gown was now not an essential garment, even with the fashionable lady. There was a marked difference between the classes, since peasants adopted neither a stiffened bodice nor the farthingale which distended the skirts of the fashionable. Moreover, they rarely wore ruffs, and, if at all, preferred the "falling" ruff.

How a widowed labourer and her daughter were dressed is described by a poet in 1568[1], to show what poverty existed, even at this time of apparent prosperity. They worked on the land in the service of a knight:

> and asken neither wages fee ne hyre
> Ne choise of time at midnight or at morning
> All were it raine or shine in dyrt and myre.
> . . . thinne was their weede [garment]
> The woman and the wench were clad in russet
> Both course and olde and worne so very neere

26. Countrywoman. Gown with basqued bodice and separate skirt; shoes raised on pattens. 1640.

[1] *Debate between Pride and Lowliness.* (Author uncertain)

  That ye might see clean through both sleeve and gusset
   The naked skinne, whereas it dyd appeare.
  . . . With homely clouts I knitt upon their head
   Simple, yet white as thing so course might be.

"Clouts I knitt" may mean "rags wound together". Neither woman had stockings or shoes.

  In the 1620s farthingales and ruffs went out. The working woman's dress came near to the informal attire of the upper classes, especially in the middle of the century, when their favourite outfit was a bodice with separate skirt, now comprising the "gown" itself. Figure 26 shows a basqued bodice and a typical wide collar with very long points known, rather misleadingly, as a "neckerchief". On a lady the bodice would have been ornamented and the collar lace edged. The woman's headwear is a simple "coif" and she wears pattens—wooden soles on metal rings, strapped to the shoes to keep them out of the mud.

  Large dowlas (coarse linen) aprons were still worn for outdoor as well as indoor work. As the girl in Fig. 28 is seen through the rosy spectacles of a love-sick shepherd, her elegance may be somewhat fanciful. She is one of those who choose

  Their sleep to lose
  And in cold dews
  With clouted[1] shooes
  To carry the Milking Pail.

   Seventeenth-century Ballad in J. Ashton's *A Century of Ballads.*

A lady of fashion in the 1680s, as well as improving her shape by a bustle, erected an elaborate headdress on a support called a commode. Hence the satirical comparison between a lady and a milkgirl:

  Whilst she in Commode
  Puts on a cart load
  And with cushions plumps her tail,
  What joys are found in russet gown
  Young plump and round
  And sweet and sound
  That carry the Milking Pail.[2] Ibid.

[1] Mended.
[2] A contemporary ballad records that her milk sold at $\frac{1}{2}d.$ a pint.

27. Haymakers. Man in shirt, breeches, sugar-loaf hat. Woman in basqued bodice, long skirt, large hat. 1640–1700.

For extra warmth the "limp hood" shown in Fig. 29 (more realistically on p. 150) was popular. The cloak continued to be the usual outdoor protection right on into the nineteenth century, red being a favourite colour in the eighteenth.

Whether separate from the bodice or not, a lady's skirt was still very often

28. Milkmaid. Patterned jacket bodice, kerchief, long decorated apron. *c.* 1670–80.

29. Woman on her knees, milking. Long skirts, apron and hood.
1640–1700.

in the seventeenth and eighteenth centuries open in front, to reveal an under-skirt. Both overskirt and underskirt were liable to be called petticoat ("coat" for brevity) and the term petticoat was not confined to an undergarment until the nineteenth century. We shall speak of overskirt and underskirt for the sake of clarity. In the years 1680–1710 there was a vogue for bunching the overskirt at the back, to add to the effect of the bustle. A similar fashion recurred, as we shall see, in the 1770s. This custom suited working women very well, as it kept the overskirt out of harm's way, and they continued with it far into the eighteenth century and took it up again later. We are indebted once more to P. Kalm for the following account of countrywomen in 1748 in the Home Counties. All, he says, had cloaks and pattens. They had adopted in a measure the tight lacing of the bodice that was in vogue at that time.

> All go laced and wear for every day use a sort of Manteau [gown] made commonly of brownish camlot [wool and hair mixture]. The same head-dress as in London . . . Paniers are seldom used in the country. When they go out they always wear straw hats which they have made themselves from wheat straw and are pretty enough.
>
> *Account of his Visit to England . . . in 1748.*

Sleeves could at last be worn short, but the billowing skirt and tight, very *décolleté* bodice look most unpractical to our eyes (see the goat-milker, Fig. 298, p. 388).

In Georgian times the gown was no longer ever an overgarment but always the dress itself, either a one-piece with a skirt open or closed, or else a two-piece (bodice and skirt.) With working women the two-piece gown that found special favour had a waisted bodice reaching to the hips or thighs, much longer than was ever popular elsewhere. This, the "jacket bodice", did not necessarily match the skirt and was worn wide open in front from the waist down (see Plate 9b.).

Women worked sometimes in the fields without any gowns at all. A contemporary in 1789 writes:

> They have stays half laced and something by way of handkerchief about their necks; they wear a single coloured flannel or stuff petticoat, no shoes or stockings . . . and their coat [petticoat] is pinned up in the shape of a pair of trousers leaving them naked to the knee.

This last account is interesting as the first evidence of an attempt on the part of women to free the legs during hard outdoor work, a true occupational adaptation.

Going without gowns, a custom seen at no other work except mining, persisted right down to the twentieth century. A painting by James Ward shows an early-nineteenth-century haymaker in only her white short-sleeved shift, her petticoat, a handkerchief, bonnet and sackcloth apron. And as late as 1873 the Rev. F. Kilvert records "old Sally Killing's" telling him:

> When she was young women never wore gowns out haymaking. If a farmer saw one of his women working in a gown he would order her to take it off. She herself had been weeks without putting on her gown from Monday morning till Saturday night.
>
> *Kilvert's Diary, 1870–1879.* Edited by W. Plomer, 1944.

George Stubbs has left us a record of farm labourers in the last quarter of the eighteenth century, but mainly of types who look as though they had enjoyed more than average prosperity. From his and much other evidence it seems that a typical outfit for the better off can be described as follows. There would be a wool or flannel gown in winter, and light-coloured calico or linen in summer, made either in one piece or as bodice and skirt (see Plate 10a). In contemporary writing the casual jacket-bodice seems to be what was meant by the often referred to "bedgown"—a garment which, like the men's "night-cap", was for informal day-time wear. It is mentioned by George Eliot, writing of the period before her time, in a vivid picture of Adam Bede's mother in 1799. She had a pure linen cap with a black band round it: her broad chest is covered with a buff neckerchief and below this you see a sort of bedgown made of blue checkered linen tied round the waist and descending to the hips, from whence there is a considerable length of linsey-woolsey petticoat.

The handkerchief or neckerchief was very characteristic—usually a large square of white linen (in Hertfordshire red or brown silk was popular) folded three-cornerwise to cover the shoulders, with its points tied or tucked in in front. The handkerchief covering the *décolletage* was fashionable with ladies for informal wear, especially in the country, until early in the nineteenth century; but with working women it continued for several decades more.

Coarse brown canvas oversleeves are shown on Stubbs's haymakers, protecting their long sleeves or their bare arms.

A very long bibless apron of coarse undyed linen was generally worn out of doors, hitched up sideways when there was much stooping to do.

Women kept their mob caps on all day. The proper occupational hat was the wide nearly flat straw, which set the fashion for "milkmaid" or "bergère" hats in town. Alternatively an urban style was copied, with a tall ebullient soft crown (Plate 10a) or else a poke bonnet. It astonished Mme. J. M. Roland, who wrote in 1784, that English women never went without a hat, which in the country:

> is mostly black for those of the common class, often gathered in behind like a bonnet, and projecting like a penthouse in front.
>
> *The Works of Jeanne-Marie Philipon Roland.*
> Trans. L. A. Champagneux, 1800.

See Plate 9b.

Sir Frederick Eden, in *State of the Poor,* sums up the clothing of Cumberland working women in about 1745 thus:

> . . . a black stuff hat.
> A linen bedgown stamped with blue.
> A cotton or linen neckcloth.
> 2 petticoats of flannel, the upper one [which would show] dyed blue.
> Coarse woollen stockings.
> Linen shift.
> Stays or rather [under] bodices.
> Their gowns are sometimes made of woollen stuff.
> A cloak.

PLATE 9

PLATE 9

(a) Woman milking. Ground length kirtle; barbette and fillet. c. 1200.

Bestiary. Bodleian Library MS. 764.

(b) George III with a Haymaker (near Weymouth). She wears jacket-bodice with non-matching "petticoat", under-petticoat, mob-cap and countrified hat. c. 1790–1810.

Engraving by R. Pollard (dated 1820) after an earlier painting by an unknown artist.

PLATE 10

(i)   (ii)

PLATE 10

(*a*) Haymakers. Men in shirts and breeches with or without waistcoat and bully-cock hat.

Women (*i*) in widely open one-piece gown with matching blue under-skirt; oversleeves;

(*ii*) in pink jacket bodice and brown skirt.

All the women in white aprons and black hats over white frilled caps.
1785.

Engraving (1791) by G. Stubbs after his painting "Haymakers" (1785).

(*b*) Milk woman with yoke. Gown with "rumped" overskirt; typical "milk-maid" hat over mob cap. 1805.

W. H. Pyne, Costume of Great Britain. *1808.*

All the garments are stated to be home-made except the hat, neckcloth, stays and cloak.

By contrast a country lass turning ladylike is described by Cowper in *The Task* (1785) as going off to sell her eggs displaying two (startlingly modern) freaks of fashion. She was "ill propped upon French heels" and:

> Her head . . . superbly rais'd
> And magnified beyond all human size,
> Indebted to some smart wig-maker's hand
> For more than half the tresses it sustains.

Round about 1800 the fashion which had set in, in the 1770s, for a Polonese had taken a hold in the country and was to last there for several decades. A Polonese was a gown (with fitting bodice) whose overskirt did not extend to the front, so once more an important underskirt was shown. Like the overskirt of a century before, it was typically gathered into a bunch ("rump't") at the back, or back and sides (see Plate 10b). By working women the same bunching was now constantly practised, even if it was only a matter of pinning up an ordinary overskirt.

In Pyne's engravings of dairywomen dated 1803–5[1] some are in old-style thigh-length jacket-bodices and others in the newer bunched overskirts. The latter were so popular with countrywomen that a true Polonese can be seen in Thomas Bewick's vignettes of 1827, some thirty years after its disappearance from high life. Even Tess of the D'Urbervilles in the mid-century had "a pretty tucked-up milking gown".[2] In several ways the worker's costume is becoming a little more convenient. The milkmaid in Plate 10b wears short sleeves, and an underskirt that well clears the ankles. Her neckerchief shields her from the yoke and the bergère hat is light to wear and shady.

Near Chichester, according to Thomas Pennant, the women were very utilitarian, especially in the matter of colour. Girls wore grey "petticoats" and older women, like French peasants today, wore black ones.[3] Our milkmaid, however, wears pink and yellow with her brown gown, and in Pyne's *Microcosm* a woman churning wears a gown with buff and white stripes.

Long white aprons continued, and indeed that particular woman wears

[1] *Microcosm.*
[2] Thomas Hardy, 1891.
[3] *Journey from London to the Isle of Wight,* 1801.

(a)   (b)

30. Yorkshire women "lowkers" (weeders). (*a*) Girl in high waisted gown, apron, oversleeves, cap and hat. (She holds a "grub".) (*b*) Woman in old-fashioned bunched overskirt and laced bodice; apron. She holds a "clam". 1814.

two. The high waists of Napoleonic days found their way into country districts by 1814 and the apron ascended to the breasts (Fig. 30a).

In 1831, in Howitt's *Book of Seasons*, we see almost for the first time a skirt only reaching the calf and a curly head without any covering at all.

For warmth a true jacket became fashionable in the 1840s and a Wessex milkmaid might have one by the middle of the century:

> The evening . . . had been warm and muggy . . . and Tess had come out with her milking hood[1] only, naked armed, and jacketless.
>
> 1891. Thomas Hardy, *Tess of the D'Urbervilles.*

Another of Hardy's descriptions of a milkmaid's attire deserves to be quoted in full. (*Romantic Adventures of a Milkmaid.*) She starts on an errand:

[1] ? A hood-shaped cap to protect the hair when the "cheek was resting against the cow", as in Fig. 18.

... a bright pink cotton frock (because winter was over); a small woollen
shawl of shepherd's plaid (because summer was not come) a white handkerchief tied over her headgear, because it was so foggy, so damp and so early;
and a straw bonnet and ribbons peeping from under the handkerchief,
because it was likely to be a sunny May day.

Hardy describes women reapers as wearing "cotton bonnets, with their great
flapping curtains". This, the true sunbonnet and an admirable occupational
garment, came into being only in Victorian times and did not long outlive
the century. It is interesting that these women reapers, like medieval and
nineteenth-century men reapers, wore leather gloves. However, their gowns
were still ill adapted, having tight sleeves and long billowing skirts which had
to be "beaten back now and then when lifted by the breeze". Older women,
Hardy says, reaped in "a brown rough wrapper or over-all, the old established and most appropriate dress of the field woman". This was possibly a
smock—men's smocks, too, were sometimes called overalls or upper-alls.

In the 1880s a pinafore-topped dress was popular in summer, worn over
a low-necked short-sleeved white blouse or shift. At about this time girls
began to wear a handkerchief tied over the head in modern "head square"
style.

Women labourers in the Fens in the 1890s were an exceptionally hard-
bitten race whose work included the arduous task of weeding in the mud.
To the astonishment of town-dwellers they wore knee-length dresses and
high leather top-boots. Indeed, their silhouette was not very unlike that of
the "land girl" in 1914. All their colours were drab, including even that of
the sunbonnet.

A somewhat down-to-earth account is also given of the Oxfordshire field-
workers of that time, remembered by Flora Thompson.[1]

They worked in sun bonnets, hob-nailed boots and men's coats, with coarse
aprons of sacking enveloping the lower part of their bodies. One, a Mrs
Spicer, was a pioneer of trousers; she sported a pair of her husband's cor-
duroys; the others compromised with ends of old trouser legs worn as
gaiters . . .

And there, in the gateway of the twentieth century, we will take leave of
our landworker, before she steps into a pair of trousers of her own.

[1] *Lark Rise to Candleford*, 1945.

CHAPTER II

SEAMEN AND FISHERFOLK

And then he hitched his trousers up, as is I'm told, their use,
It's very odd that Sailor-men should wear those things so loose.

R. H. Barham, 1842.

It would seem that there are two main principles governing the clothing of those having their business upon great waters. These are the minimum of hindrance when working, by articles of clothing, especially when working with nets, or ropes in the days of sail; and protection against the weather.

In early times the first object was achieved by sailors going naked about their work, but this method must, especially in northern waters, have been at the expense of the second principle. It is of interest to see that, from a contemporary illustration of the thirteenth century (Fig. 31), nudity appears to have been confined to the lower deck, or its equivalent in an undecked vessel, the superior orders, steersman and captain, being clad in the normal tunic, cloak and hood or cap. Some of the sailors are seen in braies (underpants).

The ancestors of these thirteenth-century sailors as displayed in the Bayeux Tapestry, which probably dates from the end of the eleventh century, had the same habits, kilting their tunics when wading ashore with an anchor; as did the passengers when embarking through shallow water. The tunics are short, above the knee, sometimes slit up the sides, worn with long hose, or often with bare legs. The steersmen or captains wear a cloak and in one case a white coif on the head; and men going aloft are naked.

Geoffrey Chaucer writing in the second half of the fourteenth century describes the shipman among his Pilgrims as dressed

In a woollen gown that reached his knee,
A dagger on a lanyard falling free
Hung from his neck under his arm and down.

(Nevill Coghill's translation, Penguin Classics, 1951.)

A knife thus suspended is observed among today's yachtsmen and small-boat enthusiasts.

31. Ship and crew, 13th century.

In 1467 the expense accounts of Sir John Howard show that a doublet, a pair of hose, and a shirt, together with a pair of "shone" (shoes) were provided for an individual described as "Cawse of the Shippe", whilst "Hoge of the Shippe" was bought a "payr hosen" for tenpence.

32. Scottish Fisherman, 1547.

A manuscript of this century in the British Museum (Cotton MS. Julius E.IV, art.6) shows a boatman clad in a very short sleeveless belted overgarment (like a jacket of the period, but without sleeves), slit at the sides, worn over a sleeved undergarment, and braies or underpants. He is bareheaded. Another fifteenth-century manuscript in the British Museum (Harl. 2278) has an illustration of three sailors in a ship setting out for the Holy Land. They have only the upper part of their bodies visible and one wears a white hood, one a red Turkey bonnet—he has a whitish tunic bound with yellow—and one bareheaded. A Turkey bonnet was a tall cylindrical brimless hat, somewhat like a fez in appearance.

Throughout the medieval period it is apparent that the seamen, fishermen and boatmen were clad in the ordinary garments of the day and in appearance did not differ significantly from the farmworker or town labourer. The kilting or tucking up of the gown when wading was an obvious adaptation, and the discarding of clothing altogether when working aloft no doubt eased the ascent and descent of the rigging and obviated fouling of blocks, etc., by the loose and ample garments of the time. However, this habit of working naked could only have been pursued in fine weather, and surely only by men more thick skinned than most of us.

With the sixteenth and seventeenth centuries we begin to see the rise of more defined occupational dress of the seamen and allied callings. Andrew Boord in his *First Boke of The Introduction of Knowledge*, about 1547, shows a Scottish fisherman clad in hose and a short loose blouse or jacket, wearing high boots, gauntlets, and what looks very like a modern sou'wester (Fig. 32). His speech contains the lines:

> For corne and for shoes our fish we do sell
> And simple raiment doth seme us full well
> Wyth dogswaynes and roudges we be content.

Dogswayne is a coverlet of coarse stuff, and roudge was another coarse material. Albeit a Scot, Boord's character was probably representative of the fishermen of the northern coasts of England. Later in the century Sir Richard Hawkins was writing of "supplying rugge gowns for my people to watch in, for in many hott countries the nights are freshe and cold" (Dudley Jarrett, *British Naval Dress*). Rugge, or rug, is a coarse woollen cloth akin to frieze.

Cesare Vecellio showed a picture of an English seaman of about 1598 in his *Habiti Antichi et Moderni* (Fig. 33). This represents a man wearing very full

33. English Sailor, late 16th century.

baggy breeches gathered in below the knee, a loose waist-length coat with a slit and lace holes in front at the neck.[1] He wears a loose ruff, like the falling ruff of the early seventeenth century, and has a shaggy brimless hat or cap. Shaped like a Monmouth cap, it appears to be a thrum or thrummed hat, made of felt or silk "with a long pile or nap".

The baggy breeches now appearing on the sailors' legs became known as "slops" or "slop hose", a name later applied to a sailor's clothes generally. (In 1756 the Navy Board set up a new department to deal with their clothing contractors—this was known as the Navy Slop Office.)

Up to the end of the first quarter of the seventeenth century the evidence for seamen's dress is scarce, and limited to odd references and to contemporary manuscripts, illustrations or woodcuts. From 1623, however, the situation is illuminated by the lists of the fixed-priced clothing contracted for by the Navy. It must be remembered here that the Royal Navy did not introduce a uniform for its officers until the eighteenth century, and the lower deck had to wait for one until the mid-nineteenth century. Although individual naval captains introduced some form of order by dressing their crews in slops of one pattern, the description of a sailor's clothes applied equally to the crew of a private ship as it did to that of a Royal vessel.

In 1663 the Lord High Admiral issued instructions for the vending of clothes on board H.M. ships, and listed the clothes allowed to be sold by contractors, and the prices. This list includes Monmouth caps 2s. 6d. and Red caps 1s. 1d., stockings, "blew" shirts 5s., cotton drawers 3s., leather shoes 3s. 6d., canvas suits 5s., and "blew" suits 5s. (Jarrett, op. cit., p. 18).

Canvas or canvice, this time as breeches, is also mentioned in 1688 in the blazon of a coat of arms, of which the supporters are two "sailors". It was no doubt this canvas or sailcloth which, when coated with tar, became the tarpaulin, short petticoats of which were worn over the slops in rough weather.

Of the armorial supporters mentioned above, one is described as wearing also a red cap and parti-coloured scarf with waistcoat, hose and shoes, while his companion sports a "short coat and stertops". Stertops or startups were a high shoe reaching above the ankle and either loose fitting or secured with laces or buckles.

An illustration in the Guildhall Library shows the Lord Mayor's Day pageant of the Fishmongers' Company in 1616 (Fig. 34). It depicts a fishing-boat with three men. The first of these fishermen is clad in a close-fitting

[1] There is a similar outfit in the London Museum.

34. Fishermen, 1616.

overgarment open at the neck to show a shirt, breeches or hose and thigh boots. He wears mittens. (Grey woollen mittens at sixpence a pair are mentioned in a Naval contract of 1706—Jarret, op. cit., p. 21). The two others appear to wear coats or jackets opening down the front.

In the sixteenth and seventeenth centuries, then, we can discern a specilization of dress appearing in the seafaring life, e.g. gauntlets or mittens and long boots for the fishermen; and "rugges" and tarpaulin petticoats as protection against the weather for the seamen. Double-soled shoes are also listed in the contract of 1706, no doubt as an extra protection against the wet environment of the wearer.

With the advent of the eighteenth century contemporary pictorial and written evidence of the sailors' clothes becomes much greater. Slops, or "slop hose", were still generally worn, and in 1736 were defined as "a sort of wide-kneed breeches worn by seamen" (Bailey's Dictionary). These were often striped, although red was a favourite colour, and had been for a long time. (In the seventeenth century Wycherley, in *The Plain Dealer*, says a sea captain may be known by red breeches, and a painting by J. White in the British Museum, of about 1600, shows a sailor in red slops—also another in blue.) Shagg and Kersey, woollen cloths, and ticken, a linen fabric, were common materials.

Jackets, waistcoats and shirts were the normal upper garments.

Smollett, who started life as a ship's surgeon, writing in the middle of the century, thus describes the sailors of his day on shore:

> He lets his jacket fly open . . . and his hair grows long to be gathered into a heavy pigtail; but when fully dressed he prides himself on a certain gentility . . . on a white stocking and a natty shoe, issuing lightly out of the flowing blue trowser . . . He is proud of appearing in a new hat and slops, with a belcher handkerchief flowing loosely round his neck, and the corner of another out of his pocket. Thus equipped, with pinchbeck buckles on his shoes . . . and perhaps a cane or whangee under his . . . arm, sallies forth. . . .
>
> He buys dozens of "superfine best men's cotton stockings", best good check for shirts (though he has too much already), infinite needles and thread (to sew his trousers with some day), a footman's laced hat . . .

The references to trousers and needles and thread are interesting. Trousers, or trowsers, were not commonly worn in the eighteenth century. Their use was restricted to labourers, sailors (Fig. 35) and soldiers, and on occasion to the country squire. Their acceptance by the majority of men did not come until the early nineteenth century.

In *Roderick Random*, published in 1748, Smollett also refers to a sailor in "check shirt and trousers, brown linen waistcoat and night cap of the same". The needles and thread show that the sailor, of necessity on long voyages, was his own sempstress, a fact evidenced also by the traditional "make and mend" of the Royal Navy. He also essayed his needle on purely decorative work and often his jacket, shirt and trousers bore evidence of his skill. In the Stranger's Hall Museum, Norwich, is a pair of short holland slops, amateurishly appliqued with the remains of an elaborately embroidered eighteenth-century waistcoat. These, we think, are certainly the work of a seaman of the late eighteenth or early nineteenth century.

The influence of the Royal Navy was becoming felt at this period. Although no uniform existed for the lower-deck ratings, various captains established a certain uniformity of dress among their crews, and the practice of Admiralty contracts for slops in the Navy also had its effect. The introduc-

35. English sailor wearing trousers, 1737.

tion of a blue coat for naval officers in 1748 undoubtedly had its repercussions on the sailor's dress in general. The *Salisbury Journal* in 1771 mentions "a seafaring man was in a blue jacket, white flannel waistcoat, and long trousers". The jacket in the eighteenth century was confined to sailors, postillions, sportsmen, apprentices and labourers. Admiral Sir Thomas Pasley, in 1781–2, refers to his "morning jacket" and "uniform jacket".

Trousers, like slops, were often striped. A print of 1788, "An English Jack Tar, giving Monsieur a Drubbing" (see Plate 11a) shows a seaman in a blue jacket, with spotted handkerchief around his neck, and blue-and-white striped trousers, ending about six inches above the ankle. He also wears a soft-brimmed hat, turned up in front.

"Jack Tar" is generally accepted as the sailor's nickname in the eighteenth century on account of the tarpaulin hats worn by them. It is a successor to the early seventeenth-century term "tarpaulin", attributable to the tarred aprons or petticoats. The petticoat, tarred or plain, was prevalent throughout the century and persisted into the nineteenth century where it is generally seen in pictures of fisherman (Fig. 36).

36. Fisherman, 1808.

The three-cornered hat, known by Victorian romanticists as a "tricorne", was the almost universal headgear of the eighteenth-century man and as such was adopted by Jack, to be gradually replaced by the end of the century by a flat-brimmed round hat.

The "tarpaulin hat" mentioned above has, in fact, no reference during this century, first appearing in print, as far as can be traced, in Marryatt in the 1830s.

The sailor's dress of the beginning of the nineteenth century shows no marked difference from his predecessors'—jacket, trousers, shirt, and generally waistcoat. Breeches or slops now appear much less frequently and seem to be becoming the wear of fishermen—Pyne, in his *World in Miniature* of 1827, shows one wearing very wide slops, very high boots and a striped stocking cap. Fairholt, writing in 1860 (*Costume in England,* Vol. 2), speaks of "loose slops, similar to the petticoat breeches of the reign of Charles II, and which are still seen on Dutch sailors, as well as upon some of our own fishermen" (see Plate 11b).

Trousers are now becoming longer and wider in the leg, generally white or striped as previously. In 1817 we read of the sailor's trousers being known as "gun mouthed"—this is a reference to the swelling of a gun muzzle and is equivalent to the later "bell bottom".

An illustration of 1827 shows a mariner "of higher rank and estimation than common sailors" (Fig. 37); he wears loose white trousers, very wide at ankles, short jacket, waistcoat, and handkerchief knotted under his shirt collar. His hat is a tall round hat with a rather curly brim—very like a normal top-hat.

37. A Mate, 1827.

Long boots of leather, calf or thigh length, were worn by fishermen, who also clung to the petticoat or apron, perhaps as a protection against their catch rather than the weather. Queen Victoria's journal for 1834, recording a visit to the seaside, mentions "six fishermen in rough blue jackets, red caps and coarse white aprons".

The knitted stocking cap, also known as a brewer's or fisherman's cap, became a popular headdress, and is still seen in a variety of patterns on the heads of modern yachtsmen.

In 1812 reference is made to an "oilskin hat" and in 1816 oilskin is referred to as a waterproof packing material. Its basis was silk or linen or cotton impregnated with boiled linseed oil. Linseed oil with the addition of pipe clay and other materials was later used in place of tar to produce tarpaulin. During the century not only hats (Fig. 38) but trousers and jackets of oilskin were produced and in 1884 reference is made to "men at the wheel in yellow oilskins". Other compositions, including rubber, also came into use as a waterproofing agent for clothes.

     (a)   (b)

38. In-shore sailors. (a) 1862. (b) 1876. Both wear sou'westers.
(a) wears "bib and brace" type trousers.

In 1826 it was recommended that the Navy should adopt "waterproof pea jackets", but nothing is known about their manufacture or material.

A picture of the mid-century shows a fisherman and two children in a boat (see Plate 12a)—the man wears a sou'wester type hat, shirt closely buttoned at the wrists, and trousers supported by braces. The elder boy wears ankle-length wide trousers, a horizontally striped waistcoat, and a knitted jersey. A writer of 1824 refers to braces thus:

About twelve years ago [i.e. 1812] I saw a British sailor walking up the High Street, Portsmouth, with suspenders to his trousers . . . the suspenders crossed each other over his shoulders . . . the impious custom has now become prevalent among our seamen.

The jersey, now universally associated with sailors, fishermen, and foot-ballers, is supposed to have been introduced in the 1860s. James Norbury in the *Journal of the Royal Society of Arts,* January 1951, however, indicates that the fisherman's jersey goes back to the late eighteenth century; and the National Maritime Museum has one of Lord Nelson's letters, dated 20th November 1804, referring to Guernsey jackets. Commander W. E. May, of the National Maritime Museum, is of the opinion that these Guernsey jackets were knitted garments, since, as he points out, later in the century the terms "Jersey" and "Guernsey" were always almost synonymous. The Manx Museum has fishermen's "ganseys" or "ganzeys", as they are also known, reputed to belong to the 1850s. The sailor's jersey is traditionally grey or dark blue. They rapidly became popular with seamen and many photo-graphs of crews of merchant ships of the last century and early in this, show them in jerseys, often with quite elaborate patterns of stitches. In some cases it was the custom to wear the name of the ship or shipping line embroidered in an arc across the chest (see Plate 12b).

During the nineteenth century the merchant seaman tended to wear clothes similar to those of the Royal Navy. As Commander May points out, the fact that Naval service was not continuous meant that sailors went back and forth between the Royal Navy and the Merchant Navy and that they took their clothes with them. When uniform for the lower deck was intro-duced in 1857 it was based on what had been the fashion for many years past. Commander May also stresses that many of the early steamships were com-manded by Royal Naval half-pay officers, and that until stopped they wore their naval uniforms. They also tended very much to introduce naval fashions into their ships. This persisted among many shipping lines, whose crews wore a modified rating's uniform.

Among the smaller ships less regard was paid to naval appearance and a photograph of a schooner of about 1890 shows two of the crew in bowler hats, one with a frockcoat, and a third member in a soft cloth cap, waistcoat, and shirt sleeves. At the beginning of the present century the skippers of Hull trawlers put on a bowler hat to enter harbour—to repeat Smollett, when the English sailor comes ashore "he prides himself on a certain gentility".

39. A girl shrimper, 1827.

Unlike the deep-sea sailor, the fisherman was not subjected to long separations from his womenfolk, and they, like their rural and urban sisters, were able to join in the work of their men (see Plate 13a). In the sixteenth century, and probably long before, they were helping with the making of nets. Together with this craft went shrimping, shellfish collecting, and helping with the landing, preparing and selling of fish.

The fisherwoman of the mid-eighteenth century had little to distinguish her from other women of the same class—a large white apron was probably her most important garment. A shrimp girl of about the same period was dressed in an open-necked bodice, overskirt hitched up around her waist showing a coarse petticoat and apron. She is barefooted.

J. S. Cotman painted a Yarmouth fishergirl, possibly at the end of the eighteenth century. She bears a flat basket of fish on her head, supported by a flat hat worn over a bonnet; her coat is thigh length, single-breasted and worn unbuttoned below the waist. Her skirt is checked, and she has an apron rolled

PLATE II

PLATE II

(*a*) Sailor, 1788. See p. 59.

Coloured print published by Robert Sayer, 1788, kindly lent by Peter Black. Photograph by courtesy of James S. Hopgood.

(*b*) Fisherman wearing what appears to be wide slops, 1842.

W. R. Dickinson, Rustic Figures. *1842.*

PLATE 12

PLATE 12

(*a*) Victorian fisherfolk.

Painting by J. C. Hook, "Luff, boy". (c. mid-19th century).

(*b*) Boatman wearing embroidered jersey, *c.* 1900.

Photograph of "Dawsey" Kewlay (1850–1904). By courtesy of the Manx Museum.

up and swathed around her waist. From the apron, apparently, hang a purse and a key. Over her coat is a wide turned-down collar extending half across the shoulders and coming to a point in front.

The wars of the late eighteenth and early nineteenth centuries made fish scarce and dear. Those fishermen escaping the press-gang were unable to venture far afield, and no doubt the demand for, and numbers of, fishwomen declined also. However, we have a picture of two of them on the Yorkshire coast in 1814 (opp. p. 80). They wear Quaker bonnets, brown dresses, and long white aprons. The aprons and dresses are mid-calf length. One of the girls has her dress bunched up, showing a red petticoat. Both wear stockings and shoes. One carries a basket of fish on her head.

A shrimper of 1827 is very similarly dressed, but her basket is supported by a waist belt in front of her and she is, not unnaturally, barefooted (Fig. 39).

40. Victorian fishergirls, 1866.

During the nineteenth century the Scottish fishergirls from Aberdeen and Newhaven with their famous striped petticoats were to be seen at the quayside of English fishing-ports.

A *Punch* drawing of 1866 (Fig. 40) shows two fishergirls wearing hoods or bonnets, jackets, aprons, and in one case a striped skirt. They are barefooted up to the knee; in fact, as the caption states, they are "clothed that indelicate that you might have knocked them down with a feather".

CHAPTER III

MINERS, COAL CARRIERS, NAVVIES

MINERS

In the early days of mining the most important minerals were iron, lead, tin and coal.

Coal, which was mined from the middle of the thirteenth century onwards was the least valuable in medieval times and required the least skill in mining. It had simply to be dug, while the others, being found in the form of ores, had to be specially treated to obtain the metal. Iron, lead and tin miners formed guilds and had many privileges.

In medieval days coal was often worked by the early monastic communities wearing monks' habits.

Mining in the sixteenth century tended to be part of the normal work done on an estate on which coal or ore was to be found, and the labourers who worked in the fields were transferred to the mines in off seasons. Their garments were still those of the farm labourer.

The famous Miner's Brass in All Saints' Church, Newland, Gloucestershire (see Plate 14a), depicts a helmet and mantling and, as a crest, the figure of a miner, with hod and pick and a candlestick in his mouth. He wears a belted doublet and knee-breeches tied neatly below the knees. This man was presumably one of the "free miners" of the Forest of Dean. His date is about 1570, as knee-breeches, then called Venetians, by the fashionable world, were not worn before this date.

> Venetian hosen, they reach beneath the knee to the gartering place of the legge, where they are tied finely with silke points [i.e. ties] or some such.
>
> 1583. P. Stubbes, *Anatomie of Abuses.*

In about 1660 Thomas Bushell, promoter of mines and mineral works, while in prison for debt, tried to persuade his fellow prisoners to join him in the working of his mines by promising that they should be "cloathed in good canvas or Welsh cottons".

Women also were employed at seventeenth-century collieries (Fig. 41).

41. Female Coal Carrier. 17th century.

In the early eighteenth century an interesting account of a lead miner at work in Derbyshire is given by Daniel Defoe in his *Tour through the whole of Great Britain*.

> From hence . . . we went to a valley on the side of a rising hill, where there were several grooves, so they call the mouth of the shaft or pit by which they go down into the lead mine . . .
>
> When this subterranean creature was come quite out with all his furniture about him, . . . our curiosity received full satisfaction without venturing down . . . First, the man was a most uncouth spectacle; he was cloathed all in leather, had a cap of the same without brims, some tools in a little basket which he drew up with him.
>
> For his person, he was lean as a skeleton, pale as a dead corps, his hair and beard a deep black, his flesh lank, and, as we thought, something of the colour of the lead itself . . . fancied he looked like an inhabitant of the dark regions below, and who was just ascended into the world of light.
>
> 1724–6.

In spite of their dirty and dangerous occupation, miners, even in the nineteenth century, do not appear to have been provided with clothing suitable for their work. In 1814 we have the picture of a rural Yorkshire collier "in customary attire" (see Plate 14b). His jacket and breeches are white bound with red, his neck tie is blue and his shoes and stockings grey. He wears a slouch hat. As he is smoking a pipe, he is probably off duty. (In the background is the Middleton Colliery railway.)

A little earlier, in 1805, W. H. Pyne in his *Microcosm* shows colliers on the surface working a machine at the pit head. Some of the men wear hats, some soft round caps, all wear breeches and some wear aprons.

Another scene in the early nineteenth century shows miners working on the surface loading coal (see Plate 15a). The men are all in waistcoats and breeches. Two wear hats and one with shirt sleeves rolled up is bareheaded. The woman wears an apron over a countrywoman's jacket-bodice and a desperately long skirt.

The following accounts come from Parliamentary Papers, 1842 (380, 382).

In the North Country coal fields, nakedness or the absence of clothes was the garb of the wretched miners working under appalling conditions in the 1840s.

In a Yorkshire coal field, an illustration shows men stark naked, or wearing caps only, hacking coal from the roof. A child is shown on hands and feet drawing a loaded "corve" (small wagon) along the tunnel by means of a chain attached to a belt round the waist. The child wears a pair of drawers only.

> Girls from 5 to 18 perform all the work of boys. There is no distinction whatever, in work, in wages or dress . . . associated with boys and men, living and labouring in a state of disgusting nakedness and brutality, while they have themselves no other garment than a ragged shift or in the absence of that a pair of broken trousers to cover their person.

The girls were known as hurriers, drawing the corves. A candlestick was stuck on the wagon by damp clay.

Women too were employed as "hurriers" (Fig. 42.).

> Betty Harris, aged thirty-seven, drawer in a coal-pit at Little Bolton, states:—
> "I have a belt round my waist and a chain passing between my legs, and I go on my hands and feet. . . . The pit is very wet where I work, and the water comes over our clog tops always, and I have seen it up to my thighs; it rains in at the roof terribly: my clothes are wet through almost all day long . . . the belt and chain is worse when we are in the family way."

In 1842 however Lord Shaftesbury—then Lord Ashley—introduced a Bill for prohibiting the employment of women and young children underground in coal mines.

The following statement was made about men working in Lancashire Collieries:

> This habit of men working without clothing . . . The reason generally given was that it was inconvenient to work with clothes on as clothes are apt to get into creases and chafe the skin . . . but I am led to the conclusion that

42. Female coal drawer in a coal pit, wearing a loose shift and
breeches, with a handkerchief tied on her head. 1842.

there is a great deal of fashion in the habit and I have myself seen men working in coal seams of 20 inches in thickness [height of tunnel] clad in flannel
singlets, trousers and shoes.

The colliers frequently wear what are called pilchers and arm patches—
sheaths of thick leather work on the arm and under the thigh to prevent the
skin from being rubbed.

A little protective clothing at last!

A woman working in the same colliery wears:

flannel shirt and trousers . . . and a small cap . . . the sex is discernible by the
small necklace of blue or red glass beads and by her ear-rings which are
usually worn.

At about the same time, in the 1840s, women were employed in the
Shropshire iron mines for carrying iron "baskets" of pennystone which they
emptied on to heaps. It was said to be "healthy light employment in the
open air."

In cold weather [they were] clothed in warm flannel dresses and great coats
like those of the men, with handkerchiefs round their necks and hats or
bonnets on their heads.

In Cornish mines women, known as "bal-maidens" (bal = mine) were employed in various processes of dressing tin and copper ores in exposed places above ground.

> They wrap their legs in woollen bands in winter, and in summer many of them envelope their faces and throats in handkerchiefs to prevent them getting sunburnt.

A peculiar headdress worn by the bal-maiden and known in some districts as a "yard of carboard" consisted of a piece of cardboard placed on the head with a curtain of print which fell down on the shoulders behind. The dress consisted of a "Garboldi", a corruption of "Garibaldi" which, in the fashionable world of the 1860s was a blouse, usually scarlet, which overhung the skirt and was worn with a belt. The bal-maiden tucked it into her skirt over which she wore a clean white pinafore when walking to and from the mine. When at work this was replaced by a hessian "trouser", a rough apron made of hemp or jute. On rough work or in the winter, cut up stockings were used as mittens. (A. K. Jenkin, *The Cornish Miner*). Bal-maidens existed between 1800 and 1870 and a few appear to have been employed in Carn Brea Mines as recently as 1912.

Managers of a sort "were recognisable throughout Cornwall by their white drill coats and high pole-hats" (1824, Hitchens and Drew, *History of Cornwall*). Others wore "rusty frock coats and tall hats".

Illumination of mines was largely done by lighted candles which might be stuck to a projection in the tunnel or more often fastened by clay to the miner's hat. This is shown in Fig. 43. This archaic method was even used as late as 1899 by the Laxey miners working in the lead mines of the Isle of Man. An ordinary light-coloured hat was coated with clay and a candle was fixed to this either in front or at the side. The hat was worn over a fine cotton skull cap. Candles were also used as time keepers as the men had no watches.

A flint and steel mill was invented as early as 1750. It was strapped to a man's chest, and by rotating the handle he produced a steady stream of sparks. The light obtained, however, was too poor to be of practical use. The Davy lamp, or Safety Lamp, invented in 1815, had to be carried by hand.

In the early days oil lamps, adapted for carrying on the cap, were used by miners in the shallow seams which were worked with open lights in Scotland and the Northumberland and Durham coalfields. Electric hand lamps

43. Cornish Miner working a winze-shaft, with a candle fixed in his hat. His shirt is dark, but trousers light. 1869.

were introduced about 1889, but it was not until 1910 or 1911 that they were in general use. The electric cap lamp was not introduced before 1928.

In the twentieth century, under some conditions, miners were clad in oil-skins including an oilskin hat. At the Bargoed coal mine near Cardiff, a miner thus clothed was photographed in 1910.

CARRIERS OF COAL

Winter . . . the friend to none but
Colliers and Woodmongers.
Dekker, *The Raven's Almanacke*, 1609.

Coal sellers in the seventeenth and eighteenth centuries are often depicted among the "Cries of London". They all carry sacks of coal on their backs, and are shabbily dressed, but in the style of their day.

In our illustration of 1689 (Fig. 44) the man wears a long loose sort of cape protecting his coat and breeches from the sack of coal on his back. In his hands he carries a measurer. On his head he wears a soft slouch hat very different from the protective fan-tail hat of the nineteenth century.

44. Coal Seller shouting his wares. 1689. See text.

Pepys, in 1661–2, writes with satisfaction of the work of the coal seller:

> All the morning in the cellar with the colliers, removing the coles out of the old cole hole into the new one, which cost me 8*s.* the doing; but now the cellar is done and made clean, it do please me exceedingly.

Carriers of coal in the nineteenth century were usually called by names which indicated the type of work on which they were employed.

(1) *The coal-backers or coal-porters* who carried coal on their backs from the ship's hold, barge or quay side, were employed in measuring and filling the sacks, then loading the wagons and attending them to the customers of the coal-merchants, their employers.

The coal-porter's attire in 1827 was: a grey smock, pink breeches, white stockings, brown spats, black boots and a fan-tail hat—or alternatively, a dark brown jacket, pink waistcoat, brown breeches, blue stockings, spats, an

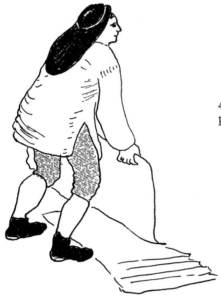

45. Coal Porter wearing a grey smock or more probably his shirt worn outside, with red breeches and a fan-tail hat. 1827.

apron and a fan-tail hat. (Figs. 45, 46.) Both these styles are depicted in W. H. Pyne's *World in Miniature*, 1827.

In 1851 his costume is described thus:

> The man wore the approved fantail, and well-tarred short smock-frock, black velveteen breeches, dirty white stockings and lace up boots.
>
> Mayhew, H., *London Labour, and the London Poor.*

By 1861 some of the men were wearing leather aprons instead of smocks and instead of breeches others were wearing trousers, often bound round below the knees with leather straps known as yarks.

(2) *The coal-heavers* worked "on board the colliers or coal ships on their arrival in the Port of London, to unload them of their cargoes". Their work overlapped with that of the coal-porters.

These men have been depicted by George Scharf the Elder, in 1841, all wearing short smocks, short boots then known as high-lows and fan-tail hats. In 1823 Rowlandson showed them wearing grey shirts, brown breeches, grey stockings and fan-tail hats, but always fan-tail hats.

In 1859 Albert Smith in *Sketches of London Life and Character* wrote:

The coal-heaver . . . knight of the fantail and shovel . . . he takes a particular pride in his legs and clothes them at times in white stockings and well-fitting shoes or boots; above droops the dingy fantail and the dusty jacket which seem but made as cushions for heavy burdens . . . for the upper part is but a mere resting place for coal-sacks.

When he is clean shaved, you can tell he is a coal-heaver, dress however he may, for a crop of coal dust still vegetates in the roots of his beard—the barber himself says that a coal-heaver is as hard to shave as a sand-bag.

(3) *The coal-whippers* had to unload the coal from the ships in baskets, containing over a ton, by means of a device which necessitated their jumping up and down.

> The dress of the whippers is of every description; some have fustian jackets, some sailors jackets, some Guernsey frocks. Many work in strong shirts which were once white, with a blue stripe. Loose cotton neckerchiefs are generally worn.

A coal whipper is stated as saying:

> I didn't buff it then, that is I didn't take my shirt off . . . it was wet through and my flannels wringing with the perspiration . . . the perspiration runs down into our shoes, and then from the dust and the heat of jumping up

46. Coal Heaver in jacket, grey breeches, blue stockings and a fan-tail hat. 1835.

and down, the feet will be galled with the small coal, so that the shoes become full of blood.

1874. Mayhew's London Characters.

(4) *The Basket-men* were the foremen of the whippers, but they assisted in the movement of the baskets after they had been raised from the hold. These men were on the plank all day and in the summer time continually exposed to the sun, so that:

> What with the labour and the heat . . . he can wear neither coat nor waistcoat—very few can bear the hat [fan-tail] on the head, so they wear nightcaps instead. The work is always done in the summer time with only the shirt and trousers on, for the basket man never takes off his shirt like the whippers.

1874. Mayhew's London Characters.

(5) One other worker must be mentioned and he is the *Carman*, "the Mercury of our Merchants". Although he was a general carrier of goods, this did include the delivery of coal to people's houses (Fig. 47):

> treasures for which the mine has been searched . . . No wonder that he walks erect, carries his whip somewhat jauntily . . . Look at his boots—heavy although they are, they are neatly laced and fit him like gloves . . . His delivery book is carried in a pocket made purposely, within the left-hand side of his jacket.

1859. Albert Smith, Sketches of London Life and Character

The Carman, however, wore a top hat. The fan-tail hat has now come to be viewed almost as the trade-mark of the men who used to deliver coal.

NAVVIES

A navvy is defined as a labourer employed in excavating for canals, railways, roads, etc.

A paviour employed in laying stones is also included in this section.

The word navvy was originally "navigator" because of their work on canals for inland navigation and this term, though now having a different meaning, was used to indicate a navvy as late as 1863.

> Navvies! Oh Lord! to think of Emily St Evremond [a singer] wasting her sweetness upon an audience of navigators.

The Ticket-of-Leave Man, a play by Tom Taylor.

47. Carman wearing jacket, waistcoat, breeches, an apron and a top hat, the coal heaver in dark shirt, breeches, apron, gaiters and a fan-tail hat. 1859.

A woodcut illustrating a seventeenth-century ballad shows two paviers (Fig. 48). (*a*) The one with pick axe and spade wears a belted coat with a ruff at his neck. His tall crowned hat, then known as a "copotain" and his knee-breeches called Venetians are better shown on his mate (*b*) who wears a doublet and a low-crowned soft hat. His high shoes, reaching above the ankle were called Startups. Besides his spade, he carries a basket of stones; as the ballad says:

A Pavier without any stones,
Oh what is he able to do?

> *The Naked Truth*, Roxburghe Ballads II, Original Broadsheet.

In a print of 1813 navvies are shown as "Stonebreakers on the Road" in Yorkshire (see Plate 15b). The bald-headed man wears protective blue sleeves over his shirt sleeves. His waistcoat is brown. The central figure has a red

48. Paviers going to work. See text. Early
17th century.

waistcoat with a blue handkerchief round his neck, yellow breeches and a slouch hat. Both men wear top boots.

In a water colour sketch by G. Scharf (the elder) in 1834, five navvies are shown digging the foundations for rebuilding the Royal College of Surgeons. They all wear waistcoats over short-sleeved shirts, some having blue and white stripes and trousers. Their caps are red or blue and one navvy wears a stocking cap, called a brewer's cap.

In another sketch of 1834 a navvy working on a huge pipe in Tottenham Court Road wears a top hat.

Navvies at this date sometimes still wore breeches instead of trousers and brewers caps, and like dustmen, they often wore smocks as a form of protective clothing.

In his fascinating book *The Railway Navvies*, Terry Coleman states that in the 1840s

> their distinctive dress was moleskin[1] trousers, double-canvas shirts, velveteen square-tailed coats, hob-nail boots, gaudy handkerchiefs, white felt hats with the brims turned up—and rainbow waistcoats.

English navvies also made thousands of miles of railway abroad, and when the news came in 1862 that many were turned adrift in France and destitute because the French refused to employ them on any other work, beggars hoping to evoke sympathy affected to be navvies by imitating their dress. The following is a contemporary account of one of these beggars:

[1] Strong woollen cloth with a very short pile.

49. Navvies. (*a*) 1846. (*b*) 1861. See text.

He goes to Petticoat Lane, purchases a white smock frock, a purple or red plush waistcoat, profusely ornamented with wooden buttons, a coloured cotton neckerchief and a red night cap [resembling a brewer's cap].

If procurable . . . also coarse-ribbed grey worsted stockings and boots whose enormous weight is increased by several lbs. of iron nails . . . and bargains for a spade for show, while he begs.

Punch has provided pictures of two navvies. Fig. 49(a) in 1846 (still called a navigator) wears a smock or possibly his shirt worn as a smock. On his head is a brewer's cap often called a night cap. His trousers are rolled up. Fig. 49(b) 1861, has his trousers secured below the knee by ties called "yarks". The roll worn across his chest may be a sack. Navvies had to be tough, but their labour in building Britain's network of railways can never be under-estimated.

CHAPTER IV

TRADESMEN AND CRAFTSMEN I

CARPENTERS AND PAPER CAPS, BUILDERS, SMITHS, TEXTILE WORKERS, TAILORS

CARPENTERS

Carpentry, always a staple industry, and possibly on account of its sacred association, is fairly widely illustrated in medieval manuscripts. Figure 50 shows an eleventh-century carpenter working on a block of wood with an adze. He wears a short tunic only. In a picture of 1320 showing the building of the ark with half a dozen carpenters at work, some, especially those at work on the ark, have their tunics shortened by having the skirt portion knotted in front; others wear girdles. The tunics are variously coloured blue, red or white. The stockings, or hose, are red or green, but some men are barelegged. All wear black shoes and all are bareheaded (St Omer Psalter, B.M. MS. YT. 14, f. 7).

50. Carpenter in short tunic and hatless. 11th century.

PLATE 13

PLATE 13

(*a*) Fisher girls, 1890.

*Detail from painting "Breakfast for the Porth" by J. C. Hook,
Birmingham Museum and Art Gallery.*

(*b*) Yorkshire fisherfolk, 1814.

Engraving after G. Walker in Costume of Yorkshire. *1814.*

PLATE 14

PLATE 14

(a) Miner in costume of the period, but he wears an unusual round cap on his head, possibly protective. A candle is held in his mouth. *c.* 1570.

Brass, All Saints' Church, Newland, Gloucestershire. Photograph supplied by National Monuments Record. Crown copyright.

(b) "The Collier"; his white suit may have been an attempt at hygiene as it required frequent washing. 1814.

Engraving after G. Walker in Costume of Yorkshire. *1814.*

The *Holkham Bible Picture Book, c.* 1330, has a number of scenes showing carpenters at work. Noah with an adze, starting work on the ark, wears
a hitched-up blue tunic, a blue hood lined with orange and a "Jew's hat".
His brown shoes with an ankle strap over a tongue are shown to be extremely supple by his position with one foot curved over the rung of a
ladder.

Joseph, who was a professional carpenter, is shown at work with an axe.
He wears a blue embroidered tunic, orange-coloured hose, short brown
boots, a "Jew's hat" and gauntlet gloves.

In all these examples no supertunics are seen, as these would probably
have been not only inconvenient but too warm.

51. Carpenters with tunics hitched up. Both hatless. Early 14th
century.

In Fig. 51, where the two carpenters are sawing through a large wood
beam, both have their tunics hitched up. (a)'s tunic is blue, with brown hose
and dark shoes, while (b)'s tunic is brown and he wears orange-coloured
soled hose (early fourteenth century).

Tunics, called "cotes" in the fourteenth century, were obviously inconvenient garments for manual work and were therefore generally hitched up
by means of a girdle or by knotting, as with land workers.

Later in the fifteenth century carpenters appear in the much more convenient attire fashionable for their day.

In an historical survey of the timber trade[1] a late fifteenth-century carpenter is shown wearing a close-fitting belted doublet, long tight hose, short boots, and a small round cap. A dagger is suspended from his belt and in his right hand he holds a saw. Aprons begin to appear at this time. In *Speculum Humanae Salvationum*, showing Solomon and the building of the Temple, the carpenter wears a knee-length buff apron, over a white shirt, orange-coloured hose with feet—no shoes and no headgear (B.M. MS. Harl. 2838, f. 7).

> What trade art thou? Why, Sir, a carpenter.
> Where is thy leather apron and thy rule?
>
> > 1601. Shakespeare, *Julius Caesar*, I. i. 58.

Master carpenters dressed in the fashion of the day, but were generally depicted holding a square or dividers, or both. A Master carpenter in 1656 is shown wearing a coat to mid-thigh with decorated button-holes down the front and slashed sleeves; full breeches, stockings and shoes with ribbon ties. He wears a broad-brimmed sugar-loaf hat. These were very fashionable from the 1640s to the 1670s in spite of the inconvenient shape.

52. Master Carpenter in fashionable clothes. 1698.

1 *Timber, Its Development and Distribution,* by Bryan Latham (C. Harrap & Co., 1957).

Sugar-loaf hats which are so mightily affected of late . . . so incommodious
for use that every puff of wind deprives us of them, requiring the employment of one hand to keep them on.

1653. John Bulwer, Artificial Changeling.

John Scott (Fig. 52), in 1698 Master Carpenter to His Majesty, wears the
new style of long coat with full, rather short sleeves and waistcoat sleeves
emerging.

Carpenters of the seventeenth century worked with or without aprons,
as is shown in the following figures from R. Holme's *Armory*. The first is
thus described by him (Fig. 53):

> A carpenter with a cap on his head, sable turned-up . . . cloathed in a short
> coat girt about the middle, grey; Breeches and Hose, russet; . . . A square
> in his right hand, and his Axe or Hatchet on his shoulder.

(Second half seventeenth century.)

The joiner wears a short apron (Fig. 54).

Eighteenth-century carpenters usually wore aprons, but nothing to distinguish them as carpenters, apart from their tools.

53. Carpenter with the signs of his trade. See
text.

54. Joiner wearing shirt and short apron, full
breeches. *c.* 1688.

In the early nineteenth century the men usually worked in shirts and breeches and large aprons (Fig. 55), some with pointed bibs buttoned to the shirt in front. Heads were bare or small skull-caps were worn (Fig. 56).

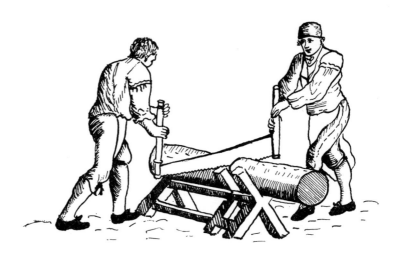

55. Carpenters in shirts, breeches and aprons. One wears a cap, as
they are working out of doors. 1807.

56. Wheelwrights at work. All wear aprons. 1807.

Soon, however, the carpenter was recognized by his paper cap (Fig. 57). This cap was also adopted by many other trades, as described in the section following.

57. Carpenter in shirt sleeves, breeches, still worn for convenience, apron and the celebrated paper cap. 1842.

58. Carpenter in short coat, apron swathed round waist as he is on his way to work, trousers and paper cap. 1867.

In the second half of the nineteenth century trousers replaced breeches (Fig. 58). Although in the 1830s and 1840s carpenters have been shown wearing cut-away tailcoats, trousers, and even top-hats, these were not the rule.

A true carpenter could always be known by his paper cap (Fig. 59). To paraphrase an old saying:

the grand distinguishing mark of a fine carpenter is the wearing of a paper cap.

PAPER CAPS

Paper caps and hats are traditionally associated with fun and games at Christmas-time. Paper caps, however, were seriously associated with certain trades throughout the nineteenth century. They were not pointed like that worn by the man in *Alice in Wonderland* (1865) who "was dressed in white paper", but square and small like that worn by the carpenter in the same book (Fig. 60). These curious little caps have consequently come to be thought of as carpenter's caps, but they were also worn by a surprisingly large number of other tradesmen, as will be seen in the following list taken from contemporary illustrations.

Braziers (1804) and (1823)

Bookbinders (1860)

Coffee-grinders (1850)

Coopers (1860)

Glass-blowers (1805)

Glaziers (1823)

Gold-beaters and polishers (1860)

Grocers (1831–4)

Hatters (1823), (1845) and (1860) (Fig. 61)

Manchester operatives (1842) (Fig. 62)

Masons (1823)

Painters (1869) (Fig. 64)

Paper-makers (1805, (1823) and today

Picture-frame gilders (1860)

Plumbers (1860)

Printers (1823) and (1860)

Soap-boilers (1811)

Stage hands (1851)

Sugar-loaf cutters (1845)

Tallow-chandlers (1823)

Tinmen (1823) and (1860)

Tobacco workers (1845)

Warp-scourers (1844)

Wheelwrights (1846) (Fig. 63)

Wine merchant's employee (1849–50)

This outburst of paper caps in the first half of the nineteenth century was probably due to the fact that paper was becoming cheap. As late as 1818, in

59. "Crusty Carpenter" talking to "facetious old gent". Carpenter known by his paper cap. 1878.

60. Carpenters wearing paper caps. (*a*) 1872. (*b*) 1860s.

order to conserve paper, it was a punishable offence to produce a newspaper exceeding 22 × 32 inches.

In 1807 a paper-making machine began to be made in England, and in 1840 a wood-pulping machine was used, bringing down the cost of paper still further, and hence a song in 1866 "The Age of Paper".

References to the paper caps are rare, but we find that Mr Jorrocks wore one.

61. Hatters in paper caps, making top hats. 1860.

62. "Manchester Operative" in short coat, breeches, apron and paper cap. 1842.

At the farther end of the warehouse, a man in his short sleeves, with a white apron round his waist and a brown paper cap on his head was seen holding his head over something. . . . The Yorkshireman . . . asking if Mr Jorrocks was in, found he was addressing the grocer himself. . . .

"Bravo," exclaimed Jorrocks, throwing his paper cap in the air . . .

1831–4. R. S. Surtees, *Jorrocks' Jaunts and Jollities*.

63. Wheelwright, in waistcoat, trousers, apron and paper cap. 1846.

64. Typical workingman's garb with paper cap, 1863. (Cartoons: Lord Palmerston as plasterer, Lord Russell as carpenter.)

Again, in 1849, the head boy in a wine merchant's shop is thus described: (Fig. 65).

> His name was Mick Walker, and he wore a ragged apron and a paper cap.
> Charles Dickens, *David Copperfield*.

A curious advertisement in the *Suffolk Chronicle and Ipswich Advertiser and County Express* of 1833, on 2nd March, states:

> Gentlemen's superfine Hats 21/- — 25/-
> Silk Hats.
> No Paper Hats sold.

So paper hats evidently belonged to manual workers, and they can even be seen today worn by workmen on building sites in Rome! In England, too, paper caps have continued to be used in industry in the twentieth century, primarily in the baking and allied food trades, where a high standard of hygiene is required. They are also worn by men working in trades where spray painting is used, such as furniture and metal trades.

What should we do without paper caps, even at Christmas-time?

65. Wine Merchant's Head Boy in shirt,
trousers, apron and paper cap. 1849–50.

BUILDERS

With the help of masons, the most glorious structures in the World have
been set up; as if their art did endeavour to imitate the Hand-Works of God,
in making little Worlds in the great Fabrick of the Universe.

1688. R. Holme, *Academy of Armory.*

After masonry was introduced into Britain under the Emperor Claudius in
A.D. 43, masons gradually became important people. Freemasons are de-
scended from the Medieval Fraternity of Masons, which flourished in the
days of monastic architecture. After having served their turn of apprentice-
ship they became free to apply for work to any body of masons anywhere.
Secret signs or passwords were given as tokens of genuineness.

In the Fabric Rolls of York Minster, 1355,[1] orders were issued for the
guidance of masons:

It was usual for this church to find tunics, aprons, gloves and clogs, and to
give occasional "drinks" and remuneration for extra work.

[1] Published by Surtees Society, Vol. 35, 1858.

The art of brick-making died out at the end of the Roman occupation and the English only started making bricks in about 1200, on a small scale, so that bricklayers as such are not found in early manuscripts.

With ordinary dwelling-houses fire was a constant danger, and in the fifteenth century brick was sometimes used to replace timber.

> Also that no chymneys of Tymber be suffred, ne thacched houses within the Cyte, but that the owners do hem awey, and make them chymneys of stone or *Bryke* by mydsomer day next commynge, and to tyle the thacched houses by the seid day, in peyn of lesynge of a noble.
>
> 1467. *Ordinances of Worcester* in *English Gilds.*

The early builders, therefore, were masons using stone.

A good example of the clothes worn by these workmen is shown in a thirteenth-century drawing of the building of St Alban's Cathedral (Fig. 66). All the men wear short tunics pulled up by girdles. The man on the wall

66. Building of St. Alban's Cathedral. See text. 1220–59.

67. Builders all wearing short tunics tucked up by the girdle or belt.
13th century.

(*right*), placing a stone, shows the front vent to this tunic-skirt and he wears
a coif, a close-fitting linen cap tied under the chin. This is also worn by one
of the men below using a winch. Both the men using choppers wear gauntlet
gloves and the one under the right-hand arch wears a hood with its cape
falling round his neck. The master builder is distinguished by wearing a long
tunic and a mantle. He is bareheaded because he is talking to the King (not
shown) (*Life of Offa*, by Mathew Paris).

Another thirteenth-century illumination shows the workmen similarly
clothed in hitched-up tunics and on their heads coifs or hoods (Fig. 67). The
man on the extreme right under the ladder has both, but his hood is thrown
back over his shoulders. All wear footed hose without shoes. These hose were
usually soled with leather.

An early fourteenth-century manuscript shows workmen in short blue
tunics, orange-coloured hose and black shoes.

Queen Mary's Psalter, showing "How Solomon the king built the Temple as David the King his father had commanded", depicts two masons at work, and one is wearing a supertunic or surcote, a loose garment worn over the tunic or cote. He also wears a hood.

The *Holkham Bible Picture Book, c.* 1330, has an illustration showing masons at work in tunics tucked up well above the knees and blue or brown hoods with short liripipes (i.e. pendant tails to hoods).

An extremely interesting manuscript of 1360, in which masons are depicted building the Tower of Babel, shows workmen wearing garments of a most unusual type, i.e. fringed footless hose, like those of the shepherds in Plate 3a. The man with the trowel suspends a container for this tool from his belt. The man on the ladder wears these strange footless hose fringed round the ankle. (Fig. 68.)

68. Masons building the Tower of Babel. See
text. 1360.

In an early-fifteenth-century scene of the building of the Temple two masons are shown wearing short blue surcotes over red cotes (previously called supertunic and tunic). They wear knee-length buff aprons, probably of leather, hose, ankle-strapped shoes and hats with turned-up brims (B.M. Harl. MS. 2838, f. 35).

Builders in the fifteenth century are more frequently shown wearing aprons and also hats, than previously.

In the splendid mid-fifteenth-century illumination showing the building of Hunstanton many builders are at work (see Plate 16a). All wear what were at this date called jackets. The jacket was close fitting, waisted and worn with a narrow belt. The length of the skirt varied, but in the unfashionable form as here it fell in loose folds to mid-thigh or knees. The man with the pickaxe wears a tall hat with rolled brim, slightly old-fashioned, and the man with the spade a style called a chaperon. He also wears stout leather boots called buskins. The man at the winch wears short ankle boots and on his head a coif. The other men are bareheaded with their hair cut in the bowl-crop style fashionable from 1410 to 1460. What is significant is that all these men wear white aprons, thus supplying some form of protective clothing during work. The master mason talking to the King is clothed in a long-waisted houppelande, i.e. gown, and piked shoes which were now returning to fashion. The King, in his long ceremonial gown and wearing his crown, watches the proceedings (*Life of St Edmund*).

> He bilt roial town
> which stant ther yit for a manier mynde
> ffor his arrivaile into this region
> which is this day called Hunstanton.
>
> B.M. Harl. MS. 2278, f. 28v.

In another miniature of the same manuscript a monumental mason who is chiselling a royal tomb wears a blue doublet, parti-coloured soled hose, one red, one white, a tall green hat and a brown apron, almost certainly made of leather (B.M. Harl. MS. 2278, f. 68v).

The next picture (Fig. 69) is a composite figure (1475) showing a worker in wood, stone and iron. His garments are obviously those worn for any of these trades. His doublet with a stand collar and laced down the front follows the contemporary style, as do his piked shoes and cap with rolled-up brim. His long apron does, however, indicate that he is a workman, even if he had not been drawn with an adze, a hammer, a trowel in his girdle and the blacksmith's anvil and tongs at his side.

In a picture belonging to the Society of Antiquaries, a number of masons are shown at work on the building of Ely Cathedral church, in about 1425, recorded in *The Legend of St Etheldreda*. They all wear white aprons, one of which is square bibbed, otherwise their costume is in the fifteenth-century style, with doublets and hose (tights) in various colours (Fig. 70).

69. A composite figure representing a carpenter, mason and smith. 1483.

70. Mason wearing doublet, hose and an apron. His hair in the
fashionable "bowl-crop" style. *c.* 1425.

PLATE 15

PLATE 15

(*a*) Surface workers. One man sifting coal wears a bibbed apron. The rest have no protective clothing. *c.* 1830–50.

Detail of a painting by an unknown British artist. Walker Art Gallery, Liverpool.

(*b*) Stone breakers on the road in Yorkshire. 1814. See p. 68.

Engraving after G. Walker in Costume of Yorkshire. *1814.*

PLATE 16

PLATE 16

(*a*) Masons building Hunstanton.
See text. *c.* 1433.

British Museum. MS. Harl. 2278.

(*b*) Brick makers. 1901–10.

By courtesy of Essex Record Office.

Masons in the sixteenth and seventeenth centuries appear to be dressed quite simply in the fashion of their day, but they usually wore some kind of protective apron.

In our next picture (Fig. 71) the mason, *c.* 1688, is described as wearing a "wastecoat [in those days sleeved], a hat, breeches, stockings and shoes". His apron from the waist is flecked and therefore probably of leather.

In a pack of playing-cards, time of James II, the ten of diamonds depicts two bricklayers building a wall. They are similarly dressed as in Fig. 71, but one has his sleeves rolled up and wears a night-cap, the soft round cap often worn for comfort during the day in spite of its name.

71. Mason in waistcoat, hat and breeches.
c. 1688.

Aprons and usually hats were worn by eighteenth-century masons.

In the nineteenth century, although jackets were sometimes worn, these were generally discarded and the men worked in shirt sleeves and waistcoats which were now sleeveless (Fig. 72). Some, however, worked in old-fashioned waistcoats with sleeves (Fig. 73), a style that was also often worn by ostlers and later by railway porters. A coloured print, after the same artist as Fig. 72, shows a mason (this time without waistcoat) wearing a short buff-

72. Mason in waistcoat, breeches, stockings and boots, plus apron and
hat. 1803.

coloured jacket, brown breeches, pale blue stockings, grey spats, black boots, slouch hat, red shirt and green necktie.

Like other working men, masons continued to wear breeches long after these went out of fashion, but in Victorian times most of them adopted trousers.

The bricklayer's labourer in 1841 is thus described in *Heads of the People*:

> His jacket of white flannel is powdered with the mingled dust of lime and brick; his stockings are white worsted, similarly spangled; his brogues, guiltless of blacking, and his cap a low flat round cap, of grey skin, does not descend low on the back of his head, so that you see his thick, bushy, lime-powdered hair curling beneath it.

Dickens in his *Sketches by Boz*, (*Seven Dials*) has an amusing description of bricklayer's labourers off duty:

> We never saw a regular bricklayer's labourer take any other recreation, fighting excepted. Pass through St Giles's in the evening of a week-day, there they are in their fustian dresses spotted with brick dust and whitewash, leaning against posts. Walk through Seven Dials on Sunday morning—there they are again, drab or light corduroy trousers, Blucher boots, blue coats, and great yellow waistcoats. The idea of a man dressing himself in his best clothes, to lean against a post all day!

1834–6.

Hardy's description of a mason in the 1840s from *Under the Greenwood Tree* is of great interest:

Being by trade a mason, he wore a long linen apron, reaching almost to his toes, corduroy breeches and gaiters, which, together with his boots, graduated in tints of whitish-brown by constant friction against lime and stone. He also wore a very stiff fustian coat, having folds at the elbows and shoulders as unvarying in their arrangement as those in a pair of bellows: the ridges and the projecting parts of the coat collectively exhibiting a shade different from that of the hollows, which were lined with small ditch-like accumulations of stone and mortar dust.

The extremely large side pockets sheltered beneath wide flaps, bulged out

73. Bricklayer in sleeved waistcoat and trousers, protected by a large apron. He wears a soft hat. 1824.

conversely whether empty or full; and as he was often engaged to work at buildings far away—his breakfast and dinners . . . he carried in these pockets.

In 1842 *The Complete Book of Trades* depicts two house-painters. One wears a short frockcoat, the other a very short jacket. Both are in trousers and both wear aprons. One is bareheaded, the other has a peaked cap.

A superior sort of mason is described by Surtees in *Hillingdon Hall*, 1844:

> Joshua (a mason by trade) . . . there was an air of respectability about Joshua, which aided by a low-crowned broad-brimmed hat, a well brushed coat, and the unusual appendage of a pair of gloves, bespoke him a remove or so from the common herd. Gloves are very unusual wear in the country. . . .

In the 1850s paperhangers are found wearing bowler hats or even wide-awakes, otherwise known as billy-cocks (low-brimmed soft hats with the brim curled up on one side). Some are in shirts only with the sleeves rolled up, some wear jackets (*Wood's Catalogue*, p. 249, No. 3355).

From Flora Thompson's reminiscences in *Over to Candleford* we have the following description of a mason in the 1880s:

> As Laura first remembered him, he was . . . a young man in the late twenties. On account of the dusty white nature of his work, he usually wore clothes of some strong light grey worsted material . . . She could see him (in memory still), a white apron rolled up around his middle, a basket of tools slung over his shoulder and a black billycock hat set at an angle on his head.

The City of Leicester Museum has a stonemason's cap of white velvet (*c.* 1860–70).

In repairs done to houses following an earthquake in 1884, builders are shown wearing jackets, but most are working in waistcoats and shirt sleeves. Their headgear varies from bowler hats to soft felts.

In the early twentieth century shirts and trousers, often secured with yarks or strings below the knee to prevent dust from being blown up the trouser leg, were the usual dress. Some men preferred breeches and gaiters, but all usually wore soft cloth peaked caps, and a sweat rag round the neck was sometimes added (see Plate 16b).

SMITHS

Blacksmiths of the eleventh century, illustrated in the Saxon Calendar (B.M. MS. Tiberius B.V.), are dressed like the labourers, in the dress of their day. The tunic is short, ending above the knee, and belted. They wear shoes but no headgear. An extremely interesting smith of 1330 shown in the *Holkham Bible Picture Book* (Fig. 74) is actually a woman who is at the

74. Female Smith making nails for the cross. Her bibbed apron is unusual at this period. 1330.

anvil making nails for the cross. Her long brown surcote worn over the kirtle to the ground is protected by a white apron with shoulder straps. She wears the usual barbette and fillet on her head over a hairnet known as a fret. Her husband, also a smith, but explaining to the Jew that he was unable to do the work owing to a bad hand, wears a blue tunic covered by an apron similar to his wife's and black boots. A brown hood falls round his shoulders and on his head he wears a white coif under a round blue hat with a red stalk, a style which indicates that he is master of his craft. Leather aprons, however, were common for smiths in the fourteenth century.

Swart smoky smiths smutted with smoke
Drive me to death with their din and their dints

. . . . . .

Of a bull's hide are their big aprons;
Their shanks are sheathed against sparks of fire.

c. 1350. B.M. MS., Arundel 292, f. 72b.

Through the next centuries leather aprons and soft caps persisted, but the caps ceased to have status significance. A smith in 1641 from a Thomason Tract wears an apron with a pointed bib and a round cap. His shirt sleeves are rolled up and his breeches are open at the knees, one of the styles worn at this date.

At a later date, *c.* 1660–80, two smiths are shown at work in Fig. 75. Both are in shirts, full knee-breeches as was the fashion, and bibless aprons to the knees with tassels at the corners. These tassels occurring on working aprons are interesting, since at this period tassels were the rage. They were added as decorations to bandstrings (i.e. collar ties), handkerchiefs, pantaloons (petti-coat breeches), sashes, purses and canes. Both men wear soft round caps, one is profusely decorated. It was a style worn for informal wear by the fashion-able world at this time.

Eighteenth-century smiths wore shirts with breeches and leather aprons (Fig. 76). If working out of doors their heads were covered, but if indoors they either worked bareheaded wearing their natural hair, or wore night-caps over a shaved head, the wig being discarded. Wigs were worn by all

75. Two Smiths at work. See text. *c.* 1661.

76. Farrier. See text. 1770s.

classes at this time and must have been far too hot to wear at work. The effect of heat is observed in the following quotation, where once again women are described as making nails. (Compare this with the fourteenth-century female smith.)

> When I first approached Birmingham, says Mr Hutton, from Walsall in 1741, I was surprised at the prodigeous number of blacksmiths' shops . . . In some of these I observed . . . females strypt of their upper garment and not overcharged with their lower, wielding the hammer with all the grace of the sex . . . "they are nailors".
>
> *Hone's Table Book II.*

Coppersmiths of 1804, shown in Pyne's *Microcosm*, wear short coats, breeches and small round caps (Fig. 77). The invaluable leather apron is used as a lap for a sheet of metal. It was also used as a pad for the horse's hoof by the farrier in Fig. 76 in 1770, and similarly again in 1807 (Fig. 78). This drawing also shows the fringed leather apron worn by the blacksmith holding the horse. Both these men wear small round caps.

Through the nineteenth century the leather apron continued, generally with a substantial bib, and by 1840 trousers replaced breeches (see Plate 17a). In

77. Coppersmiths at work. See text. 1804.

Fig. 79 the smith still wears a small soft cap. A stout leather apron is worn by the blacksmith in Landseer's painting "Shoeing the Bay Mare" in 1844.

Flora Thompson, recalling village life in the 1890s, says:

> The smiths left anvil and tools and forge and fire . . . and hurried out (to see the Meet) to a little hillock . . . where they stood . . . with their fringed leather aprons flapping about their legs. . . . It was still the custom in that

78. Farriers at work. See text. 1807.

79. Smith in strong leather bibbed apron. 1847.

trade for unmarried workmen to live-in with the families of their employers; and at meal-times, when the indoor contingent was already seated
... "the men", as they were always called, would appear, rolling their leather
aprons up around their waists as they tiptoed to their places at table.

Flora Thompson, *Lark Rise to Candleford*, 1954.

TEXTILE WORKERS

In the textile trade up to the nineteenth century the spinning, carding and
much of the weaving was done by women, a large proportion of whom
were simply housewives working at home.

Their clothes were consequently in the style of their period, which in
medieval days meant that the kirtle and or gown was long to the ground and
often trained, in spite of its inconvenience (Fig. 80). After the thirteenth
century these women generally wore aprons. With the exception of young
girls, their heads were always covered by a veil or coverchief (a draped headwear falling round the face and back or other headgear).

80. Young girl in long kirtle, spinning. No headdress indicates that
she is not a married woman. 1320.

In Fig. 81 the spinner has pulled her veil in under the chin to get it out of
the way, but her kirtle trails on the ground.

The weaver's veil in Fig. 82 is worn in the usual way.

In the sixteenth century we find women working at primitive factories,
the most famous being that known as *Jack of Newbury's Clothing Factory*.

> A hundred women merily
> Were carding hard with joyfull cheere
> . . . . . .
> And in a chamber close beside
> Two hundred maidens did abide
> In petticoats of Stammel red
> And milkwhite kerchers on their head
> Their smock sleeves like to winter snow
> That on the Western mountains flow
> And each sleeve with a silken band
> Was featly tied at the hand.
> These pretty maids did never lin [leave off]
> But in that place all day did spin.
>
> 1597. T. Deloney's Ballad.

81. Married woman in veil (= headdress), long kirtle and apron.
Early 14th century.

82. Weaver in veil and long kirtle. *c.* 1360.

In the seventeenth century two men employed in spinning and weaving are shown at work (Fig. 83). Both are dressed alike in short doublets and breeches and both wear tall-crowned hats called sugar-loaf hats. Neither have aprons, but according to Pepys weavers were among those who had a fondness for blue or green aprons. In a street fight in London in 1664, between weavers and butchers, he says:

> At first the butchers knocked down all the weavers that had blue or green aprons, till they were fain to pull them off and put them in their breeches.
>
> 26th July 1664.

In the eighteenth century both men and women were employed in textile factories. Hogarth shows men and women at work in 1747; both sexes wear the fashion of their day and the only difference between the apprentices and the master is that he wears a "tricorne" hat, while they are bareheaded. The women, as was the rule, wear caps.

The *Universal Magazine* of 1748, showing "the Method of Winding and Twisting of Silk for the Weavers", has an illustration of women at the

83. Two men weavers. Both in contemporary style clothes. 1636.

machine. Their skirts are bunched up to hip-level, showing the underskirt, which is short—well above the ankle—and their caps are tied under the chin.

In 1799 we have a fascinating list of clothes allowed to spinning girls "in proportion to their labour" working in a York Charity School.

> Spinners from four to six hanks a day had a Stuff gown, two linen Bedgowns, Two Shifts, Two pair of Shoes, Two checked handkerchiefs [i.e. headker-chiefs], Two blue aprons, a straw hat, Two pair of stockings, Three ounces of Worsted, shoes mended twice, 1 Wolsey Petticoat.

Additional grants were made according to the number of hanks spun in a day.

Six Hanks — a checked apron.
Seven hanks — a cap, a coloured shawl, a pair of pattens.
Eight hanks — a green riband round the Hat,
a pair of worsted mittens.
Ten hanks — a better shawl, a wolsey petticoat, one shift, one white apron.
Eleven hanks — one cap, a stuff petticoat with the gown.
Twelve hanks— one checked apron.
a black bonnet.

Stays are allowed to those who have regularly spun seven hanks per day for one year. Cloaks are lent and when the girls go to service, are given to them if they have behaved well in the school.

The knitters are also supplied with each a Gown, a Handkerchief, a Cloak for their Sunday dress.

1799. Mrs Edwin Gray, *Papers and Diaries of a York Family 1764–1839*.

In *The Cottage Industry in Yorkshire* in 1814 a young girl is shown at a spinning-wheel. She wears simple clothes of her date; a white bodice with a pink-and-white squared neckerchief, a green skirt and a white mob cap and an apron (Fig. 84).

It is interesting to compare this illustration with Fig. 81, about 450 years earlier.

Wensley Dale knitters in 1814, from *Costume of Yorkshire*, are shown in Plate 17b. They are all in unfashionable country clothes. The woman, standing, wears a long-waisted jacket over a short skirt, and an apron. She also has a soft hooded scarf under her hat. The book states:

84. Young girl spinning. See text. 1814.

In any business where the assistance of the hands is not necessary, they uni-versally resort to knitting . . . A Woman . . . walked to market three miles away to do her shopping with the weekly knitting of herself and family packed in a bag on her head, knitting all the way. . . . She was so expeditious and expert, that the produce of the day's labour was generally a complete pair of men's stockings.

A contemporary writer has this to say about knitting:

Knit stockings are made with needles of polished iron . . . In England knitting is not much carried on as a trade, but in country places most female servants are expected to be able to fill up their time in this way. . . . The Scotch are said to make the best stockings of any people in Europe, and they sell at enormously high prices, from thirty shillings to four or five pounds a pair.

1811. *The Book of Trades*, Part IV.

Knitting-pads were often worn by Scots women knitters. The pad, made of leather, and perforated with holes to support a long knitting-needle, was fastened by a belt round the waist of the knitter.

In 1818 a man at a hand loom wears a tailcoat, tight pantaloons, cravat, shoes and no headgear, but his smart suit is protected by an apron from the waist (R. Phillips' *Book of English Trades*).

A poor Spitalfields weaver, working at home is thus described in 1841:

> There are two looms in the apartment, at one end of which is seated the father, a jaded man in a worsted nightcap and a pair of grey stocking sleeves. At the other loom is employed a sickly boy of ten years of age, clad in a calico nightshirt and a pair of corduroy trousers suspended by a piece of list running transversely over his shoulders.
>
> *Heads of the People*—Section by Arthur Armitage.

From early times children were employed in these Textile Factories:

> Spinning the hard silk and winding it employs a great number of hands of all ages.
>
> 1811. *The Book of Trades*, Part III.

In Manchester the textile workers, both women and children, in 1842 wore over their ordinary clothes long pinafores with short sleeves and tied at the back of the neck (see Plate 18a).

TAILORS

Tailors and dressmakers, who used the materials made by the textile workers, followed the fashions of their day and were sometimes extra smart. An amusing example is given by the writer of *Debate between Pride and Lowliness* in 1568. A tailor, riding in a group of country folk, gives himself away by having a threaded needle stuck in his coat; otherwise he passed for a "knight or squire":

> Piked he was and handsome in his weede:
> A faire blacke coate of cloth withouten sleve,
>   And buttoned the shoulder round about;
> Of xx s a yard, as I beleeve,
>   And layd upon with parchment lace without.
>
> His dublet was of sattin very fine,
>   And it was cut and stitched very thick:
> Of silke it had a costly enterlyne;
>   His shirt had bands & ruffe of pure cambrick.

His upper stocks of sylken grograne
   And to his hips they sat full close & trym,
And laced very costly every pane.
   Their lyning was of satten as I wyn.

His nether stockes of silke accordingly;
   A velvet gyrdle rounde about his waist
I . . . Sawe where a needle sticked on his brest
   And at the same a blacke threed hanging by.

Throughout the following centuries fashionable tailors dressed like the gentlemen of their day. A slight exception is shown in Hogarth's engraving of 1735 (Fig. 85), where the tailor wears, for comfort's sake, a banyan (an

85. Tailor measuring for gentleman's suit. 1735.

PLATE 17

PLATE 17

(*a*) Smiths working in shirt sleeves, waistcoats and trousers
with aprons. They both have round black caps. 1840s.

Detail of coloured engraving Smith's and Farrier's Shop or Veterinary Forge
*published by Darton. By kind permission of the Museum of English Rural Life,
Reading.*

(*b*) Wensley Dale knitters. See text. 1814.

Engraving after G. Walker in Costume of Yorkshire. *1814.*

PLATE 18

PLATE 18

(*a*) Women factory workers, dressed in the style of their day, with protective aprons. 1842.

After a drawing by T. Allom in Lancashire, its History, Legends and Manufactures *by the Rev. G. N. Wright. 1842.*

(*b*) Cross-legged tailor of 20th century.

Photograph from the Bagshawe Collection. By courtesy of T. W. Bagshawe.

elegant negligee) and a night-cap. Generally speaking, however, these workers, who were helping to build up the fashions, demonstrated that:

One had as good be out of the World as out of the fashion.

1696. Colley Cibber, *Love's Last Shift.*

The traditional image of the tailor, as a man in his waistcoat, sitting cross-legged at work, is just as true as the picture painted above. The one describes him when cutting and sewing, the other when measuring and fitting his client (see Plate 18b).

CHAPTER V

TRADESMEN AND CRAFTSMEN 2

BUTCHERS, MILLERS, BAKERS, COOKS, LIQUOR TRADE, STREET VENDORS

BUTCHERS

As with other trades, no protective garments appear to have been worn by early medieval butchers (Fig. 86). In an eleventh-century manuscript a butcher, dressing the huntsman's meat, is shown wearing the ordinary clothes of his time, a short tunic, shoes and no headgear (B.M. MS. Claudius B IV).

86. Man in long tunic with two vents, coif on head, slaughtering pig. (St. Swithin's Psalter "November"). 1150–60.

Later, in the fourteenth century, two butchers are depicted; one, who is killing a pig, wears a long tunic hitched up by a belt, a coif on his head, but he is barefooted. The other, who is laying open the carcass of a pig, wears a short tunic, but shoes and no coif (Queen Mary's Psalter, 1320).

Towards the end of the fourteenth century we find butchers wearing aprons. The butcher on a misericord at Worcester Cathedral, about to axe an ox, wears an apron over his fashionably low–belted doublet and long hose (1397) (see Plate 19a opp. p. 128).

In the sixteenth century we have the "Inventory of John Powle butcher, made 27th February, 1590".

> *His apparayle*
> 3 bands [i.e. collars]
> a gowne
> 2 clokes
> a pair of breeches
> 2 pair of stockens and a hatt
>
> Sum £3. 4. 0.

Evidently a high-class tradesman.

When at work, however, upper garments were usually discarded and the butchers worked in shirt sleeves.

> And work in their shirts too, as myself, for example, that am a butcher.
>
> 1591. *2 Henry VI*, IV. 7, l. 57.

Aprons, however, symbolized work and were therefore considered taboo in London for butchers on festive occasions in the early seventeenth century.

> Ordinances for the Butchers 19th August 1607.
>
> *49 Item.*   It is ordered that noe persons using . . . the saide art or mystery nor his nor theire nor any of their servantes shall hereafter stande or goe abroad in any open streete or lane within the Citty of London or one myle of the same Cittye upon any Sonday or other festivall day with any Aprone about hym.
>
> *Livery*
>
> *52 Item.*   for that decent and comely apparell is to be used by the Citizens of soe noble a Cittye as London is. It is therefore ordered that every person and persons being or that hereafter shall be in the livery of the Company of Butchers whensoever he shall weare his livery gowne and whood, shall weare therewith a rounde Cappe of wooll and not a hatt. And that every person being . . . Maister or Warden of the saide art or mistery or any of their Assistants shall sit in the Courte and in all other Assemblies in this Common Hall[1] in a gowne and a Cappe and neither in cloake nor hatt. And that every freeman . . . come before the Maister and Wardens of the saide art and mystery sitting in the saide Hall or Courte . . . shall come before them in a gowne and not in a cloake.

[1] Butchers' Companies existed as early as 1355, but the butchers were incorporated by James I in 1605.

Apart, however, from the forbidden apron on "festival days" the apron for butchers became an essential accessory from the seventeenth century on, and the hall-mark of his trade was the steel slung from its tie.

In Fig. 87, 1641, the butcher wears a short apron from the waistline of his doublet. The apron has a pocket. His breeches and doublet are in the fashion of his day and his cap is the "rounde cappe of wooll".

87 (*a*) Butcher and (*b*) brewer, both wearing protective aprons. 1641.

Protective sleeves, according to Pepys, were now almost a distinguishing mark of butchers. Describing the fray between London butchers and weavers, in which the butchers got the worst of it, he says:

> The butchers were fain to pull off their sleeves that they might not be known.
>
> 26th July 1664.

A butcher of 1688 wears a doublet, full knee-breeches, protected in front by leather apron, and on his head a small hat.

In the eighteenth century butchers are shown wearing aprons and soft round "night-caps".

In "The Country Butchers Shop", late eighteenth century, (painted by J. Ward and engraved by S. W. Reynolds), the butcher is shown outside, leaning against a window-sill loaded with meat. He wears a dark apron from the strings of which dangles his steel. The apron covers his breeches, but has no bib. He wears a sleeved waistcoat, stockings and buckled shoes; on his head a large dark round hat. In another of Ward's paintings the butcher's apron is blue. From this date to about the 1890s butcher's aprons were generally blue, though sometimes white.

By the nineteenth century protective sleeves were usual. These covered the coat sleeve from the wrist to above the elbow. They were white or blue and washable. Many, however, worked in their shirts with sleeves rolled up above the elbow (Fig. 88). Blue aprons were coming into fashion and also aprons with pointed bibs buttoned to a coat button.

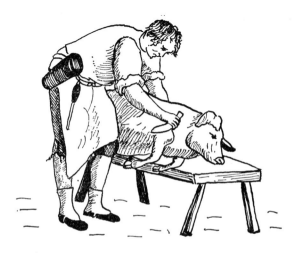

88. Butcher working in shirt, breeches, apron and spats. 1805.

Slaughtermen in 1805 are shown in Pyne's *Costume of Great Britain* attired thus:

Waistcoats striped red and white.

White shirts with sleeves rolled up.

Brown breeches and red fishermen's caps.

They are provided with two aprons, the upper is black and knee length, the under one appears to be of raw hide and has a triangular bib buttoned to the waistcoat. They wear leg shields (splashed with blood) and resembling hockey pads.

The butcher boy (Fig. 89) in 1824 wears a sleeved waistcoat which was now out of date and only worn by working people. His short boots, known

89. Butcher's boy delivering meat. 1824. See text.

as highlows, were worn mainly by countryfolk. His attire contrasts well with the fashionable gentleman beside him.

The butcher in 1828 (Fig. 90) wears a blue coat, a white apron, a red brewer's cap and black top boots with brown turnover tops. His steel is, of course, in evidence. He obviously enjoys a smoke. (The waiter is all in brown with a white apron.)

The following is part of a letter from Benjamin Robert Haydon to Miss Mary Russell Mitford, 18th August 1826:

> The other night I paid my butcher . . . and he drew up his beefy shiny face, clean shaved, with a clean blue cravat under his chin, a clean jacket, a clean apron, and a pair of hands that would pin an ox to the earth if he was obstreperous.

Through the first half of the nineteenth century the brewer's cap and blue coat became conspicuous features of the butcher's outfit. "He dressed in the usual blue garb of the butcher", is Mayhew's description of a hawking butcher in 1851. Top-hats were worn at this date (Fig. 91) and later bowler hats were correct (Fig. 92).

Towards the end of this century, however, headgear appears to have been discarded by many butchers, until the famous straw hat appeared on the scenes. In the 1890s:

> Mr Rooksby, like all butchers of the period wore blue overalls, but no hat: no butcher wore a hat in those days and together with Bluecoat boys, were the only males one saw abroad with uncovered heads. This was rather remarkable in an age when every man of every class looked upon it as an unspeakable lapse from grace to walk the streets hatless.
>
> F. Willis, *A Book of London Yesterdays*. 1960.

But going hatless did not last as far as butchers were concerned. By the turn of the century the straw boater hat was adopted by all butchers for summer wear and was even used as a tradesman's sign (Plates 19b and 61a) (opp. pp. 128 and 368).

90. Butcher wearing protective sleeves. See text. 1828.

91. Butcher in double-breasted cutaway coat, blue apron, trousers
and top hat. 1851.

In the first decade of the twentieth century, apart from the wearing of
frockcoats, butchers were using protective clothing in addition to their now
customary striped aprons. The frockcoats, made of serge, blue[1] jean or

1 Butcher's blue is a lighter shade of indigo.

92. Butcher in horizontally striped apron
and bowler hat. 1893.

bluette,[1] were well provided with pockets, two behind, two side pockets, one outside breast pocket and a ticket pocket. Protective sleeves were usually worn with these. Market porters wore long round smocks or "frocks" of white duck or plain blue (Fig. 93). Footwear was amply provided for, as will be seen by the illustrations in Chapter XIV (p. 345).

Last of all, for his all-important apron, he had a wide choice; these included "fleshers" of cotton or wool, white aprons of jean, drill or century cloth, macintosh aprons for market wear, black or yellow oilskin, slaughterhouse aprons, plain or with bib, and finally the best known of all, the butcher's striped apron, the blue and white stripes being set horizontally.[2] The correct butcher's outfit was thus described by a local family butcher today: "A butcher wore a straw hat in the summer, a bowler in the winter and a striped apron. A fishmonger's stripes are vertical, but a butcher's are

[1] Bluet, bluett, or bluette is a kind of woollen cloth of bluish colour.
[2] Today the fashion has changed, but in the North most butchers still prefer their stripes to be horizontal.

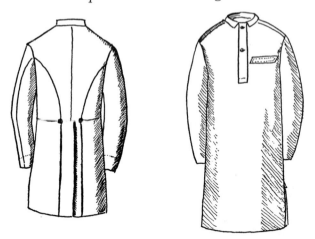

93 (*a*) Butcher's frock coat. (*b*) Market Porter's smock. 1909–12.

horizontal." When asked why these conventions, he thought for a time and then summed it all up with: "Well, you see, it's the proper rig."

MILLERS, BAKERS AND COOKS

There are three trades in the pursuit of which the worker is liable to become dusted over with flour—those of the miller, the baker and the cook. In consequence all three tend to wear white; and the interests of hygiene are served at the same time.

As to the miller, a glance must suffice. Chaucer introduces him thus:

> Ful big he was of braun and eek of bones; . . .
> A swerd and bokeler bar he by his syde; . . .
> . . . he hadde a thombe of gold, pardee.
> A *whyt cote* and a blew hood wered he.[1]

The "white cote" would, at this date, probably be an overgarment to the knee with wide sleeves—the cote-hardie of ordinary wear—but the whiteness was distinctive.

In a seventeenth-century ballad the miller's proverbial thumb and his "dusty necke" are mentioned, but not what he wore.[2] However, the "meal-

[1] *Canterbury Tales, c.* 1387. Edited by W. Skeat, 1894.
[2] Pepys' Collection, I. 206. B.L.

man" as he appeared in 1647 is shown in Fig. 253, and he proves to be one of the earliest tradesmen to adopt the apron. He has it again in the 1731 edition of Comenius's *Visible World*.

On very large estates a miller would be one of the lord's employees and so was supplied with his clothing. Thus at Ingatestone Hall, Essex, in Tudor times, the miller received a "livery" of mottled "grey marble" cloth like the other servants.[1]

In the nineteenth century millers typically wore smocks (white or off-white). A writer in *Hone's Table Book* of 1827 remembered when the *Miller of Mansfield* was played in a somewhat impromptu manner in a Wiltshire malthouse:

> The bell rang, the curtain went up, but before the miller could appear a *smockfrock* was called for from . . . the frocked rustics in the gallery and . . . a youth pulled off his upper-all, proudly observing that the player should have it because his was a sacred persuasion.

By the end of the century the millers changed their smocks for overalls, or went back to the "white coat" of Chaucer's day.

Compared with millers, bakers and cooks have always had to contend with more heat and aim at more cleanliness in harder conditions. For a long time bakers and men cooks dressed alike and will therefore be taken together. Women cooks, on the other hand, are dealt with in Chapter VII.

Until well into the eighteenth century there were men of both these callings working in three different settings: the private home, the shop, and the street.

In all large private houses the men in the kitchen and bakery would be provided with their clothing—a "livery", though not an ornamental one.

The bakers and cooks who were independent maker-retailers ran bakers' shops and the equally ancient cooks' shops or eating-houses. As early as about 1170 we read:

> There is in London upon the river's bank . . . a public cook-shop. There daily . . . you may find viands, dishes roast, fried and boiled . . . the coarser flesh for the poor, the more delicate for the rich such as venison . . . sturgeon . . . guinea fowl.
>
> W. Fitz Stephen, *Descriptio Londiniae*.[2]

[1] F. G. Emmison, *Tudor Secretary*, 1961.
[2] Translation in Historical Association Leaflet 94 (1934).

Both bakers and cooks also sold their products in the streets, and indeed the muffin-man survived into the present century. The cooks sold such things as "hot sheeps' feet" (fifteenth century), meat- or rabbit-pies, soup and, in the 1830s, hot plum puddings for the men of Smithfield market. Naturally there was friction between the two equally powerful Companies—the Bakers' and the Cooks' (chartered respectively in 1486 and 1482, but both founded much earlier).[1] An Ordinance of the Cooks' Company dated 1670 notes that:

> Severall Members of the Company of Bakers of London have for severall years baked pyes, puddens and other bake-meates and things properly belonging to the Cooks' trade and doe daily blow hornes, ring bells and make cryes by their boyes about the streets of the Cittie . . . and subberbs . . . to the great detriment of the members of this Company.
>
> F. T. Phillips, *A Second History of the Worshipful Company of Cooks of London.* 1966.

It was a rule of the Cooks' Company that no girl should be apprenticed.

94. Baker and baker's man. No aprons. Early 14th century.

For cooks, a cloth, grey or white, tucked into the belt to act as apron was the distinguishing mark in the Middle Ages—at a time when aprons of any kind were little used by men (see Plate 20). Having to contend with splashing, cooks were driven to adopting them earlier than bakers (Fig. 94). Both men would wear the garments typical of their period, but without any overgarment because of the heat. The head would be bare or covered by an ordinary coif or other light indoor headgear.

1 The Bakers' fraternity had received recognition by Henry II.

95. Queen Elizabeth I's cook unpacking a picnic lunch. Smart doublet,
ruffs at neck and wrists; small apron protecting trunk hose. 1575 (?)

In the well-known fifteenth-century illustrations to *Canterbury Tales*[1] the
cook is already in a true apron, long and white, and wears it even on horseback. In 1568 a baker, also on the road, but seeming "to be of towne" because
"handsomely apparelled in a very seemely gowne", wore "a white knitt
cappe". This white headgear was evidently functional, for the writer goes
on: "I judged him a Baker by trade."[2]

In Fig. 95, Queen Elizabeth's own master cook is seen unpacking a picnic
lunch of cold capons, pigeon-pie, "saulsages", etc. His dress is chic, but his
apron, if diminutive, is real.

In R. Holme's illustrations (1688)[3] it is still the cook and not the baker who

[1] *Ellesmere Chaucer in Facsimile* (Manchester University Press, 1911).

[2] F. Thynn, *Debate between Pride and Lowliness.*

[3] *Academy of Armory.*

96. (*a*) Cook wearing "sleeves and apron". (*b*) Baker with peel, his
waistcoat sleeves rolled up. Both wear special caps. 1688.

is aproned (Fig. 96). The baker wears his waistcoat without the coat, for
coolness. The sleeves of the waistcoat but not the shirt are "stripped above
his elbows", i.e. rolled up. The description of the cook starts: "Cooke with
cap, sleeves and apron". This is an early reference to a cook's wearing oversleeves. An alternative to rolling up the shirt sleeves, these become common
from now on. The explanation:

> For cooks, sleeves must be kept long, against splashing from hot liquids and
> from contact with hot oven doors.

J. Fuller, *Kitchen Management*, 2nd edition, 1966.

Comparing two editions of Comenius's *Visible World*, we find the baker
has acquired both cap and apron between 1664 and 1731. A long, bibless,
characteristically white, apron was also worn from late seventeenth century
onwards by street vendors of all cooked foods and bakery. Figure 97 shows
how it could be combined with the wearing of an overcoat. "Colly Molly
Puff" himself was known to Addison, and is mentioned in the latter's tirade
against criers, in the *Spectator* (No. 251) in 1711.

In the eighteenth century it was not yet *de rigueur* for cooks, even in
France, to wear headgear. However, like bakers, they generally put on the
rather shapeless velvet or white linen object worn by all classes indoors, and
called a nightcap (Fig. 98).

In the nineteenth century, with the decline in home baking, the baker's delivery man or boy grew into prominence as quickly as he is disappearing today (see Plate 21a). He thus swelled the ranks of those carrying bakery and cooked food through the streets, and like them wore not only the apron but sometimes now a white jacket. He wore an ordinary hat or else a white cap, which, out of doors, would be very distinctive (Fig. 99). Pyne paints a somewhat odd example in his *World in Miniature* (1827). This "baker's man", with a white cap and an off-white jacket over his yellow waistcoat, pushes a little bread cart with the help of two harnessed dogs.

97. "Colly Molly Puffe" the pastry man. Overcoat fastened back, apron underneath. 1689.

Working bakers' headgear now ranged from none at all (Mr Bun in "Happy Families", drawn *c.* 1851, has an apron only, no cap) to a variety of shapes in the 1850s and 1860s. They settled down finally in favour of the flat type known in the trade today as the tam-o'-shanter style. This latter, beloved by the French *pâtissier*, is eminently practical for carrying trays of pastries on the head.

98. Baker. "Nightcap" and long apron. 1811.

George Dodd, in describing a biscuit factory at Gosport in 1845, shows that hygiene in clothing was beginning to assume importance:

> The men engaged are dressed in clean check shirts, and white linen trousers, apron and cap, and every endeavour is made to observe the most scrupulous cleanliness.
>
> *British Manufactures*, Ser. V.

Meanwhile there were changes in kitchens, for, as *The Complete Servant* tells us, by about 1825:

> In England men cooks are kept only in about 300–400 great wealthy families and about 40–50 London hotels.

The writers add the important point:

> The man cook in the establishment of a man of fashion is generally foreign.

PLATE 19

PLATE 19

(a) Butcher wearing apron over fashionable suit. On his head a round cap. 1397.

Misericord, Worcester Cathedral. Photograph by courtesy of S. Whiteley, Hatch End, Pinner.

(b) Butcher in straw boater hat as worn from 1890s.

Photograph from Author's collection.

PLATE 20

PLATE 20

(*a*) Cook (*b*) Turnspit. Each has a cloth tucked into his belt to
serve as apron. (Fowl and sucking-pig on spit.) *c.* 1340.

British Museum MS. Add. 42130 (Luttrell Psalter).

99. "Hot Loaves!" Vendor in white cap and jacket. (Portico of St. Martin-in-the-Fields church in background.) 1805.

The protagonists are now the head cooks in rich households, clubs and fashionable restaurants. The importation of French chefs began in Regency days. The great Antoine Carême was employed by Lord Stewart, who took him to the Embassy in Vienna in 1820–1. It was during that time that Carême, catching sight of a girl's cap that was white and *stiff*, slipped a round of cardboard into his own cap to give it a smarter appearance. The traditional *"bonnet"* (night-cap) of cooks, he said, gave them *"l'air de malades"*. The innovation drew a compliment from Lord Stewart himself. Under the name of *toque* a stiff cap was at once adopted by the whole *"brigade de cuisiniers"* in Vienna, later in Paris, finally in London.

Its stiffening had come to stay, but the toque underwent various transformations in cut, starching, pleats and height.[1] At Burghley, when the kitchen staff turned out for inspection on the occasion of a visit from Queen Victoria in 1843, their caps were the round white flat-topped "tam-o'-shanter". A cook ceremonially roasting an ox at Buckingham in the same

[1] The above account of Carême is based on an article, *Nos Coiffes et Carême*, by J. Germa of La Société Mutualiste des Cuisiniers de Paris.

year had a peaked cap. In 1846 *Punch*, illustrating the Mansion House kitchen, shows a cook in a tall smooth-pointed "dunce's" cap. Other smart cooks had a skull cap or a "pork-pie" with a tassel, as in Fig. 100 (also as late as 1878). The tall "cauliflower" or "French" shape of today seems to have been unfashionable or even unknown in the nineteenth century.

100. Cook at Messrs. Staples of Aldersgate. Tasselled pork-pie cap; long apron. 1850.

For the biographical details and the quotations which follow we are indebted, except where otherwise stated, to Professor John Fuller's book *Kitchen Management*, mentioned above.

The head cook at the Reform club in 1841 wore a flat white cap; but the reign of that uncrowned king of chefs, M. Soyer, dawned there a few years later. This Frenchman, who set a standard for English club and hotel catering, had the eccentricities of genius, and wore various bizarre costumes. But even when in ordinary white jacket and apron he always affected a flamboyant creation which approximated to a tasselled beret in *black velvet* (Fig. 101)! He chose it perhaps for the very reason that it would be "less likely to be cool and comfortable in wear for the working chef at the stove". Only the very "top man" could afford to wear such a thing. This black cap has been retained at the Reform Club, and was adopted at the Mansion House and two or three famous hotels and restaurants, just for the head man—and in each case he is known as the "master cook", not "chef", to emphasize that English cooking is now on the map.

101. Mons. Soyer (Chef) at Reform Club wearing dress clothes and his special black velvet hat; assistants in light jackets and "nightcaps"; all in aprons. 1847.

Soyer's underlings, if we may trust the draughtsman of Fig. 101, wore white caps of still another form—exactly like the real nightcaps that were popular in bed at just this period. They do not seem even to be starched.

Thackeray describes a fashionable chef in 1852 as: "sporting a rich crimson velvet waistcoat . . . a variegated blue satin stock . . ." but redeeming his garish appearance with "a white hat worn on one side of his long curling ringlets".[1] We are left guessing as to its shape. But the tam-o-shanter seems to have been winning, and also getting wider, in the later part of the century —at least for the head cook. It was worn by a French chef giving lessons to an English girls' school in 1897; also by various celebrities in the 1890s (Fig. 102). Moreover, the Universal Cookery and Food Association, founded about 1885, took as a symbol of their membership in a 1906 "Souvenir", a figure with a similar plain flat cap.

A hint of what was coming was given, however, back in 1892. In this year C. Herman Senn founded the first cookery class for boy apprentices in London. The lads wore bibbed aprons, the teachers overalls fastening behind.

[1] *A Little Dinner at Timmins's.*

102. Chef in wide "tam-o'-shanter"-shaped cap etc. 1896.

But it is the teachers' caps that are prophetic. For the first time they are cylindrical and taller than a "pork-pie".

Then at the opening of the twentieth century a startling evolution took place. The crown of the tam-o'-shanter became gathered in folds as in Fig.

103. Chef in "plaited tam-o'-shanter"-shaped cap, white "French style" coat, etc. 1905.

103 (plaited), and then the pork-pie threw up a similar folded crown, but this time vertically. Having hybridized a "plaited tam-o'-shanter" with a "pork-pie", you get a "cauliflower" (Fig. 104).

COOKS' AND CHEFS' CAPS.

The "Tam-o'-Shanter" Shape.

The "Plaited Tam-o'-Shanter" Shape.
(The Crown Plaited into the Band.)

104. Cauliflower shaped chef's cap, and the earlier toques from which it evolved. (Manufacturer's Catalogue, 1906.)

The "Pork Pie" Shape.
(With Double Band.

The "Cauliflower" Shape.
(With Double Band.)

The hybrid showed vigour, and soon after 1914 the fashion shown in Plate 21b flowered in its extreme form.

And so was completed the essentially elegant attire of the twentieth-century chef:

> High white starched cap or toque, with double breasted jacket topped with white neckerchief, his blue and white check cotton trousers protected by the white apron, into the string of which is tucked the "rubber" or kitchen cloth.

A few practical details may be filled in. The neckcloth had originally the purpose of absorbing the sweat, but has now turned into a carefully adjusted cravat. The jacket preferred is the cross-over design ("French style"), which cannot leave a gap in front (Fig. 103). The sleeves are slit at the wrist so that the cuffs can be turned back; as mentioned above the cook does not roll up his sleeves. As to the apron:

> Reversing the apron once is permissible and by adjusting the number of folds [over the waist string] stains can be hidden;" [but] "the practice of folding to camouflage staining to such an extent as to make the apron ludicrously short cannot be too strongly deplored.

The kitchen cloth has to be "worn as well as used" and must be scrupulously clean.

All in all it is a well-adapted costume; but note also:

> there is no doubt that working dress (apart from its functional purpose) plays an important part in establishing morale and in heightening or diminishing job prestige. The chef's dress must be worn with pride and maintained with care.

LIQUOR TRADE

This section deals mainly with brewing, but wine-making will be mentioned briefly first.

An eleventh-century manuscript gives a charming picture of gathering and treading grapes, the men in tunics and the woman in a long kirtle and

105. Gathering and treading grapes. See text. 11th century.

106. Men treading grapes. See text. *c.* 1320.

coverchief or veil on her head (Fig. 105). Another in 1320 shows two men treading grapes, having their tunics hitched up high enough to expose their braies, which are also pulled up like babies' napkins (Fig. 106). The following quotation shows the superior garments worn by the vinter (merchant) as compared with the ordinary clothes of the "vitayler" in the sixteenth century:

> . . . A Vitayler did retaile,
> Bought by the barrell and solde by pint and quart,
>   And had his living by that travayle
> . . . clothed after citizen,
> Neither in slovenrie, ne yet in pride.
>   . . . . .
> And after them there came all in a rowt
> . . . all likely men, and neither knave nor lowt

One of whom was

>   a Vintner
> That had full many a hoggeshead looked in
> . . . A Spanish cloke he wore fine with a cape,
> . . . A fine French cappe on his head accordynge
> . . . And one [on] his finger were a myghtie ring.
>   1568. *Debate between Pride and Lowliness.*

107. Ale-wife in long embroidered kirtle. Early 14th century.

The workers in the brewing trade selected are the brewers, the coopers who made and mended the casks and the draymen who drove the brewers' carts. Tavern-keepers are omitted except for the ale-wife, who in medieval days was also herself a brewer. At this time every tavern brewed its own ale and the brewers were generally women, who were known as ale-wives. After each brew the ale-stake, a pole topped with a branch or a bush of leaves, was put out to indicate that the tavern was ready for customers.[1]

Fig. 107 shows the ale-wife of the fourteenth century in a very long kirtle embroidered round the neck, and the usual veil on her head, but no apron—a woman of some standing.

108. Ale-wife, serving a customer. See text.
? *c.* 1500

---

[1] Hence the saying "Good wine needs no bush".

A misericord, probably of *c.* 1500 (Fig. 108) shows a more workaday ale-wife, with her customer. Her kirtle, with bodice laced in front, has a shorter skirt and she wears an apron.

In the seventeenth century we have a picture of a brewer in doublet and ruff, full oval breeches with sash garters below the knees—all in the fashionable style of his day, but he wears a protective apron (Fig. 109).

109. Master brewer in fashionable clothes. See text. 1625.

Fine clothes were appreciated even by brewers' servants. An amusing eighteenth century anecdote is given by Ashton of a young man who became the servant of

> a brewer of Lynn who wanted a lusty man to carry beer to the marsh and to Wisbeach; but Tom [the servant] would not hire himself until his friend persuaded him and the master promised him a suit of clothes from top to toe.

Figure 110 shows two wearing "tricorne" hats bound with gold, but they protect their elegant clothes with aprons.

In Pyne's *Costume of Great Britain* (in 1805) brewers are shown wearing buff jackets and waistcoats with knee-length leather aprons. Their stockings

110. Brewers' Servants. See text. 1700–50.

are white or striped blue and white, worn with buckled shoes. Some have
blue neckties, others red with spots. All wear billycock hats.

All the brewers working in a factory in 1845 in Dodd's *Manufactures,
Series V*, are shown wearing aprons with high square bibs covering their
ordinary clothes, but the man filling moulds with a scoop full of hot sugar
is stripped to the waist. All their heads are covered with a varied assortment
ranging from dark tam-o'-shanters, paper caps, to the famous brewer's cap
which became so popular with other trades and also with children on seaside holidays. The brewer's cap was knitted, coming to a point, often with a
tassel and generally red. This red brewer's cap and leather apron identified
Mr Bung in "Happy Families".

The next on our list are the *Coopers*.

"A Cooper" in 1640 from the "Cryes of the City of London" is depicted
in doublet, breeches, a slouch hat and a leather apron, which protected him
from knife cuts and sparks. R. Holme in 1688 describes a cooper thus:

> A cooper in his Waistcote and Cap, Breeches and Hose Russet: with an
> Adds lifted up in his right hand and a Driver[1] in his left, trussing up a Barrel
> with fire out of the top of it . . .

Trussing up a barrel= "Putting it together from Boards or Staves within a
hoop". Heating the staves of the barrel, makes them "pliable" and "bow to
the hoops".

Hogarth in 1751 shows a cooper smoking a pipe outside an inn; he has no
coat, his shirt sleeves are rolled up and his apron with a triangular bib is
fastened to his shirt button. Tucked into his apron band is a pair of pliers.

[1] A mallet.

All through the nineteenth century the coopers wore aprons (Fig. 111) with bibs, square or pointed, and by the 1830s the more fashionable trousers were beginning to replace breeches. Jackets were usual, but smocks were occasionally worn and the brewer's cap was very popular.

Draymen. It was the eighteenth century that witnessed the founding of most of the large English breweries, and transporting of beer, which had been carried out previously by hand barrows, was now largely done by horse-drawn carts with two wheels. The dray was a four-wheeled vehicle, but the drivers of either were called draymen and the drayman's assistant was known as the *trouncer*. Messrs Whitbread have supplied the following account of the clothes worn by their employees in the eighteenth century.

111. Cooper making a barrel, working in shirt sleeves, bibbed apron, brewer's cap and still wearing breeches. 1824.

112. Two draymen in jackets, leather aprons, white stockings, buckled shoes and slouch hats. 1805. Cf. Fig. 110.

The clothes of the drayman and trouncer . . . consist of a long coat, breeches of beige moleskin, a hard wearing cloth. . . . The waistcoat is of a deep wine colour with long sleeves of a thinner, lighter material—in a style similar to the garment worn by hotel porters. A leather apron, white stockings and buckle shoes with red heels complete the outfit. The drayman wears a broad brimmed beaver hat, while his trouncer wears a red knitted cap as part of his uniform, to guard against the cold (see Plate 22.)

Hogarth's drayman in 1751 wears a tricorne hat. The rule seems to have been that in the eighteenth century the draymen wore hats and the trouncers caps of the brewer's cap style. A lampoon on the occasion of the visit of George III and Queen Charlotte and daughters to the Whitbread Brewery in 1787 was written by Dr John Wolcot (Peter Pindar) as follows:

. . . Whitbread . . .
Poor gentleman most terribly afraid
He should not charm enough his guests divine

He gave his maids new aprons, gowns and smocks[1]
And lo! two hundred pounds were spent in frocks[2]
To make th' apprentices and draymen fine.

In the nineteenth century the draymen began to wear jackets, reinforced at the shoulders and elbows (Fig. 112 and 113). Boots instead of shoes were usual. A drayman is shown in 1815 wearing a yellow jacket, breeches, blue-and-white striped stockings and a leather apron. On his head is a low

113. Two draymen wearing jackets, leather aprons, hobnail boots and tall-crowned hats. See text. 1820.

"topper". In one of Pyne's illustrations in 1827 an ale brewer's drayman wears a soft round black hat, but the Porter brewer's drayman has a red brewer's cap. Draymen from now on often wore a brewer's cap and those that stuck to breeches wore gaiters as well (Fig. 114).

The distinction in dress between a master brewer, a drayman and a trouncer is shown in an interesting lithograph of 1842.[3] The master at the door of the brewery was dressed like a gentleman, that is in a blue cut-away tail-coat, red waistcoat, brown trousers, a top-hat, but also a white apron. The

[1] Shifts.
[2] "Slop-frocks" or smock-like overalls.
[3] Truman, Hanbury, Buxton & Co. Album.

114. Drayman in brewer's cap and wearing
gaiters. 1855.

drayman wore a brown jacket, blue breeches, a bibbed leather apron and a
low topper. The trouncer was similarly clothed, but as usual wore a red
brewers' cap.

A drayman's jacket was often made with a special pocket to hold his
delivery book:

> He makes a display of his delivery book with its brass clasp carried in a pocket
> made purposely within the left hand side of his jacket.
>
> 1859. *Sketches of London Life and Character.*
> Edited by Albert Smith.

A drayman studying his delivery book is shown in Fig. 115 (1871–3).

By now trousers, not breeches, were usual and strong wooden-soled
boots. This drayman's long bibbed apron protects his shirt, and his jaunty
brewer's cap gives a finishing touch to this studious figure.

115. Drayman studying his delivery book and wearing a brewer's cap, bibbed apron, trousers and stout boots. 1871–73.

STREET VENDORS

My maisters all attend you,
 if mirth you loue to heare:
And I will tell you what they cry
 in London all the yere.

1612. *Turner's Dish of Lenten Stuff.*
Ballad in Pepys's Collection (I. 206 BL).

At least until the eighteenth century a typical citizen of a big town would do much if not most of his shopping in the open, and street vendors formed an important class even to the end of the nineteenth century. Many of the same goods are on record as being "cried" in the streets of London for over five hundred years.

Typical travelling pedlars and chapmen will not be discussed, since there was little that was adaptive in their dress: we will limit ourselves to local vendors, and must also ignore the many street characters who served but did not sell.

Vendors of bakery and cooked dishes have been dealt with (pp. 124–129) and other vendors are mentioned in Chapter XV, where the way they used their clothing in carrying is referred to.

Besides the more coherent groups such as costers, the present section deals with a miscellaneous assortment such as men and women selling singing-birds, tinder-boxes, "Worsterchyr" salt, ink, news-sheets, ironmongery, even brick dust, and—from the eighteenth century onwards, flowers and lavender.

Since an ambulant salesman must make his presence known, the streets were once as noisy with the cries, bells and horns of vendors as they are today with traffic. Addison protested:

> There is nothing which so astonishes a Foreigner and frights a Country Squire than the *Cries of London.* . . . A Freeman of *London* has the Privilege of disturbing a whole street for an hour together, with the twancking of a Brass Kettle or a Frying Pan.
>
> 1711. *Spectator,* No. 251.

Already in the early fifteenth century, street salesmen were bombarding people in Cheapside with offers of "Mackrel", "Velvet, Silke and Lawn" and "Rashers Green".[1] In the reign of Charles I they were a group conspicuous enough to inspire a series of prints, "The Cryes of the City of London", which was followed by many others later.

It may be said of all these that their typical costume at any period would be old-fashioned for its time and shabby, but it nearly always included an apron even when the goods were merely pins or almanacks. A lady in the 1870s sketched a dozen different vendors who still frequented St John's Wood, London, in her day. Nearly all of them are in aprons, but sur-prisingly enough not the girl laden with carcasses, who cried: "If I'd as much money as I could tell, I'd never cry out young lambs to sell."

In the nineteenth century a smock sometimes took the place of an apron with the vendors of such things as clothes-pegs, brooms and mats, who came in from the country homes where these things were made.

Exposed to all weathers, street traders went in for a good deal of headgear. Men had hoods in the Middle Ages and always hats later; women had a coif,

---

[1] J. Lydgate, *London Lickpenny or Lackpenny.*

PLATE 21

PLATE 21

(*a*) Baker's delivery man. Tailcoat, top hat, apron. 1805.

W. H. Pyne, Costume of Great Britain. *1808.*

(*b*) Chefs wearing the "Cauliflower" or "French" hat in its extreme form; white jacket, neckcloth, kitchen cloth "worn" tucked into apron string. 1965.

Photograph: The Guardian, *5th July, 1965.*

PLATE 22

PLATE 22

Drayman, holding horse. He wears a red waistcoat and brown
leather apron. The trouncer on the left wears a brown apron
and a red brewer's cap. 1792.

"A View of the East End of the Brewery" [*Whitbread's*] *by G. Garrard.
Photograph kindly given by Messrs. Whitbread, London, E.C.1.*

cap, handkerchief, and/or "limp hood", surmounted by a large felt or straw hat: either might have a pad on top of all (Fig. 282, p. 368).

Feet must have been constantly wet and muddy. Pattens, though seen occasionally on the women, would be unpractical for long hours of walking or standing. Most vendors could afford neither good footwear nor over-shoes.

The types who emerge with enough distinctness to be worth a few further remarks are the water-sellers, the hawkers proper, the costermongers and the milk-sellers.

Water-sellers were essential street traders nearly all through history. Our example of a London "Tankard Bearer" in *c.* 1640 wears a special type of pinafore fastened on at the top corners and hanging straight down from the chin—an excellent splash-board. His belt supports a money bag (Fig. 116).

116. Tankard-bearer. Towel worn as pinafore and another hanging behind. Purse on belt.
c. 1640.

On the other hand, the two water-carriers in Fig. 117a and b have no protective clothing at all. Living three and a half centuries apart, their equipment is nevertheless exactly the same—a pony, bearing leather saddle-bags full of water, which the man, apparently indifferent to splashes, would dispense with a leather "scoop".

117. Water-carriers each with leather scoop and pony bearing saddle
bags of water. (*a*) *Luttrell Psalter. c.* 1340. (*b*) 17th century.

When Tempest published his "London Cryes" in 1688 Lauron's drawing
of an old man carrying pails on a yoke and wearing a large apron tucked
into his belt is given its original title "New River Water" (Fig. 118). In a

118. Seller of "New River Water". 1688.

later edition, *c.* 1750, when presumably more houses had water laid on, this same individual is redesignated a collector of kitchen refuse! But despite "Company's water" we read that in the 1830s in Hampstead:

> The water of Shepherd's Well is . . . in continual demand . . . a few of the villagers . . . make a scanty living by carrying it to the houses for a penny a pailfull.

1830. Hone's Tablebook, I, 382.

The illustration to the article here quoted shows a typical yoke and pails, but the man has no apron.

By the nineteenth century *hawkers* proper were a rather special breed of men (with a few women), defined by H. Mayhew in 1851 as itinerants from the country, selling game, poultry, etc.[1] The retailing of game in the streets was legalized, under licence, in 1831.

---

[1] And originally foreign hawks—hence, possibly, the word "hawker".

His (a hawker's) customary dress is a smock frock covering the whole of his other attire except the ends of his trousers and his thick boots . . . indeed he often . . . assumes the dress of a country labourer . . . Forty years ago it was customary for countrymen . . . to bring their birds to London to hawk them. . . . These mens' smock frocks were a convenient garb, for they covered the ample pockets . . . beneath, in which were often a store of game . . . all poached.

1851. H. Mayhew, *London Labour and the London Poor.*

119. Hawker from the country selling birds' nests, snakes, etc. Smock, "Italian-looking" hat, bare feet. 1865.

A hawker whose portrait appears in Mayhew's book (see Fig. 119) was "a gipsy-looking lad" who collected from Essex, and sold in London, "birds' nesties" of linnets, thrushes, moorhens, etc., with their eggs ("they're for hatching under bantam fowl");[1] also snakes at 5s. a pound and frogs and wild flowers. His appearance was "picturesque"—a smock "with side pockets", an "Italian-looking hat" and bare feet.

Another hawker was the rabbit-seller, who carried his goods hung on a pole. He wore a thick blue or green apron or a piece of sacking swathed

[1] The man's own words quoted by H. Mayhew.

round the waist "to catch the blood dripping from the carcasses". (This last in 1884.)[1]

The true London *costermongers*, according to H. Mayhew, comprised the street sellers of fruit, vegetables, fish and shellfish; thus they had special importance, since they transported perishables from market to consumer with a minimum of delay. Men, women (the proverbial fishwives) and girls, they were so numerous and so clannish that their history is easier to trace and their dress, especially in the nineteenth century, more stylized than that of other vendors.

In "London Cryes" depicted in the 1640s there is still little to characterize the men except their aprons. Women crying "Flounders" and "New Walle Streete Oysters", etc., wore the full-length skirts and collar-like kerchiefs of their day, but all without trimmings; their aprons are roughly tucked sideways and the crowns of their hats flat for basket-carrying. One of them tucks her skirt up as does the orange-seller fifty years later in Fig. 120. Many of the latter's contemporaries have gowns with overskirts that were open in front, and thus all the more easily gathered for protection into a bunch at the back, exposing the shorter underskirt to the hard wear (cf. p. 46). None have adopted the fashionable bustle underneath. A cape, or an old coat of their husbands' seem all that the women could afford for warmth, and these, helped out later by shawls, continued in use to the end of the nineteenth century.

Paul Sandby's water-colour drawings of 1759 reveal the coster's character and garb with a pungent realism. The men are always shabby, even ragged. Most of them wear short aprons—a surprising exception being the seller of "Tripe and Neat's Feet". The women are still in foot-length skirts, but sometimes solve the problem by frankly turning and pinning up the hem in front, or in festoons all the way round, as does the spoon-seller in Fig. 121. Sometimes instead of a laced bodice they simply wear their stays (as did countrywomen at times) and make up the deficiencies with a tucked-in neckerchief and the short sleeves of the underlying shift. All have voluminous blue or white aprons and sometimes both. (See also Fig. 266—after another draughtsman—on p. 354.)

Francis Wheatley's "Cries of London" present a contrast, not merely because painted in the 1790s—his girls are undoubtedly glamorized. How-

[1] O. J. Morris, *Grandfather's London*.

120. Costergirl. Full skirt turned up, sides drawn together at the back;
shorter underskirt; limp-hood under hat. 1688.

ever, they show the working woman's predilection for a two-piece gown
comprising a long jacket-bodice and separate skirt. This was seen both
earlier and later. Wheatley's "Mackerel Seller" wears an apricot-coloured
skirt and a yellow jacket-bodice with its flaps pinned back out of the way.
Often there is an open overskirt, and again this is gathered up into a bunch
at the back in what had actually been a fashionable style in the 1680s and
1770s (compare Plate 10). A white apron, neckerchief and mob cap are still
usual and a bergère straw hat increasingly popular.

In the early nineteenth century a folded kerchief worn over the head like
the head square of today was not unknown with costers, but bonnets and
hats were preferred. Sleeves shortened, the waistline rose (some ten years
later than in the *beau monde*) and we arrive at a style like that of the milk-
seller shown in Plate 55. She still affects the open overskirt style, and this
lasted with women of her type right on into mid-century, as our next

121. Spoon-seller: skirt (red, lined white) pinned up; a white apron over a blue; hat tied over mob cap; cape strapped on. Tinker in bibbed leather apron (banging a pan; pair of bellows tied on behind). 1759.

example shows. The bunch at the back would now be highly unfashionable.

"Kathy", the subject of the portrait in Fig. 122, was a Covent Garden woman in 1841. Notice that she wore a hooded cape, headkerchief, mob cap and hat all at once. The hat was one of

> those nameless species of straw hats, scorched brown by the sun and flatted in the crown by the pressure of her market basket.

She had a loose gown of striped linsey woolsey, open to show her underskirt or petticoat.

> Her petticoat was short and of black quilted stuff. . . . Alternatively, and mostly on Sundays, Kathy sported a red stuff petticoat and an open cotton gown of a large chintz pattern, which was always looped up behind, and secured from the muddy contaminations of the street by a corking pin.
>
> 1841. Mrs S. C. Hall in *Heads of the People*.

122. "Basket woman", Covent Garden. Hooded cape, head-kerchief,
hat and mob-cap. 1841.

By the 1850s the costers' dress had become highly distinctive. An oyster-man, or a fishmonger calling for orders, might wear an ordinary frockcoat, waistcoat and blue apron; a fish-porter wore jersey, breeches, thigh boots and a fan-tail hat; but the true coster's get up, combining "durability with quaintness", was remarkable enough to deserve the following quotations from H. Mayhew's *London Labour and the London Poor* (1851). Some of the features show in Fig. 123.

> A well-to-do coster, dressed for the day's work, wears a small cloth cap a little on one side . . . close fitting worsted tie up skull cap, . . . ringlets at the temples. . . . Hats they never wear . . . excepting on Sundays—on account of their baskets being frequently carried on their heads,[1]—coats seldom . . . waistcoats of broad ribbed corduroy with fustian back and sleeves, being made as long as a groom's and buttoned up nearly to the throat.

Reflecting the eighteenth century and foreshadowing the festal attire of

---

[1] Costers had always worn hats in the past, but clearly the topper, now the normal style of hat, did not lend itself to their use.

123. Coster, jaunty cap typical of costers. (Other vendors wear toppers). Conspicuous waistcoat with metal buttons; trousers nearly cover the boots. 1865.

a "Pearly", buttons were a great feature of this waistcoat and its pockets. With light-coloured corduroy, brass ones with sporting designs were liked, and with dark corduroy, mother-of-pearl. The kerseymere trousers were bell-bottomed. An advertisement, from one of the five London tailors who alone made the costers' garb, read: "Pair of out and out fancy kicksies cut to drop down over the trotters." But his boots ("trotter cases") were one of the coster's chief prides and they were often "tastily ornamented". Above all there was his brilliantly patterned silk neckcloth, always known as a "King's man".

The women were not outdone. They wore

> a black velveteen or straw bonnet, . . . and a net cap, fitting closely to the cheek . . . the silk "King'sman" covering their shoulders. . . . The petticoats are worn short ending at the ankles . . . just high enough to shew the whole of the much admired boots.

Costers are described by D. C. Calthrop[1] as still dressing very much in this remarkable manner as late as the 1890s, when "Albert Chevalier and

[1] *English Dress*, 1934.

Phil May introduced them to public notice". Even in 1903 *Punch* has a draw-ing by G. Browne showing just the same outfit on a typical barrow-boy.

Milk sellers. There remain the folk who sell or deliver milk. In the country their dress would conform to descriptions in Chapter I, aprons or smocks being usual. But a milk-boy going some distance in winter might appear as in Fig. 124.

124. Country milk-boy: brown caped greatcoat and muffler, battered
black billy-cock hat. 1815.

In London the retailing of milk in the streets had started at least by the beginning of the seventeenth century, and the cries "Milk below!" "Mio", etc., and the sight of the yoke and pails were familiar till late nineteenth century. Most of the sellers were women, who even in London would often have done the milking themselves 4–6 a.m. (In 1805 there were cowkeepers with farms in Paddington, Knightsbridge, Tottenham Court Road, Mile End and other unlikely-sounding "suburbs".) Apart from an extra ample white apron and a special fondness for the bergère or milkmaid's straw hat, they looked much like other vendors cf. Plate 10b. Two independent prints of the 1820s give them black hats rather like toppers (see Plate 23a).

Even in 1851 there were men selling skim milk at special pitches in the city, and these were generally ex-milkers and wore smocks.

In 1864 for the first time milk was brought into London by train and the whole trade began to be organized on a bigger scale. The roundsman was born. Milk went out from depots to be delivered at people's homes by schoolboys with clean Eton collars, pushing mail-carts, or by men in bibbed blue aprons with wooden yokes or with prams. Then near the end of the century these gave place to men in belted white overalls with hand-carts and to high-class milkmen and the direct employees of the wholesalers, both of whom drove milk-floats. All the men wore bowlers or top-hats, but these last two types were specially smartly dressed. A master milkman would have a "blue, close-fitting monkey jacket, and apron to match",[1] and employees of the big pioneer firm had uniform white jackets with blue collars and cuffs (see Plate 23b). With these

the top hat stayed firmly in place until exchanged for a peaked cap in 1902.[2]

But right to the end of our period their vital aprons were, as far as colour went, *au choix*—blue, white or striped. It was a few years later that in this particular firm the blue-and-white striped apron was finally enforced and the roundsman's public image crystallized.

A blue and white livery was selected for its overtones of purity.[3]

[1] O. J. Morris, *Grandfather's London.*
[2] *Express Story 1869–1964* (published by Express Dairy Co. Ltd., 1964).
[3] Ibid.

CHAPTER VI

HOUSEHOLD SERVANTS—MEN

Introduction

Domestic service comprises a variety of occupations and those employed in it form a larger group than their lack of social organization would suggest. Until recent years, even for the smallest farmer's or tradesman's home, their number could generally be counted in ones and twos, while in upper-class medieval households it often ran into scores or even hundreds. It has been estimated that in the eighteenth century domestic servants constituted the largest social group in England, and among them men were in the majority.

Though the nature of their work has seldom prevented servants from wearing clothing fairly typical in style for their period, their dress has often been to some extent distinctive and has shown within the group a meaningful variety. Factors influencing it in opposite directions have been, on the one hand, the dictates of convenience and suitability, often backed by Sumptuary Laws against extravagance; on the other hand, the desire of the servant to avoid a menial appearance, and the desire of the master to display his wealth on the backs of his liveried staff.

Wherever there is more than one servant in a household there will be diversity in their dress, partly because of division of labour and partly because the servant's appearance must express, on purely social grounds, his position within the servant hierarchy itself.

What seems to have been true throughout history is that domestic servants tended more than other workers to ape the upper classes in their dress, owing partly to closer propinquity and partly to the custom for master and mistress to give them their cast-offs. Upper servants such as valets and ladies' maids got most of the good cast-offs, but where staffs were large the question of who got what would be ruled by protocol:

> "There," said a gentleman one day to his father's butler, "there is a pair of boots for you."
> "Thank you sir," replied the man, "but *they* belong to the footman."
> 1874. H. Mayhew, *London Characters.*

In earlier days garments were often left to servants in their masters' wills. A surgeon in 1591 bequeathed:

> To John Dighton my servaunte my blacke cloth cloake layed with lace and faced with velvett, my blacke satten Dublett and my rounde velvett [trunk] hose.[1]

A wealthy steward or bailiff left, in 1582, clothes to a servant of his own and also "To John Kemp, the boy of my master's kitchen a black cap, two pairs of handruffs".

Whatever its cause the servants' tendency to dress above their station has been criticized by their "betters" for at least five hundred years.

> Of servynge men I wyll begyne
> For they goo mynyon trym
> Off mete and drynk, and feyr clothing
> By dere God I want none.
>
> *Fifteenth century song.*[2]

Randle Holme in 1688 writes:

> Nay it is a hard thing to distinguish a master from his man, but only that he goes after, and stands with his head uncovered before him.
>
> *Academy of Armory.*

Again in the eighteenth century:

> The Valet de Chambre cannot be distinguished from his master but by being better dressed.
>
> Soame Jenyns in *World IV.*

The women were as bad as the men:

> Apeing all the fashions of those they live with . . . mobs to go under the chin are all exploded; silks and muslins and tasty slippers supplant the stuff cotton gowns and strong soaled shoes, formerly used.
>
> 1791. *London Chronicle.*

And it was—

> a hard matter to know the Mistress from the Maid by their Dress; nay very often the Maid goes much the finer of the two.
>
> 1725. Defoe, *Every Body's Business . . .*

---

[1] Quoted by Sidney Young in *Annals of the Barber-Surgeons,* 1890.
[2] F. Fairholt, *Satirical Songs and Poems on Costume,* 1849.

Or—

> Things have lately come to such a pretty pass that even one's maidservants
> can walk into any corset makers' and buy a figure fit for a lady of the highest
> respectability.
>
> 1847. *The Greatest Plague of Life* . . . Ed. by H. and A. Mayhew.

In the chronological treatment which follows, menservants will be dealt
with first, then women. Cooks in the kitchens of larger establishments have
generally been men, especially in the earlier centuries. These men cooks will
not be considered here, but taken along with bakers (pp. 122–134), owing to
their affinity with these in the matter of dress.

Medieval Upper Servants

For medieval and Tudor times most of our information relates to the very
large households kept by the nobility. Among their resident "servants" many
were themselves noblemen or gentry, for example the marshal, steward,
master of the horse, even clerke of the kitchen. These in their everyday dress
had little to distinguish them from their employers. The same applied to
those who valeted their master, generally the chamberlain and his assistants.
In Fig. 125 the men in attendance contrast strongly with the "working-class"
people in the same manuscript, for the former have adopted the new fashion
and wear tight doublets ("gipons") instead of loose tunics; also elegant little
shoulder capes.

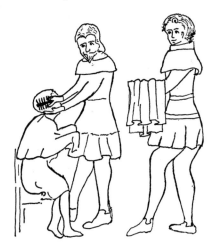

125. Chamberlain (?) and assistant valeting
their master (who wears a towel to have his
hair combed). Fashionable doublets and
shoulder capes but no headgear. *c.* 1360.

The same applied to the page, who would be a boy of gentle birth who gave service in exchange for a noble upbringing. His clothes were provided by his master. A record has come down to us of how Chaucer himself at the age of 17, in the household of Prince Lionel, was supplied with a paltock,[1] shoes and a pair of black and red hose.

126. Attendant, fastening on his master's armour. Doublet with sleeves puffed above, its skirt fashionably short but simply cut. *c.* 1470.

Yemen[2] ushers, etc., and those in the upper ranks connected with stables and gamekeeping would again have dressed like others of their own class.

"Courtesy books" were published in the fifteenth century laying down rules of protocol and procedure for all the servants, and from these and illuminated manuscripts a little information can be gathered on three points connected with their dress.

(1) At a time when everyone wore a hat, bonnet or cap indoors and actually at meals, it was *de rigueur* for even the most superior servants to go bareheaded in attendance.

[1] A type of doublet, not, as has been stated, a cloak.
[2] Approximate equivalent of *yeomen*.

127. Servants at Marriage Feast at Cana. One wears, over the shoulder, a napkin which passes under the dish he carries. *c.* 1330.

No groom's head to be covered serving at meals yemen ne yemen Jentilmen ne Jentilman the Stewarde.[1]

In Plate 24a the man serving, who is distinguished by his long gown, is probably a high-ranking servant. Even the marshal himself, when waiting on the lord and his guests, would wear no headdress, unless it were a coif, like the skull cap that a monk was allowed in church. But we are told that a "gentleman usher", at least if his master was no more than a baron, might address him with his hat on when out of doors.

(2) The wearing of a napkin by a waiter, a custom surviving to this day, was already traditional by the fifteenth century.

[1] *A 15th century Courtesy Book.* Edited by R. W. Chambers, 1914.

PLATE 23

PLATE 23

(*a*) Milk-girl. Stays, over décolleté white shift; blue apron; short skirt; top-hat. 1820.

Drawing and Engraving by T. L. Busby dated 1820, in Costume of the Lower Orders *by T. L. Busby. 1835.*

(*b*) Milk roundsman. White coat, blue apron, top-hat with rosette badge. Late 19th century.

Photograph in Express Story. *1864–1964. By courtesy of the Express Dairy Co. Ltd.*

PLATE 24

PLATE 24

(*a*) Marshall (?) in long gown and assistant in short one, serving at marriage feast. 1377–1399.

British Museum. MS. Roy. 1 *E IX.*

(*b*) Member of the Cabal Ministry. Petticoat breeches like those of the 18th century running foot-men. Shoulder-knot of ribbons. (An elegantly dressed negro messenger just visible.) *c.* 1670.

J. B. da Medina, "The Cabal Ministry of Charles II". Lord St. Oswald's Collection, Nostell Priory, Wakefield. (Detail.) c. 1670.

128. Waiter "wearing" napkin. Cf. Fig. 127. 1841.

A General Rule to every gentleman that is keruer (carver) to ony maner Lord:— A towel must be layed on his shoulder when he shall bryng his lorde brede.[1]

Compare figures 127 and 128. Again:

Duties of a Panter or Butler:—Put a towel round your neck, for that is courtesy and put one end of it mannerly over your left arm.[2]

Evidently this towel partly served the purpose of the white gloves worn by some waiters today, for the passage goes on:

Take one end of the towel in your left hand . . . together with the salt cellar and . . . the other end in your right hand with the spoons.

In Fig. 127 the napkin passes under a dish. In the fourteenth century the custom was not fully established—sometimes there are no napkins at all, and

[1] Ibid.
[2] From John Russell's *Book of Nurture* in *Babee's Book*. Edited by E. Rickert, 1923 (modern ized spelling).

129. Cup-bearer to Sir Geoffrey Luttrell wearing napkin round the
neck; loose surcote over tight-sleeved cote. *c.* 1340.

in the Luttrell Psalter (*c.* 1340) those serving cooked food do not have them,
but the cup-bearer has a typical fringed towel round his neck (Fig. 129).

(3) The use of livery was more extensive in early than in late medieval
days. At first the colours of a great family might be worn on occasion by
almost anyone who did anything for it (serving, fighting, even selling), and
this included the superior gentlemen servants. They wore these colours in hat
or hood or even gown.

Sumptuary Laws in the reigns of Richard II and Henry IV endeavoured,
at first unsuccessfully, to limit livery to resident menial servants.

Medieval Menial Servants

Indoor grooms (later called footmen), outdoor grooms and kitchen staff
mostly lived in, and had their clothing provided. Those of them who went

130. Servants at marriage feast. One climbs stairs in ankle-length tunic. One with rolled up sleeves, the others with ornate cuffs to their tunics. 1150–60.

abroad with their master or came before his guests would then wear either his full livery colours or else just have his crest worked in silver on the breast, sleeve or shoulder of their outer garment. When not of livery colours, the cloth would be grey or russet, as was usual for working men. As to style, this conformed to prevailing fashion—convenience no object. The twelfth-century waiter in Fig. 130 has to mount a staircase, both hands engaged, without tripping over an ankle-length tunic. Even the water-drawer has no apron, but these were worn in the kitchen in the fourteenth century (Fig. 131).

Typical fifteenth-century clothes are mentioned in Sir John Howard's household account-book,[1] which records in 1465 the purchase for Jenyn of the stable of a doublet and "a payr of hosen [tights] and iii shepes scynnys to make hym a jakett", also "i payr of botuys". "Gownes of tawney and rede" were bought for the henchman. The botuys were riding boots (botews).

[1] *Manners and Household Expenses in the XIIIth and XVth Centuries.* ed. B. Botfield (Roxburghe Club, 1841).

131. Carver in the kitchen. Apron-cloth tucked into belt; chaperon style of headgear. *c.* 1340.

That the shape of a servant's gown could be in the height of fashion is evidenced by a poem of 1411:

> Now have these lords but little need of brooms
> To sweep away the filth out of the street,
> Since the long sleeves of impecunious grooms
> Will lick it up.
>
> T. Hoccleve, *The Regemente of Princes,* Edited F. Furnivall, 1897.

Outdoor grooms and postilions rode in the usual flowing garments without special riding boots (Fig. 132).

Sixteenth Century

The chief changes in fashion in the sixteenth century were reflected at all levels. When in about 1550 "tights" gave place to trunk hose, servants seldom wore these with exaggerated padding, but one of Queen Elizabeth's attendants in Fig. 133, from George Turbervile's *Noble Arte of Venerie,* wears them in the extreme form. Note the royal crest embroidered on his doublet.

In 1570 the alternative of breeches with separate hose (stockings) began. Though grooms and other servants in Tubervile's book are all shown in

132. Groom in short tunic, very light ankle boots, hat over coif.
13th century.

133. Attendant on Queen Elizabeth I wearing late-style trunk hose
much inflated above, narrow below, ending under the knee. Both
attendants in livery with royal badge on their doublets. 1575 (?)

trunk hose, one or two of the gentlemen already wear breeches. By 1588 footmen, too, had taken to these, as is shown in Fig. 134. It might be said that the knee-breeches, so characteristic of footmen right down to the present day, took their origin in the late sixteenth century.

A servant still wore reminders of the claim a master had on his support in battle. Besides his sword and dagger, the various alternative coats which he wore over the doublet had a somewhat military air. There was the buff-jerkin (leather) or the basecoat (its "skirt" reaching to the knees) or the "loose coats which they call mandilions, covering the whole body . . . like bagges or sacks". Mandilions are stated by R. Holme (1688) to have resembled, in Elizabeth's reign, the military overcoat called a cassock. They were not, however, confined to soldiers or servants. What Daniell Batchiler, Sir Philip Sidney's little page, is wearing at his master's funeral would probably be called a short cassock (Fig. 134).

(a)　　　　　　　　　　(b)

134. (a) Page to Sir Philip Sidney at his master's funeral. Short "cassock"; high boots of soft leather. (b) Footman. Breeches, light cape, hat in hand. 1588.

As an extra garment, especially in winter, the gown was still worn by servants, while it was going out of fashion with their masters. But Queen Elizabeth reinforced the Sumptuary Laws and

> it was not lawful for any man[1] either servant or other to wear their gowns lower than the calves of their legs except they were above threescore years of age.

The cloak was less worn than by the gentry and mostly as a summer garment.[2] The footman in Fig. 134 in ceremonial attire does wear a cape-like cloak.

Striking hats and caps were so much the rage in late Tudor times that "every servynge man . . . even all indifferently, dooe weare of these hattes" (1585. P. Stubbes, *Anatomy of Abuses*).

As regards materials, white broadcloth was usual for trunk hose. Blue watchet was adopted for the other garments of nearly all servants and apprentices (who often lent a hand with domestic work). This convention for blue lasted from early Tudor till late Stuart times and throughout that period blue was avoided by gentlemen. In Dekker's *Honest Whore* (1604) a master, after disguising himself by exchanging his cloak for the blue coat of his serving-man, says:

> You proud varlets, you need not be ashamed to wear blue when your master is one of your fellows.

Again:

> Since blue coats have been turned into cloaks we can scarce know the man from the master.
>
> 1607. T. Middleton, *A Trick to Catch the Old One.*

The colour is mentioned again in Shakespeare's touching picture of the efforts of some servants to look their best on the return of their master with his bride. The head man gives orders:

> Let their blue coats [be] brushed and their garters indifferently [plainly] knit

and let them wear

> their new fustian and their white stockings.

---

[1] Meaning below the rank of gentleman.

[2] But the Bishop of Winchester in 1535 rode forth with a dozen lackeys in gay velvet cheyney cloaks with large velvet capes.

Some of them were not able to appear at all because:

> Nathaniel's coat, sir, was not fully made, And Gabriel's pumps were all
> unpink'd i' the heel.[1] There was no link to colour Peter's hat, And Walter's
> dagger was not come from the sheathing.
>> *Taming of the Shrew,* IV. i.

If an employer had a family crest, this would distinguish one blue livery
from another. F. Thynn (?) describes a knight travelling with five servants
all wearing "for cognizaunce a pecock (as me thought) without a tayle".[2]
When sham hanging sleeves came in, as ornaments for jerkins, it was on
these that the badge was blazoned (one's "heart on one's sleeve").

Where the livery had a distinctive heraldic colour, tawney was specially
favoured by dignitaries of the Church. The Duke of Gloucester exhorts his
serving-men against Cardinal Beaufort's thus:

> Draw, men, for all this privileged place;
> Blue coats to tawney coats! Priest beware . . .
>> *1 Henry VI,* I. iii.

At Ingateston Hall the livery was of grey frieze in winter and fine grey
marble cloth in summer. Even the miller got his livery.[3]

With special roles went some distinctions in costume. The steward's
insignia are mentioned under seventeenth century. A bailiff would be almost
ornately dressed. One such bequeathed to his master's daughter:

> Gold buttons, after strawbereyes' fashion hanging, upon my new Spannyshe
> lether jerkin.
>> 1582. Transcripts of Wills, Canterbury. E.R.O.

The falconer, a very eminent member of the staff, wore tasselled gauntlet
and a hat with plumes (Fig. 258, p. 341).

The napkin was part of the outfit of those who waited at table. All three
gentlemen serving the Queen at a picnic scene in Turbervile's book are shown
carrying one. The apron was still little in evidence, but her butler drawing
wine wears one (Fig. 135), and so did men serving it in inns:

[1] Red heels were the fashion.
[2] *Debate between Pride and Lowliness,* 1568
[3] F G. Emmison, *Tudor Secretary,* 1961.

135. Queen Elizabeth I's butler at a hunting picnic. Small apron over his trunk hose. 1575. (?)

2nd Drawer [of wine]: Here will be the Prince [Hal], and Master Poins anon, and they will put on two of our jerkins and aprons and Sir John must not know of it.

2 Henry IV, II. iv.

Aprons or no, there was a regard for cleanliness and neatness in servants' dress. John Harington, once tutor to James I's daughter Elizabeth, put forward among rules for good management that a servant should be fined 6*d.* for a dirty shirt on Sunday or a missing button.

Less is known about the general manservant in a small household than about the staffs of large. For him, suffice it to quote some of the list he was to learn by heart when travelling on horseback, "that he shall not forget his gere in his ynne behynde him". Besides writing and mending materials, harness, etc., there were

Cloke, nyght cap, kerchief, boget [budget or bag], sporres [spurs] and shoes, hat, gloues, sword, dagger and purse.

1523. J. Fitzherbert, *Boke of Husbandrye.*

Seventeenth Century

In the seventeenth century a nobleman's hoards of servants were still ruled over by a steward and other gentlemen.

> And by this staff[1] of office that commands you, this [gold] chain and double ruff, symbols of power . . .
>
> c. 1630. Massinger, A New Way to Pay Old Debts.

The page would still be a gentleman's son, "but none under the degree of a Lord would have such a servant".[2] The Earl of Bedford's steward records spending in 1670 and 1681:

> for two shirts for the little page 7s. 6d.,
> for two periwigs for my lady's page £2. 0. 0.
> for scouring his clothes 1s. 0d.[3]

This page's stockings, hat, shoebuckles and the buttons for his cuffs are all mentioned at various times. R. Holme says of pages: "their habit is Trunk Breeches", and he figures a page in the trunk hose typical of a century earlier. Thus it may already have been stylish for a page to be somewhat picturesque, like our "Buttons" of yesterday. The one shown in Plate 30a, however, is in the height of fashion for his own day.

Liveries became more and more glorious. To attend a wedding in 1623 the Duke of Bristol had more than thirty "rich liveries made of watchet velvet with silver lace up to the very capes of their cloaks".

The outdoor garment was called a "trencher cloak" (servants were trenchermen, i.e. resident).

In a ballad of the time (Roxburghe, I, No. 188) a servant praises his own fortunes compared with those of a husbandman. At court he can wear:

> A shirt as white as milk
> And wrought of finest silk.

However, in the woodcut he is depicted wearing a "flat-cap". This style was introduced by Henry VIII, but owing to Elizabethan Sumptuary Laws insisting that working townsfolk should wear such caps (of wool), they were

---

[1] The Lord Steward of today, responsible for the Royal household management, still bears a ceremonial rod.

[2] R. Holme, *Academy of Amory*, 1688.

[3] Quoted in M. Harrison and O. Royston, *How They Lived 1685–1700.*

abandoned by the gentry, and by mid-seventeenth century were seen only as part of livery.

Remarkably enough, some of the aristocracy insisted that as a mark of respect the coachman should drive them without his hat on. It is recorded that at his fall Lord Bacon was censured for this practice.

In the seventeenth century for the first time "military and civil uniforms diverged, the latter retaining the name livery".[1] But a medieval custom remained—any servant, even when his master was merely out shopping or calling, would escort him wearing a sword.[2]

136. "Serving Man". Loose coat with hanging sleeves. Second half of the 17th century.

Liveried servants had informal clothes for use behind the scenes; "the footman's undress jacket of linen" is mentioned in 1641.[3] When his employers went into mourning he was supplied with a black coat.

The lower grades of "serving-men" wore over the doublet and breeches a characteristic loose coat hanging straight down to mid-thigh with loose or with hanging sleeves (Fig. 136). In the form of a "gabardine" this had been

[1] J. Laver in *Country Life Annual 1951*.

[2] Weapons and extravagances of dress were, however, frowned upon in households with special standards of humility and economy, like Charterhouse Hospital, a home for the poor. Here not only the "Poor Brethren" but the "Inferior Officers and Members" were forbidden to wear:

"Any weapons, long hair, coloured boots, spurs, feathers in their hats, or any Russian-like or unseemly Apparel."

[3] Contemporary account quoted in *Domestic Life in England . . .* by the Editor of the *Family Manual . . .*, 1835.

quite fashionable before 1560, but was now a garment for working people solely.

Where there was only one indoor manservant quick changes might be necessary. A young mistress before one of her first dinner-parties turns the kitchen boy into a footman:

> Where's that knave Pipkin . . . bid the fellow make himself handsome, get
> him a clean band [collar] . . . Sirrah, get a napkin and wait today.
>
>   1605. Dodsley's *Collection of Old Plays*. Edited Hazlitt.

The staff of inns cannot fully be dealt with here, but it is worth remarking on the strange appearance of a waiter in one of the Roxburghe Ballad woodcuts (Fig. 137). He wears ankle-length trousers—a garment never seen on the upper classes at this time, though sometimes on rural labourers. Over his shoulder is again the traditional napkin.

Eighteenth Century, Upper and Liveried Staff

In the eighteenth century superior servants such as the butler and the valet (who took the place of the "gentleman in waiting" early in the cen-

137. Waiter at inn, in the trouser-like garments worn only by humblest menial workers; napkin over shoulder. (He apparently holds client's stick as he hands him a mug.) 1620–1630.

tury) dressed much like their employers. The somewhat crude Tony Lumpkin did put his man Diggory into livery and thereby drew the cry from a sophisticated valet:

> Do you make no difference between a fellow in livery and a gentleman's gentleman?

Diggory, in soliloquy, returns the sneer with

> How genteel he looks in his master's old clothes.[1]

The gentlemanly appearance of upper servants could lead to embarrassment. After a visit to the Duke of Newcastle in 1780 a foreigner wrote:

> Ten or twelve servants out of livery attended on us, which would naturally make it difficult for a stranger to distinguish between guests and servants.
>
> J. W. van Archenholz, *Picture of England.* Trans: 1791.

Pages of superior social standing, who were now rarer than formerly, often did wear livery, but in a rather special style of their own.

A rapid growth of the commercial middle class resulted in an "extraordinary number of domestics" of the liveried and lower ranks, especially in towns. Countryfolk

> seduced by the appearance of coxcombs in livery . . . swarm up to London in hopes of getting into service where they can live luxuriously and wear fine clothes.
>
> 1771. Smollett, . . . *Humphry Clinker.*

The family coach, now well established, served admirably for the display of livery. "Every trader, every broker and attorney, maintains a couple of footmen, a coachman and postillion" (ibid.). In such competition, says a writer in the *London Chronicle*, 1762, "I have known many a Doctor and Apothecary starve themselves that they may maintain their footman".

A livery suit, in the family's colours if any, consisted of coat, waistcoat, tight breeches and a hat, all in contemporary style. The fitting coat was increasingly replaced by the "frock",[2] whose turn-down collar and cuffs would have a contrasting colour. Breeches were of similar cloth or of a piled cloth, either "shag" or plush.

---

[1] J. O'Keefe, *Tony Lumpkin in Town*, 1782.
[2] Quite distinct from the frockcoat of the nineteenth century.

Overcoats (surtouts) took the place of cloaks, and coachmen, especially, affected the type called "wrap rascal", often with multiple capes overlapping each other to shed the rain.

Hats, at first slouched, later three-cornered, were generally black and made of "Caroline" beaver.

All parts of the outfit were elaborately ornamented.

> Livery? Lord, madam, I took him for a captain, he's so bedizened with lace! And then he has tops on his shoes up to his mid-leg . . . and has a fine long periwig tied up in a bag.
>
> <div align="right">1707. G. Farquhar, <i>The Beaux' Stratagem</i>.</div>

The *Morning Post* (1777) described Lord Derby's footmen in their "red feathers, and flame coloured stockings" as looking like something in opera. But the peak was perhaps reached about the end of the century when an American wrote:

> The livery of the footmen was gaudy and fantastical in the last degree. They wore lace [braid] not only on the borders but on all the seams of their garments and their large cocked hats were surrounded by broad fringes of silver and gold.
>
> <div align="right">1820. B. Silliman, <i>A Journal of . . . the years 1805–6</i>.</div>

An interesting "vestigial structure" was the "shoulder knot" of ribbons or cords. This had been in general wear in the seventeenth century, but was now a mark of livery only (Fig. 138, cf. Plate 24b). The expression "a knight of the shoulder knot" is used to denote a footman in O'Keefe's *Doldrum*, 1796.

The wearing of a sword by servants, as a frequent threat to peace,[1] was at last prohibited by law in 1701; henceforth to carry a sword became the mark of a gentleman.

R. Dodsley in his satire *The Footman's Friendly Advice to his Brethren* . . . (1731) sums up the footman thus:

> Internal qualities conduce to greater ends
> Than . . . powder'd Wiggs, clean Shirts and such like do;
> Yet these are necessary, and 'tis fit
> That those whom Time and Business will permit

---

[1] John Evelyn, on a journey in 1675, himself saw a servant, in a frenzy of jealousy, endeavour to fall upon his own sword and, when deprived of this, seize a fellow servant's sword and attempt murder.

138. Servant with livery shoulder-knot—derived from a by-gone
fashion. (Cf. Plate 246.) 1747.

Appear before their Masters always clean and neat.
But don't ye run into affected Ways . . .
Be decent, clean and handsome but not nice.

The postilions were an important element in the grander equipage. Their
suits, in 1757, cost the Duke of Bedford nearly £5 each in contemporary
money.[1] Made of the orange cloth of the Russell's livery, each was "richly
laced with gold and velvet" and had nearly a hundred gilt buttons.[2]

[1] £5 in 1757 would be a carpenter's wages for fifty working days. It would buy food,
fuel and clothing worth about £30 in 1954.
[2] G. Scott Thomson, *The Russells in Bloomsbury 1669–1771*, 1940.

It is a relief to learn that additional "work clothes" were provided for liveried servants:

> Bring 3 Linnen washing frocks[1] for the 3 men servants such as you used to bring; let them be big enough, the last were too tite upon 'em.[2]

The coachman needed his frock "to put on over his cloaths when he rubs the horses down".[3] A gentleman records in 1734 buying a "white frock" for one of his footmen "to powder my periwigs in".[4] Worsted stockings, heavy shoes, leather or cloth breeches and coarse shirts were supplied by the Duke of Bedford to every footman for rough work.

Running Footmen

The eighteenth century was the heyday of the running footman. His antecedent was the groom who ran beside his employer's horse (as "trotter" in the thirteenth century) and we read that in 1500

> Mony of hem foteman ther ben
> That rennen by the brydels of ladys.
>   *Boke of Kurtasye* (E.E.T.S.), 1868.

In 1608 the running footman was nicknamed "Linnen stockings and three-score miles a day" and in 1688 what is described under the head "footman" by R. Holme is clearly one of these:

> generally for ease of speedy going clothed in light thin cloaths, all in white, as doublet, slashed or open, breeches or drawers, and stockings of the same, thin soled shoes called "pumps". These men run by their Lord's coach or horse's side.
>   *Academy of Armory.*

The white stockings and pumps persisted as dress wear for footmen right down to the present day.

In the eighteenth century the running footman went in front of the coach, chiefly to make a show, and a very fine show it evidently was. His costume, though for once comfortable—e.g. the heel-less light pumps—is also quite spectacular. A description dated 1730 runs:

---

[1] Smocklike overalls.
[2] *Purefoy Letters 1735–1753*. Edited by G. Eland, 1931.
[3] Ibid.
[4] Fitzwalter's Account Book, 1734-5. Essex Record Office.

Fine Holland drawers and waistcoat, a blue silk sash fringed with silver, a velvet cap with a great tassel; and a porter's staff with a large silver handle.

The Weekly Journal.

A white jacket was the usual outer garment: "white dimity [cotton] fringed with black" was how William Hutton remembered one in 1741.[1]

Looking back on his youth in Ireland in the 1760s, John O'Keefe recalls a costume so similar that it must have become almost a uniform for running footmen—the same white jacket, blue silk sash, velvet cap with silver tassel and the long staff.[2]

The runner's breeches till mid-century were of the kind called "petticoat breeches" (see Plate 24b). The fashion for these, introduced from France in 1658 and affected by Charles II, was abandoned by the upper classes after about fifteen years; but owing to their extreme width (they were like full divided skirts) they were favoured by running footmen for a century. If worn without drawers beneath, they were sometimes for decency kept down by a deep gold fringe—but alas not always:

> Village Maids delight to see the Running Footman fly bare-ars'd o'er the dusty road.
>
> 1725.[3]

Negro Servants

The expansion of overseas trade and exploration caused a fashion to spring up for the employment of negro footmen and pages.[4] Paid no wages, in the early part of the century they even wore a badge of slavery in the form of a silver collar (see Plate 25). Advertisements such as the following from *The Times*, 1794, were all too common.

> *Absconded.* An . . . indented black servant lad named Toney, aged about 19 . . . very black and slender made. He went off in a striped dressing jacket, Nankeen [a yellowish cotton] waistcoat and breeches, ribbed cotton stockings, shoes and plated buckles.

The clothes here described were probably the man's "undress" wear. His livery would have made him too easily recognizable. A Negro's livery was

[1] *Book of Recollections.*

[2] *Recollections of the Life of John O'Keefe*, written by himself, 1826.

[3] Quoted from a writer of 1725 by E. Bovill in *English Country Life*, 1963.

[4] Dr Johnson employed a negro servant and the Duchess of Devonshire had a black page of eleven years old.

generally very smart and might comprise some exotic feature such as a feathered turban (see Plate 25).

In the nineteenth century the fashion for employing Negro servants gradually died out, but they could still be seen on grand carriages in the 1830s.

Eighteenth Century Small Households

Needless to say in many households where there were only one or two menservants these might not wear livery at all.

The advertisements that follow give an idea of the clothes worn by un-classified men "servants". Clothing, apart from underwear and shoes, was generally provided for them, whether livery or not, so that abscondence meant theft as well as default.

> *Servant absconded* [wearing] his own brown short hair; buckskin breeches' white swanskin[1] lapelled waistcoat, light-coloured cloth cape-coat.
> 1765. *Ipswich Journal.*

> *Servant Run away* in brown clipt wig, a duffel [coarse woollen] coat, a drill Frock [the "undress" summer coat of the period].
> 1795. *Ipswich Journal.*

Nineteenth and Twentieth Centuries

Early in the nineteenth century gentlemen's everyday fashions changed abruptly—trousers came in, and owing to a tax on powder, wigs went out. An eighteenth-century appearance, however, was faithfully preserved in livery, and this underlined the difference between the "upper" and "lower" servants.

Upper Servants

The valet or gentleman's gentleman, needless to say, followed the vogue. There is a hint, however, in the caricature shown in Fig. 139 that he did not dare to be quite as fashionable as his master. Neither of them has yet gone into trousers, but only the valet still wears a wig. As time went on a gentle-man's clothes became less formal; the valet's tended to lag behind so that he became, like P. G. Wodehouse's Jeeves, the more formal of the two.

Butlers also aimed at a gentlemanly appearance, but tended to affect a

---

[1] A sort of flannel used by working men.

139. Prince Regent with his valet, who is similarly dressed except for
having a queue wig instead of his own hair. 1812.

mildly old-fashioned dignity. Surtees, in 1831,[1] describes one butler in the
fashionable tight pantaloons, while another is quite of the old school, in knee
breeches ("shorts"), and:

> a blue coat with velvet collar and metal buttons . . . white silk stockings
> . . . a white waistcoat and a [shirt] frill as big as a handsaw.

This was exactly what a gentleman wore as formal evening dress twenty
years before, or as court dress in the butler's own day. Even in 1847 a
coloured print by W. M. Thackeray shows a butler in evening dress still
wearing breeches (Fig. 141). However, he would always be more up to date
than the liveried footman, as well as quieter in his colours. In Thackeray's
print his evening coat is blue grey, his waistcoat white, his breeches black;
the footman's coat is green with red tabs and gold edging, his waistcoat and
breeches red. But butlers might let themselves go when it came to day-
waistcoats, as is only too clear from the following:

[1] *Jorrocks's Jaunts.*

a rich, . . . all the colours of the rainbow reflecting, vest, set off with metal buttons.

1854. R. S. Surtees, Handley Cross.

By the late 1870s butlers' smart evening wear had taken on an almost modern appearance—black trousers, white "boiled" shirt and white waistcoat. Again the note is formal—even when his master dined alone the butler might wear a white tie (Fig. 140). In the twentieth century his afternoon

140. Butler in formal dress clothes although his master dines alone.
1879.

toilet was indistinguishable from his master's evening dress—except that he wore white gloves. Even in the 1870s the conservative rural butler was still clinging to breeches and white stockings.

Butlers' pantry clothes included a large square-bibbed apron. The Cardiff Museum has an example, in linen, dated 1839. Green baize aprons were adopted later. "A spruce green gambroon [cotton mixture] butler's pantry jacket[1] with pockets" (1831–4) was another adjunct.[2]

[1] A *jacket,* i.e. short unskirted loose coat, was adopted by the gentry only in the second half of the century.

[2] Surtees, *Jorrocks's Jaunts.*

In 1826 Creevey writes of visiting the Earl of Darlington:

> I wish you could have seen the servants . . . the four servants out of livery
> [i.e. upper servants] had brown coats and gold embroidery and frogs exactly
> the same as the King's dress uniform. The six or seven livery servants were in
> bright yellow dress coats.

It must have been highly unusual for upper servants to be put into a uniform
and Creevey hints that this was a vulgarity of the upstart Countess.

141. Evening guest, footman and butler. Footman in typical livery,
i.e. 18th century style. Tail coat not squarely cut away and
having stand collar; long waistcoat; breeches; ruffled shirt (coat
green, breeches red, edging and buttons gold, stockings white.)
Butler dressed like the guest except for wearing breeches and a grey
coat instead of black. 1847. Compare Fig. 142 *a* and *b*.

Footmen

For more than half the century the better-class footman's indoor livery resembled the court dress of the early decades. Designed on purely eighteenth-century lines, it comprised a knee-length coat, worn open or nearly so, a long waistcoat, knee-breeches often made of plush, stockings (conventionally of white silk), and for evenings buckled shoes or pumps (Fig. 141). Except for being further cut away, in a curved line, the coat was in a style typical of the 1770s, trimmed with metal buttons and often braid (compare Fig. 141 with 142a and b). The traditional shoulder knot persisted, often composed of long gold "lace" (cords) hanging even to the elbow,

(a)   (b)

142. For comparison with Footman in Fig. 141. (*a*) Gentleman's day dress. *c.* 1775. (*b*) Court dress, 1831. Each consists of tailcoat, not squarely cut away, and with large cuffs and stand collar or none; long waistcoat; breeches, ruffled skirt, buckled shoes—all like the footman's livery. In (*a*) the colour is also bright (green and silver). In (*b*) note the "flash", a bow on the coat replacing the bow on the queue wig of the previous generation.

FLUNKEIANA.

John Thomas. "YES, I MUST LEAVE. YOU SEE, MARY, MY DEAR—THERE'S TOO MUCH RED
IN THE LIVERY, AND THAT DON'T SUIT MY COMPLEXION—NEVER DID!"

143. Footman's livery with shoulder-knot. 1857.

sometimes with one of the ends sewn into the facing seam while the others
were finished with "aigulets" (tags). See Fig. 143. The employer's crest, once
embroidered on the coat, was now relegated to its buttons, and a Birmingham
manufacturer was said to hold 10,000 different dies at once, for stamping
these.

A "sword-slash" would still be left in the overcoat so that the man could
get at his non-existent sword, and sometimes even in the 1880s a "flash"
(bow or rosette) might be put at the back of the neck of his coat to represent
the bow on his non-existent wig (Fig. 144). Another interesting "vestige"
was the thin cord worn over the left shoulder by royal footmen when
travelling. Like that of the Household Cavalry today, this was a relic of the
string that carried a flask of powder for their one-time pistols.

144. Footmen of a magnate. Livery in typical 18th century style
including bow at back of neck representing the bow of long extinct
queue wig. 1880. Compare Fig. 142b.

The wig itself lingered on well into the century and was then replaced by
powdered hair, which lasted, for smart footmen, until its end. With an
imperfectly trained young man, as described by Surtees in 1854,[1] this might
degenerate into

> a quantity of flour concealing the natural colour of his wild matted hair.

Even in 1937 an ex-footman recalls that in his boyhood, when called upon
suddenly "to go on the carriage" in the footman's place, he, too, had to
resort to flour. The said footman himself was allowed £2 a year for "Violet
powder".

Another anachronism was the style of hat. In the early decades this would
have a cocked bicorne or tricorne brim, often trimmed with gold lace,

[1] *Handley Cross.*

exactly like the hat that was normal for gentlemen in the 1740s. This gave place in the 1830s to the universal silk top-hat. If the master came of an armigerous family or was an officer in the sovereign's or a foreign embassy's service, the livery hat bore a distinctive rosette-like cockade; at a wedding this would be white.

Waistcoats (vests) were very often striped—horizontally for indoor servants and vertically for outdoor. Surtees pokes fun at a rural footman whose stripes went the wrong way.[1]

Washable white "Berlin" gloves were worn outdoors and indoors alike.

After the 1860s the squarely cutaway day dress coat, ceasing to be fashionable wear, had become correct for day livery (Fig. 145). Its tails shortened and eventually it turned into coatee. However, many footmen in their best still wore the original shape of coat even in the 1870s.

From about 1870 a well-dressed footman might at last wear trousers, and these would match the coat. The coat itself shed most of its furbelows. At last its only insignia of servitude were its brass buttons (nearly all of them functionless), its "evening-dress" appearance and finally its colour.

Overcoats right down to the feet were the fashion in the 1880s and 1890s and a head footman might be dignified by one of these (Fig. 146). An actual specimen in the London Museum is nearly five feet long.

Colour in the livery of old families was fixed by verbal tradition. That it should be recorded in print in "all future editions of the Peerages and Baronetages" was recommended ineffectively in a letter to the *Gentleman's Magazine* in 1784, which maintained that the colour of the servant's coat, as a cognizance, was of as much consequence as the crest. A chart showing various livery colours of the early nineteenth century may be seen at Bristol Museum.

With the "new rich", colour schemes for liveries were left to what often proved too fertile an invention. It was orthodox for the different garments of the suit to present some contrast, and this opened the way to a garishness which worsened with the introduction of aniline dyes in the 1860s. In a satire of 1847, the ambitious wife of a lawyer, engaging her first footman, writes in her diary:

> The livery I had made was one of the sweetest things when it was new. Every
> article of the entire suit was of a different colour. I ordered . . . the love of a

[1] Ibid.

white coat and a pet of a canary waistcoat and a perfect duck of a pair of bright crimson plush knee what d'ye-callums.

H. and A. Mayhew, *The Greatest Plague of Life.*

Surtees' befloured footman was another example. "A clumsy looking youth

145. Footman. Tailcoat now squarely cut away. Light colour for morning wear. 1869.

(*a*)　　　(*b*)　　　　(*c*)　　　(*d*)

146. (*b*) and (*d*) Head footmen of two households in foot length overcoats and cockaded top hats. (*a*) Second footman in breeches. (*c*) Second footman in trousers. 1883.

in a gorgeous suit of state livery", his coat was bright orange coloured, his waistcoat had broad blue-and-white stripes and his breeches were of scarlet plush. Small wonder at one of J. Leech's "Flunkeiana" (*Punch*, 1857) see Fig. 143. However, by 1897 gaudy colours were clearly not in good taste. The *Tailor and Cutter* writes of such liveries:

> Garments made from every conceivable shade, yellow, green, salmon, blue, plum . . . gaudy but ugly, showy but cumbersome, costly and well nigh useless, eccentric if not grotesque. The sooner some of these are presented to family museums the better.

A few of our public museums have, indeed, reaped some of the crop.

Footmen of the wealthy had both dress and undress livery and all had informal clothes as well, e.g. the "curious yellow jean jackets of the 1860s" remembered by Lord Frederic Hamilton.[1] A footman would clean the knives in

[1] Lord Frederic Hamilton, *The Days before Yesterday*, 1920.

an overall, a waistcoat, a fustian jacket and a leather apron, with a white apron to put on occasionally when called from these duties.[1]

Coachmen and Grooms

> Every genuine coachman has his characteristic costume. His flaxen curls or wig, his low cocked hat, his plush breeches and his benjamin surtout,[2] his clothes being well brushed and the lace buttons in a state of high polish.[3]

Even in the 1860s a very smart coachman would still wear a wig. His livery, while agreeing with the footman's in colour and "old-fashioned" style, differed in several points. His overcoat like the footman's had a shoulder knot, but was generally longer and heavier and often caped. As such it gave its name "box coat" to a fashion for the gentry. The *West End Gazette* of 1877 records some conventional distinctions that seem to be made purely for distinction's sake. A footman's greatcoat had pockets on the pleats only and had plain stitched seams, but a coachman's had pockets on the hips only and double-stitched seams.

As we have seen, the stripes of a livery vest must be horizontal for a footman, but vertical for a coachman and grooms.

The association with horses made coachmen stick to breeches, jackboots or gaiters all through the century. The outfit in the later years is well exemplified by a livery suit of Mr Gladstone's coachman now preserved in the Cardiff Museum.

In 1912 it could still be written:

> Modern coachmen . . . wear the tall hat, the bright buttons, doeskin breeches and top boots characteristic of the . . . riding dress of the gentleman of the beginning of the 19th century.
>
> M. W. Webb, *Heritage of Dress.*

Postilions were still a great feature of the high-class family coach. Lord Frederic Hamilton writes of his boyhood in the 1860s:

> The crimson barouche with the six blacks and our own black and crimson liveries made a very smart turnout indeed. . . . It was my consuming ambition to ride leader postilion and above all to wear the big silver coat-of-

[1] S. and S. Adams, *The Complete Servant,* 1825.
[2] A loose overcoat worn by working classes.
[3] S. and S. Adams, *The Complete Servant,* 1825.

PLATE 25

PLATE 25

Negro page-boy. Fancy turban, silver collar (would be engraved with employer's name); livery shoulder-knot.
1732–34.

Engraving by W. Hogarth. Harlot's Progress II. (Detail.)

PLATE 26

PLATE 26

(*a*) Page and "Tiger".
Page in typical pageboy's livery.
"Tiger" in elegantly waisted blue coat, red waistcoat, white corduroy breeches, gold banded grey cockaded top-hat, and top boots. 1848.

J. Couts, Guide to Cutting. *1848.*

(*b*) Chauffeur in livery coat, breeches and leggings like a groom's. *c.* 1920.

Photograph kindly lent by Mrs A. Mansfield.

arms our postilions had strapped to the left sleeves of their short jackets on a broad crimson band.

1920. *The Days Before Yesterday.*

Tigers

> His tiger Tim was clean of limb
> His boots were polished his jacket was trim
> With a very smart tie in his smart cravat
> And a little cockade on the top of his hat.

1837. R. Barham, *Ingoldsby Legends.*

In about 1830 a light "gentleman's cabriolet", driven by its owner, attained great popularity. Displayed on a platform behind was the equipage's Tiger—a type immortalized in Dickens's Mr Bailey. He would be a diminutive youth wearing a specially dashing livery of riding-dress (although he was not riding). His coat was either a little tight tunic like a jockey's, or a long-skirted coat as in Plate 26a, or else a frockcoat with conspicuous trimmings. A letter purporting to come from a youthful lady's maid in an upstart Bloomsbury family appeared in *Punch* in 1841. A member of the staff she describes was

> Theodore—in the morning he's a tigger drest in a tite froc-cote, top-boots buxkin smawlcloses[1] and stuck up behind Master Ahgustusses cab.

Chauffeur and Hall Staff

In the twentieth century the coachman's mantle fell on the chauffeur, who recognized the heritage by wearing riding breeches and gaiters for another twenty years (see Plate 26b).

Descendants of the footman are the liveried doormen and hall porters of public buildings. Their braided and distinctively coloured coats, with contrasting collar, epaulettes and stamped buttons, also the doorman's cockaded topper, are all relics of the past. At the British Museum the doorman of 1840 wore "Windsor uniform"—blue coat with red-and-gold collar and cuffs (see Plate 27a). Like the "Windsor livery" still worn in the royal household, this was almost identical with semi-court dress as worn from George III's reign to the end of Queen Victoria's. The Museum livery changed only in the 1950s to navy blue, and the special insignia are now confined to buttons, collar and hatband.

[1] Breeches.

147. Cook, Footman, Housemaid and Page. Page in typical short,
tight tunic with rows of buttons. 1847.

Pages

The page, who has perhaps undergone more changes than any others
of the domestic staff, became by Queen Victoria's reign a boy of neither
noble nor exotic origin. He retained, however, his smartness, his smallness
and his ranking as an upper servant. From mid-nineteenth century to the
end of our period his livery suit was a tight little coat reaching only to the

waist, like an Eton jacket, and pantaloons or long trousers. In the days of Tigers one boy might play both parts. Of Theodore, mentioned above, we learn that

> in the evening he gives up the tigger and comes out as the paige, in a fansy iacket, with too rose of guilt buttings . . . and being such a small chap you may suppose they [the ladies] can never make enuff of him.

The custom of giving him, on his padded chest, one, two, or frequently three rows of buttons with as many as eighteen in each row gave him his popular name of "Buttons" (Fig. 147 and Plate 26a).

> The jacket was a claret, with three rows of sugar loaf buttons so close together as a rope of onions.
>
> 1847. H. and A. Mayhew, *The Greatest Plague* . . .

Shoulder bands were given a new usefulness—they helped the boy not to lose his white gloves.

From about 1890 a pillbox cap replaced his topper.

Unliveried Outdoor Servants

For undergrooms, stable-boys and ostlers a loose brown "jacket" is described as early as 1788. An alternative was a waist-length coatee like a

148. Groom. Light jacket, breeches, gaiters.
c. 1840s.

jockey's. Grooms had breeches, with leggings, gaiters or top boots, smart white "starchers" (cravats) and gay waistcoats.

Ostlers at inns sometimes wore a garment shown in Fig. 149—a cross between leggings and trousers, buttoned down the side from waist to ankle.

When working in the stables a man might still don a washable overall shaped like a smock (see Plate 27b).

149. Ostler at inn (holding a sieve). Combined trousers and leggings. 1828.

Waiters

The costume of waiters in hotels and restaurants differentiated itself during the century. Content before to wear ordinary costume with an apron and the traditional napkin, he now took on a more formal appearance and, like footmen, affected the fashions of a bygone day. In 1822 Cruikshank depicts him in a rather low-down inn wearing a blue jacket, a white apron and the now outdated brown breeches; in a smarter inn at the same date he was wearing a cutaway tail coat and coloured waistcoat, but again breeches and white stockings. Mr Pickwick saw him (not at his best) in the Great White Horse, Ipswich, "with a fortnight's napkin under his arm and co-eval stockings on his legs".

In 1841 P. Prendergast[1] points to some nice distinctions which are confirmed by G. Scharf's drawings. "Waiters in hotels, and inferior inns and coffee houses" wore

> a decent suit of black and a white neckcloth, and but for their white cotton stockings, might almost be mistaken for clergy. At an eating house, on the other hand, they might wear a black neckcloth and either a blue coat with brass buttons or a striped linen jacket . . . called a duck-hunter.

Valuing smartness above comfort, most waiters in the 1840s clung to the high stiff-winged collars that had pilloried the fashionable between 1810 and 1830 (Fig. 128).

By the 1870s waiters had come down in favour of the "decent black" for most purposes. Formality was emphasized by the coats having tails, even in day-time, and although a light colour was permissible in the mornings this might be associated with the prevailing white bow-tie. An apron could be worn at a restaurant even by a waiter in a boiled shirt.

In the 1880s a light-coloured washable tail-less informal jacket appears for morning wear, perhaps for the first time, and finally at the turn of the century gave place to the hygienic white coatee of today.

General Servants

In the typical small middle-class household where there was only one male servant his costume varied.

In the country, combining as he often did the roles of "groom and game keeper in the morning and butler and footman in the afternoon", Surtees describes such a man as wearing "an old white hat, a groom's fustian stable coat cut down into a shooting jacket, red plush smalls and top boots".[2]

The general factotum Sam Weller

> was provided with a grey coat, a black hat with a cockade to it, a pink striped waistcoat, light breeches and gaiters.

"Dress is another bogy", writes an ex-manservant in 1925.[3] "Some years ago men [in high-class households] had to go to church in livery . . . Servants in a small establishment are more prone to indulge in the fashion of the day."

---

[1] *Heads of the People.*
[2] *Jorrocks's Jaunts,* 1831–4.
[3] W. Lanceley, *From Hall-boy to House-Steward.*

150. General manservant, serving at breakfast. White jacket and apron. 1848.

There was, indeed, a general decline in the wearing of livery from mid-nineteenth century onwards and this is partly explained by Mayhew in his *London Characters*. He says that despite the lavish supply of livery clothes and good wages which "these difficult-to-be-got servants can bargain for", nevertheless—

> The 19th century considers livery a badge of servitude . . . certain it is, a man for livery is scarcer than he was. . . . In what are called single-handed places it is even more difficult to get a man to wear livery . . . He likes . . . to consider himself on the level of a butler.

Now, on top of this, he has come to like more washable and comfortable clothing. Figure 150 shows an early example of the popular light coat.

In summary it might be said that the keynote to the costume of domestic servants, except when out of sight, has been in the past formality and ornament. What the footman wore at home was like his master's dress at court; what the waiter wore at lunch was like his customer's dress at dinner; but now the truly decorative servant, the period piece in his livery, is dying out —historical pageantry and display are giving place to democracy, hygiene and convenience.

CHAPTER VII

HOUSEHOLD SERVANTS—WOMEN

Defoe writes in 1725:

> I was once put very much to the Blush, being at a friend's House and re-
> quir'd of him to salute the Ladies, I kis'd the Chamber-Jade into the bargain,
> for she was as well dressed as the best. Things of this kind would be avoided
> if our Servant Maids were to wear livery as our Footmen do, or if they were
> obliged to go in a Dress suitable to their Station.[1]

The idea of livery for women domestics never took on and there was
scarcely any regulation costume for them until the reign of Queen Victoria.
Up to that time—when the demand for dining-room and drawing-room
servants began to exceed the supply of men—the women were either too
high in rank to wear clothing that stamped them in any way as servants, or
else were largely behind the scenes, where their dress need not be standard-
ized.

LADIES' MAIDS AND HOUSEKEEPERS

In the higher ranks belong ladies' gentlewomen or waiting-women (later
"ladies' maids") and housekeepers. Employed in upper-class households, they
were themselves, in the earlier centuries, of gentle or even noble birth and a
lady's maid was a confidante of her mistress. They naturally dressed very
much as she did, with at first nothing to distinguish them except an avoidance
of display. In Fig. 151 and Plate 28a both mistress and maid are in their
kirtles. The maid in Plate 28a, attending Pharaoh's young daughter (indicated by the crown), is shown without any headdress, to suggest that she is
a young girl. Even these gentlewomen had at least part of their clothing provided for them and this continued to be true until the nineteenth century.

---

[1] *Everybody's Business is Nobody's Business.*

The account-book of Prince Lionel's household in 1356–9 records the purchase for "Philippa Pan", probably a "Panetaria" or mistress of the pantry, of a fur-lined bodice. In addition, it has always been the custom for the mistress to give her cast-offs to her lady's maid.

151. Lady's maid doing her mistress's hair (cf. Fig. 125). Ground length kirtle, veil head-dress. *c.* 1340.

An etching by Hollar (see Plate 28b) gives us a comparison between a lady's maid and her mistress in about 1635–40. The maid's costume combines fashionable cut (her basqued bodice is as "new" as her mistress's stomacher front) with less richness in the material and an absence of lace on the neckerchief. The coif she wears was usual for ladies, but perhaps not quite as smart as her mistress's coiffure. She was allowed shoes in the same style as Madam's, but the master shoemaker whom the lady is addressing was not to make them himself:

My shoes are neate I sweare
Now bid your man go make my maid a paire.

PLATE 27

PLATE 27

(*a*) Doorman to British Museum at Montague House, in his Windsor livery (see text). Tailcoat, breeches and loose leggings. 1840.

Elijah Shaw, Portrait of William Scivier. 1840.

(*b*) Groom in smock-like overall, white "starcher", peaked cap, top boots. 1846.

J. F. Herring, "Gretna Green" (detail). Walker Art Gallery, Liverpool.

PLATE 28

PLATE 28

(a) Foreground: Pharaoh's daughter and her maid, both without headdress being young girls. (The princess has a crown.) Midwife attending Moses' birth and other women have veils. All in ground-length kirtles. 1377–1399.

British Museum MS. Roy. 1 E IX.

(b) Lady and shoemaker, her maid and his assistant. Maid's dress fashionable but her neckerchief and headgear simpler than her mistress's. c. 1630s.

Etching by W. Hollar, "Crispin and Crispianus". British Museum.

In *The Gentlewoman's Companion* (1675), Hannah Wolley advises chamber-maids to "dress well, that you may be able to supply the place of the waiting woman should she chance to be ill". Mrs Wolley also rebukes the indigent gentry for often neglecting the education of their daughters so that they "lacked the accomplishments of a waiting woman or a housekeeper". Possessed of these they "might have inclined ladies to covet their company . . . had respect from other servants, worn good clothes and received a considerable sallary".

By the eighteenth century these advantages might even be the good fortune of a farmworker's daughter, as is told by S. Richardson of his heroine "Pamela" (1740). Training her up in her early 'teens "her good lady gave her learning, . . . cloaths and linen and everything that a gentlewoman need not be ashamed of". When at the lady's death Pamela foresaw that she would have to return home, she felt obliged to "put out the ear rings from her ears" and get herself "equipp'd in the Dress that will become my condition". "For how should your poor Daughter look", she writes,

> With a silk night-gown [i.e. a loose day dress] silken petticoats, cambrick head-cloaths, fine Holland linen, laced shoes that were my lady's and fine [silk or cotton] stockens!

When she had donned a humbler outfit it so transformed her that the house-maid did not recognize her on the stairs.

Highmore's illustrations to *Pamela* (1745) show that the housekeeper, in her tied mob-cap and decorative apron, was also dressed as a lady might be at home (Fig. 152).

Two satirical sketches (Fig. 153 and Plate 29a) show that ladies' maids in the early nineteenth century made a lively response to changes of fashion as regards silhouette. However, they still favoured, indoors, the tied mob-cap that was by then very informal wear for ladies, and their aprons tended to be more workaday and might even be black.

Out walking with her mistress in 1866 a young lady's maid is nicely shown in *Punch*, over the caption "Protector and Protected". Unlike the lady, she wears no fur, she has less trimming on her cap and none at all on her dress; but she is well and fashionably turned out. If more charming than her mistress she cannot be blamed for that, and combining quietness with elegance she is a perfect example of her kind.

152. Housekeeper. Kerchief mob cap and decorative apron, like the informal wear of her mistress. 1745.

153. Lady's maid in fashionable high waist and mob cap like her mistress's. Occupational apron. 1810.

ORDINARY RANKS OF WOMEN SERVANTS

The chambermaids, kitchen staff, nursery maids, dairymaids, etc., of large households, like the general servants of humbler ones, wore outer garments that were shaped in contemporary style, but plainer and made of cheaper cloth such as coarse worsted "stuff" or coarse linen.

Some of their clothing, at least until the eighteenth century, was supplied to them. In 1481 the household account-book of Sir Thomas Howard records:

Maude of the Kechin. Schone, [shoes] viii d.[1]

---

[1] *Howard Household Account Book*. Roxburghe Club, 1845.

Again:

> I did pay Letice her full year's wages . . . being four nobles, an apron and a
> pair of hose and shoes.
>
> <div align="right">1594. <i>John Dee's Diary.</i>[1]</div>

Medieval Times

The long kirtles of the Middle Ages trailed on the ground while these women did their work. They wore long sleeves, very tight below the elbow, and, in the fourteenth century, had flapping veils even when stirring a cauldron of food (Fig. 154). Long bibless aprons, often with a band of embroidery across the top, were worn by servants, but seemingly less often than by typical peasants. However, throughout all the centuries an apron was donned by almost any servant when she cooked. The frivolous type in Fig. 154 is an exception. In the *Holkham Bible Picture Book* the innkeeper's wife is shown wearing gloves at home. She takes one off, leaving it hanging from her wrist when she tends the infant Christ (Fig. 155).

In Plate 29b the woman on her knees is probably a domestic servant of ordinary rank. She wears no "gown" over her white kirtle, but like the ladies she has an elaborate headdress. However, in a similar scene in the second half of the fifteenth century, while the ladies wear the enormous butterfly headdresses then in vogue, it is perhaps significant that the three servants have low-crowned "bonnets" instead.

When waiting at table a maid would wear no headdress at all and again no "gown" until the latter part of the century.

A rare record exists of how a chambermaid of this period would look when beating mattresses. She has the usual veil on her head, but has hitched up her kirtle to ankle length and wears blue gauntlet gloves.[2]

Sixteenth Century

A sixteenth-century general servant is well shown in contemporary illustrations to J. Heywood's *The Spider and the Flie* (1556) (see Fig. 156). She had a typical full-length kirtle; but with her sleeves rolled up, an apron, a ribbon to bind her hair, and no headdress, collar, ruff, stomacher or farthingale, she

---

[1] *English Diaries of XVI, XVII and XVIII Centuries.* Edited by J. Aitken, 1941.
[2] B.M., MS. Tib. A VII, Trans. by J. Lydgate, 1426.

154. Cook in veil and ground-length kirtle; unusual in lacking apron.
Early 14th century.

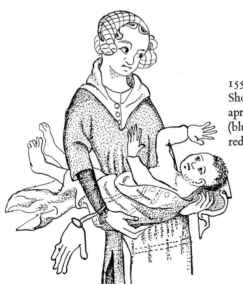

155. Inn keeper's wife tending infant Christ.
Short-sleeved surcote (brown), kirtle (blue),
apron (white with red embroidery), hood
(blue, lined red), net-like headdress (white and
red); white glove hangs from right wrist.
c. 1330.

looks very practically dressed compared with the ladies of her day. The long apron, which she sometimes tucked up, would be made of coarse linen or worsted. This was, of course, quite different from the decorative apron fashionable in the second half of the sixteenth century and again in the eighteenth century. The decorative type was made of transparent cambric, later muslin, or of silk. Such an elegance as that, offered actually as a bribe by her mistress, is greeted rapturously by the maid in Dekker's *Shoemaker's Holiday* (1600).

> By my troth yes! . . . A cambric apron, gloves . . . O rich! A cambric apron!

A model country servant of 1575 is described by Thomas Churchyard as she cleans the house:

156. Maid sweeping away flies. Skirt long but natural in shape and sleeves short; apron; hair bound with ribbon only. *c.* 1556.

And at her gyrdle in a band
A jolly bunch of keyes she wore
Her petticoat fine laest before
Her taile tucke up in trymmest gies
A napkin[1] hanging o'er her eies
To kepe of(f) dust and drosse of walles
That often from the windows falles.

        ("The Spider and the Gowte" in *Churchyardes Chippes*.)

This maid made her own smocks (chemises), and, as well as a holiday gown, her wardrobe comprised:

Two fayre new kirtles to her backe
The one was blue the other black . . .
She had three smockes, she had no lesse
Four rayles and eke five kerchers fayre
Of hose and shoes she had a payre . . .
She would go bare-foote for to save
Her shoes and hose for they were deere.[2]

Seventeenth Century

Figure 157 shows an early-seventeenth-century housemaid. Her white apron is again tucked aside in the manner favoured by anybody who has to stoop in an apron of this length. Note her falling ruff and lace cuffs, the dainty fashion of the period, but in moderate form. The wearing of fripperies by servants was severely discouraged by James I, and the Common Council of London had to enact that maids were to wear "no lawn, kambrick, tiffany, velvet, lawns or white wires on the head or about the kerchief, koyfe . . .", but only linen, and that not to exceed 5s. the ell. Their ruffs were not to be more than 4 yards in length before gathering. Nor were they to have "any fardingale at all, . . . nor any body (bodice) or sleeves of wire, whalebone or other stiffing saving canvass or buckram only".[3]

Plate 30a shows a servant in 1686 who was 96 at the time of the portrait. Her coif and kerchief belong to the period of her youth and their complete lack of trimming are in keeping with her "station".

1 This prototype of the "head-square" is nowhere else mentioned to our knowledge before the eighteenth century.

2 Spelling partly modernized. Rayle = neckerchief worn shawlwise.

3 Quoted by W. Herbert in *Livery Companies of London,* 1837.

157. Maid in dress of the period; falling ruff, slashed sleeves, "cornet" on head); large apron. *c.* 1625–30.

Eighteenth Century

In illustrations to eighteenth-century chapbooks, based mainly on rural life, maids and women cooks have skirts which hang without hoops or are bunched behind for protection; they generally wear mobs or "limp-hoods" instead of the latest style in caps, and their function is always denoted by an apron.

Very different is the impression we get of domestics in town (see Plate 30b). The keen demand for servants in the eighteenth century resulted in high wages and an outburst of sartorial extravagance. A parson's daughter from the country might be poor enough to seek a domestic job possessing only a small bundle of linen and "one cotton nightgown (day dress) two shifts, one white and one coloured apron, two handkerchiefs and a half, and one pair of lac'd shoes".[1] But the urban mistress of such a one wrote "she had not liv'd with me three weeks before she sew'd three Penny Canes round the bottom of her Shift" to serve as a hoop-petticoat.[2]

Defoe declares in 1725[3] that when a country wench goes into service:

[1] D. Defoe, *Everybody's Business* . . . 1725.
[2] Mrs Centilivre, *The Artifice.* 1722.
[3] D. Defoe, ibid.

her Neat's Leather Shoes are now transform'd into lac'd Shoes with high Heels: her Yarn Stockings are turn'd into fine worsted ones with silk Clocks; her high Wooden Pattens are kick't away for Leathern Clogs; she must have a Hoop too . . . and her poor scanty Linsey Woolsey Petticoat is changed into a good Silk one 4 or 5 Yards wide.

Her wearing of cottons and printed linens was deplored because of the cost of washing, and a letter to *The Times* in 1795 complains of the waste of flour entailed in the starching of servants' white dresses and muslin kerchiefs. For Defoe the worst of it was, first, that

> they grow proud and for fear of soiling their gay garments avoid all manner of household business,

and secondly, there was the risk of mistaking them for their employers (see p. 195). "Mentor" in the *Gentleman's Magazine* in 1800 even bemoans

> the prostitution . . . and female depravity occasioned by the great increase of dress in female servants.

Doubtless the picture has been exaggerated. An outfit probably typical for the average London maid in the last quarter of the century was a long

158. Chambermaid at an inn. Dress fashionably high-waisted and with train; white kerchief; white apron with tiny bib; mob cap plain. 1804.

frock of calico or linen, perhaps bunched in polonaise style, with a black worsted petticoat underneath for warmth, a long white apron, a muslin kerchief over the shoulders, always either a fashionable trimmed cap or a less formal but beribboned mob-cap and shoes of Spanish leather, cloth or silk. As a concession to the practical, the skirt might clear the ankles.

Nineteenth and Twentieth Century Dresses and Aprons

In the nineteenth century a maid's dress, while following the broad dictates of fashion, varied widely with her duties and her employer's residence and status.

159. Office cleaner with unfashionable silhouette. Open gown (green, with slight train) over pink underskirt; yellow and red kerchief tucked into checked apron; mob cap with red ribbon. 1804.

160. Maid-of-all-work, cleaning. Old fashioned jacket bodice; skirt pinned up all round; checked apron; pattens to keep feet dry. *c.* 1829.

From 1795 to 1820 lines were classical. Waists were high and all women domestics would tie their apron strings just under the breasts, which made the bib, if any, ludicrously small (Fig. 158).

> The servant girls they imitate
>   The pride in every place, Sir
> And if they wear a flower'd gown
>   They'll have it made short waist, Sir.
>   1805. Popular song, printed by J. & M. Robertson, Glasgow.

An office cleaner, as portrayed in a satirical print of 1804, has indeed a high waist, but is modestly dressed in the style of about 1796 (Fig. 159). She wears a green short-sleeved gown, with a slight train, open in front to show a long pink underskirt. Her red-and-yellow neckerchief with its ends tucked

161. Smart housemaid. Waist-line, sleeves, elaborate cap and dainty
slippers all fashionable; bibless apron. *c.* 1829.

in at the waist, her mob-cap with red ribbon and her long (though bibless)
blue-and-white check apron are all garments typical of the working woman
for some decades before and after this time. Aprons worn in public were
generally white. The *Cook's Oracle* (5th edition, 1823) allows a "female
servant 4 check and 2 white aprons".

Where footmen were employed, the "housemaid" was in the background,
and as regards her clothes *The Complete Servant*[1] enjoins on her only that
after she has cleaned the fireplaces she should don a clean apron to make the
beds. But that there was a constrast between a maid-of-all-work and a smart
housemaid is shown in caricatures by Heath in 1829 (Fig. 160 and 161). Both

[1] 1825. S. & S. Adams.

162. Parlour maid. Fashionable skirt with bustle; apron; smart cap. 1836–7.

have the new, natural waistline, but the maid–of–all–work wears an uncommonly short skirt, and the hip-length "jacket" and outmoded mob-cap then typical of working women. The high-class housemaid is fashionable all over. Maids in the country would probably look more like the former than the latter.

Leigh Hunt,[1] describing a maidservant of about 1800 comments on her changing in the afternoons, a habit which was gradually established as maids, later "parlourmaids", took on the duties of footmen. "She changes her black stockings for white, puts on a gown of better texture and lays aside her neckhandkerchief for a high-body (bodice)." (Neckerchiefs had by now gone out of fashion.)

In the 1830s "the very servant girls" did their best to wear bustles (Fig. 162). Jane Welsh Carlyle writes:

> Eliza Miles told me a maid of theirs went out one Sunday with three kitchen dusters pinned on as a substitute.[2]

[1] 1820. *Essays, The Indicator.*
[2] Jane Welsh Carlyle, . . . *Letters*, arranged by Trudy Bliss, 1950.

PLATE 29

Caricature, W. Heath.

PLATE 29

(*a*) Lady's Maid lacing up her mistress. Caricature of ultra-fashionable small waist and effervescent headgear; apron.
c. 1829.

(*b*) Birth of St Edmund. Midwife (seated) and servant (kneeling) wear long kirtles and horned head-dress; no gowns. 1433.

British Museum MS. Harl. 2278.
(*John Lydgate's Life of St Edmund*).

PLATE 30

PLATE 30

(a) Domestic servant, Bridget Holmes aet. 96. Plain open gown with underskirt; neckerchief and coif in the fashion of her youth and very plain.
Page boy smartly dressed in the fashions of the day. 1686.

John Riley, Portrait, "Bridget Holmes, aet. suae 96". Reproduced by gracious permission of H.M. The Queen.

(b) "An English Family at Tea" *c.* 1720. Parlourmaid in fashionable wide skirts and "pinner" cap, with the lappets pinned up; functional white apron.

By unknown British artist. Reproduced by courtesy of the Trustees of the Tate Gallery.

163. Housemaid, early morning. Baker—"How them curl-papers do
become you Miss Molly!" 1848.

In a satire of the 1840s a lawyer's young wife engaged her maid on condition that there were to be "No ringlets, followers or sandals".[1] (Except for the
ankle-lacing, Molly, in Fig. 163 seems to go in for all three.) Evidently
sandals, which resembled dancing-shoes, were a town-dweller's depravity,
for Dickens describes a maid-of-all-work in the country as wearing a "pro-
digious pair of self-willed shoes";[2] and a vicar's wife of the time complains
that the thick soles of her maid's shoes caused a "hideous clatter and wore out
the carpets".[3]

[1] H. and A. Mayhew, *The Greatest Plague* . . . 1847.
[2] *The Battle of Life*, ed. 1846.
[3] G. S. Layard, *Mrs Lynn Linton—Her Life, Letters and Opinions* (1901).

Maid's skirts, though often a little shorter than a lady's, of course followed the trend towards widening, through the 1840s, 1850s and 1860s (Fig. 164 and 165). Finally "even servant girls cleaning doorsteps" wore crinolines.

> We wonder what our mobcapped grandmothers would say if they could rise from their graves and see housemaids in hoops.
>
>   1860. R. Surtees, *Plain or Ringlets*.

The neckerchief, given up by ladies long before, continued for servants' "undress wear" (Fig. 163), going with a coloured washing-dress and an apron often coloured, sometimes bibbed. When bustles were revived in the 1880s, in exaggerated form, the apron was ingeniously adapted to the situation (Fig. 166).

Towards the end of the century black for afternoons became *de rigueur* for parlourmaids (see Plate 31). The custom of "changing" for the afternoon persisted into the twentieth century, even for the maid-of-all-work, if resident,

164. *Lady:* Mary I thought I told you not to wear your hoop till you had done your rooms, because you broke the jugs and basins with it! *Mary:* Oh, Mum! You see the sweeps were coming this morning and really I couldn't think of opening the door to them with such a figger as I should ha' been without my crinoline! *Punch* 1863.

165. Parlourmaid in afternoon black dress with crinoline; starched white apron and fancy cap. *c.* 1860.

166. Cook. Apron adapted to the wearing of a bustle. Ribboned cap. 1880s.

167. Nanny in cap and apron with frilled straps. 1899.

168. Cook in shapely overall. 1910–12.

in a middle-class home. Mary, a Yorkshire maid that one of us can remember would exchange her printed or striped cotton for a black dress and her rough apron (and its superimposed canvas) for a starched white one.

In the 1890s it was correct for the smart apron to be bibbed (see Plate 31) or even frilled like the Nanny's in Fig. 167; after that it became smaller and smaller and, especially with waitresses, was often reduced in the twentieth century, like their caps, to a mere wisp. But in the first decade an advertisement ran as follows, suggesting the persistence of a pinned-up bib:

> How nice when going to answer the door
> To be robed in a Pimpernel Pinafore.
>
> *c*. 1912. Advertisement—John Peck & Co., Liverpool.

Washable protective sleeves for cooking or rough work were sometimes worn, or even (strictly in the kitchen) an all-embracing but shapely overall (Fig. 168).

169. Hotel housemaids. Bibbed and unbibbed starched aprons; caps; fashionable sleeves to dresses. 1892.

Nineteenth and Twentieth Century Caps

In the earlier decades maids' mob-caps tended to be replaced, in formal wear, by the daintier day-caps then in fashion, perched near the back of the head; but, generally without their strings, mobs continued for ordinary work to the end of our period. In about 1860 the wearing of indoor caps by ladies at last began to die out and the starched caps, featured to this day by maids and waitresses, are an anachronism, like the wearing of eighteenth-century costume by nineteenth-century footmen. One of the last styles to be worn by ladies had long streamers, generally hanging untied behind, and this became correct for maids with their afternoon dress for many decades (Plate 31). In the mornings, caps of various shapes were adopted (Fig. 169).

In the twentieth century the cap tended to diminish in size, but Mary, mentioned above, still wore a mob-cap in 1914, and even in the afternoons only exchanged it for another one that had a black ribbon.

In otherwise servantless homes there was often a little "step-girl", who came daily to clean the doorstep, wearing half a sack for an apron. She and the genuine charwoman were the only female servants who did not wear what had become customary to other grades for fifty years—a vestigial cap. The modern servant's costume converges unwittingly towards theirs in its tendency to reduce or even abandon this time-honoured insignium of domestic service.

CHAPTER VIII

TRANSPORT

RAILWAYS

Railways grew with the nineteenth century and so, having no earlier tradition behind them, they were free to develop as they thought best the dress and uniforms of their employees. Early in their history the companies adopted uniforms, being, perhaps, the first purely commercial undertakings to do so. (The Insurance Fire Brigade's uniforms were adapted from the dress of the Thames watermen; and by the first quarter of the century these brigades were really a public service, despite their commercial backing.)

During the nineteenth and first half of the twentieth centuries until Nationalization, a pride in and loyalty to the particular company which employed them became deeply engrained in the railway workers and the uniform they wore was an outward and visible sign of that pride and loyalty. In turn the companies knew the value to themselves of a smart uniform; not only in terms of prestige but also as a means of fostering and maintaining morale and efficiency among their staff. In 1856, for instance, the Taff Vale Railway enjoined every employee "to come on duty daily clean in his person and clothes, shaved and his boots blacked".

The founding of our railway system can be taken as the opening of the Stockton and Darlington in 1825, and at the time of the Rainhill Trials four years later the engine crews of driver and fireman were generally dressed in the familiar garb of the day, frockcoat or cutaway dress-coat, trousers and top-hat. In some cases the coat was replaced by a short jacket and one illustration of 1829 shows a fireman wearing a flat round hat.

In 1841 the Sheffield, Ashton-under-Lyne and Manchester Railway provided its drivers and firemen with a uniform of "dark green cloth with red edging" and with "glazed hats", but the following year the board ruled that "engineers, firemen, and other servants belonging to the locomotive department were to find their own clothing, hats, etc."

In 1848 the Great Western drivers and firemen were wearing blue trousers, white shirts or blouses, black neckcloths and peaked blue forage caps. From this date onwards the standard engine-driver's cap appears to have been the forage cap, generally dark blue, and Alken's picture of "The Driver of 1852" (see Plate 32a) shows such a cap worn with white trousers and a heavy short jacket with wide lapels, something like a pea-jacket, but single breasted.

By the end of the nineteenth century the driver's uniform had settled down to a jacket and trousers and forage cap or cheese-cutter cap (Fig. 170). Over-

170. A Railway Guard wearing "cheese cutter" cap. 1852.

alls or dungarees, waterproof coats, leather gaiters, and waterproof leggings were all introduced for outdoor staff by the early twentieth century. Large oilskin capes are mentioned as early as 1847. Brakesmen of the London & North Western Railway in about 1846 were issued with a "greatcoat of stout milled cloth and check Kersey lining".

Guards and station staff coming into close contact with the travelling public were put into uniforms more eye-catching than the locomotive branch, although the porters, by the nature of their duties, were clad in more workaday garments than the station-masters, ticket collectors, and train guards.

Ticket collectors of the London & North Western in 1846 wore a "superfine green frock coat with plain Prussian collar" and "superfine trousers, green". The contractor's prices for these were 49s. 0¾d. for coats and 21s. 9½d. for the trousers.

Green frockcoats were also worn by the Great Western at the same period. A lithograph by W. J. Linton shows a guard of the Great Western Railway wearing one piped with red. He also wears a shoulder belt and pouch and a top-hat. Later, in the 1860s, Frith's painting of Paddington Station shows the guard wearing green coat and trousers with a silver stripe. The cap and wrists of the coat are also silver laced.

Alken's painting "The Guard of 1852" (see Plate 32b) shows a London & North Western guard wearing a green frockcoat like the ticket collector, but with grey trousers. He is a splendid-looking specimen and from his pose seems to be aware of it. His head is surmounted by a saucy gold(?)-laced forage cap with a button in the centre of the crown; his collar is also laced and he carries across his manly bosom a shoulder belt of enormous size bearing a pouch and a buckle in proportion. His neck is encircled by a red stock. In one hand he holds a paper—presumably a way-bill, in the other is elegantly poised a pencil. He casts a disdainful look at a porter unloading a luggage van. He is obviously conscious of that 49s. 0¾d. superfine coat he is wearing.

During the 1860s a guard of the London & South Western railway was painted wearing a mulberry-coloured double-breasted frockcoat with silver buttons, a forage cap with patent leather peak and silver piping and lacing, and again a shoulder belt and pouch. At this time other companies' guards wore red coats and black trousers.

Station-masters do not seem to have been so often painted or described as guards and one wonders if they were less familiar to the public or less distinctive in their dress. Certainly the morning-coat and top-hat which has now crystallized into the main-line station-masters' ceremonial uniform would excite little remark in a period when every other man wore them. At the beginning of the twentieth century assistant station-masters were issued with uniform including a cheese-cutter cap laced with gold.

In 1846 we read that the London & North Western porters were wearing green cord jackets with an embroidered badge and green cord waistcoats with fustian sleeves. Both garments had metal buttons. Five years earlier the Sheffield, Ashton-under-Lyne & Manchester line dressed their porters in dark green velveteen suits with red cloth collars, and dark green caps lettered "Porter No. —". On the arm were worn badges similarly lettered. The Great Western Railway porters at about this date also wore green jackets, together with black forage caps piped with red bearing "G.W.R." on the band. A badge or armlet on the jacket sleeve bore the same legend. In the case of the Great Western Railway the porters seem to have worn drab corduroy trousers. They also sported a waistcoat and neckcloth over their shirts. The South Eastern Railway porters at the opening of Charing Cross station in 1864 wore sleeved waistcoats, shirts, trousers and peaked caps.

171. Guard, Bath Station, 1886.

At the end of the nineteenth century the common form for station plat-form staff was frockcoat or jacket, waistcoat, shirt, collar and tie, trousers, boots, cheese-cutter cap (Figs. 171 and 172). Sleeved waistcoats or short jackets were worn by porters. It is interesting to note the survival as part of the porters' dress of the sleeved waistcoat, which, once common, had died out generally by the middle of the eighteenth century.

172. Railway Porter, 1910.

By the early years of the twentieth century the main-line companies each had clothing regulations and catalogues almost as comprehensive as those of the armed services. The North Eastern Railway, for example, in 1905 issued a volume of 126 pages listing details of dress issued to all grades of staff from the Agent, assistant (Bradford) to Yardmen (permanent way). The preamble states that "all grades in receipt of uniform must keep the same in good order and appear neat and clean on all occasions".

In general, issues of clothing were made to the staff on 20th March each year, with a winter trouser issue on 1st November. They had a suit every year and an overcoat or waterproof every two years. A nice gradation of quality and weight of cloth according to the grade or duties of the employees is specified for jackets, trousers and greatcoats.

This most detailed list covers, with illustrations, such items as "Fire Brigade Captain's Brass Helmets, Metropolitan Fire Brigade pattern"; "waterproofs, cashmere dry heat vulcanized", and "Motor bus drivers special stout rubber blackproof waterproof, full length, as supplied by A. W. Gamage". Winter clothing included in most cases a double-breasted frock-coat or jacket, which in summer was replaced by a single-breasted jacket.

The uniform remained the property of the company and the regulations stated that "all grades when leaving the service are required to give up the whole of their clothing".

In 1914 the newspaper *Railway News* celebrated its jubilee and among other items gave a list of typical uniform issues in that year, including "Stationmasters—summer coat and vest, winter coat and vest, trousers, top coat, mackintosh, hat or cap" (according to grade); and "Porters—jacket, sleeved waistcoat, cord trousers, pea jacket, cap, 2 neckties".

Some of the records of the old companies pose sartorial questions that will never now, alas, be answered. Why, in 1893, did the directors of the London and South Western order

> that the whole of the Company's staff wearing uniform (except Station Masters and Policemen) are to be supplied with neckties of a red material, which must always be worn by them when on duty . . . Superintendents, Station Masters and Travelling Inspectors must . . . see that the Directors' order with reference to these red neckties is strictly carried out.

Do we detect here the first rumblings of the Socialist State and listen to the still-distant siren of British Rail diesel—or did the directors of the London & South Western merely seek to introduce a welcome touch of colour among the Gladstone bags and milk churns, in a kindly effort to bring good cheer and gaiety to their customers?

And why, oh why, in 1905 did the North Eastern Railway decree, in a special footnote following the prescribed dress for lavatory attendants and lavatory towel lads that "Lavatory Attendant W. Robson, Bridlington, is supplied with Passenger Guard's Uniform"?

Railway Policemen

It is not realized, perhaps, by every traveller that the familiarly uniformed police officer standing on the station platform or in the forecourt is not a member of the local force but a railway policeman, whose duties are concerned with the preservation of order and prevention of crime on the railway's premises.

The railway policeman is as old as the railways themselves and originally his duties included the patrolling of the lines and the control of traffic on them. To this end the policeman was provided with a flag and at set points on the line, such as tunnel entrances, he would signal "All clear" or otherwise to approaching drivers. From the early policeman has evolved not only the present force, but also the whole elaborate system of modern railway signalling and traffic control.

In the early days the police of the Great Western Railway were, according to Brunel, dressed like the Metropolitan constables. In 1846 the London & North Western uniform was a green cut-away tailcoat, costing 23s. 8d., with

173. Railway Policeman signalling "All Right" at a tunnel entrance. 1844.

metal buttons and an embroidered collar, green trousers and a greatcoat with an embroidered badge. The Superintendent wore a superfine frock coat, also green, with rich silver collar, silk skirt linings and silver buttons. This cost 75s. 11d. Presumably both wore top-hats. An illustration from the *Illustrated London News* of 1844 shows a constable standing at the entrance to a tunnel signalling "All right" with his flag (Fig. 173). He wears a top-hat, dark tailcoat, and white trousers strapped under his boots. An undated lithograph by A. B. Clayton, perhaps of the 1830s or early 1840s, shows a policeman wearing a black top-hat, brown tailcoat, white gloves, pale blue trousers, and black shoes. His company is not recorded, but may have been the London and Southampton, which is said to have worn coats of a chocolate-brown colour.

Apart from the variations in colour all the companies seem to have followed the Metropolitan police uniform, although the Great Western Railway appear to have abandoned the top-hat before the Metropolitan Force and changed to caps in 1860.

In 1885 the railway policeman was wearing a belted coat, trousers, and helmet. By 1900 the familiar blue seems to have been universally adopted.

In 1905 the North Eastern Railway police were issued with a coat, mid-thigh length, to be worn with a leather belt in winter, and a shorter jacket with no belt for summer wear. In some cases short leather leggings were worn, presumably to protect the trousers on outdoor duties.

A touching echo of the past is contained in a letter written in 1881 from King's Cross station and signed by about twenty policemen. It reads:

Mr. Thomas Williams.

Sir,

    We the undersigned beg to ask for the back of our great coats to be lined as we have felt the late severe weather very much in between the shoulders and down the back. Hoping you will kindly take this into consideration,

We remain,

Your obedient servants,

The document is endorsed by Head Office to the effect that unlined overcoats cost 20s. 6d.—lined ones would be 21s. 9d.

It is satisfying to know that the gallant constables got their linings to warm them in between the shoulders during any subsequent severe weather they may have met with.

CABBIES AND CADS, BUS AND TRAM CREWS

The hackney coach, mentioned by Pepys in the seventeenth century, was the ancestor of the modern cab, and the short-stage coach plying between the City and the outer suburbs in the late eighteenth and early nineteenth centuries was the forerunner of the London bus.

The seventeenth-century dress of the drivers of coaches was probably little different from that of other working men of the day—doublet, or coat, breeches and stockings, a cloak or overcoat and a wide-brimmed round hat. To these garments would be added a whip and most probably a pair of jack-boots with large bucket tops to enclose the knees (Fig. 174).

174. A Hackney Coachman, 1680s. The "coachman" rode the horse, hence the spurs and short whip.

In the eighteenth century the garments worn were a frock—that is a loose-fitting coat with a flat turned-down collar, often made of fustian—breeches, jack-boots, and a caped greatcoat, probably with a belt or half-belt (Fig. 175). A round or three-cornered cocked hat, perhaps decorated with gold lacing, was the usual headgear. That the coachman affected a certain style in the wearing of his hat is evidenced by the *London Evening Post*, which refers in 1758 to "gold laced hats slouched in humble imitation of stagecoach men". Rowlandson's picture of Blackfriars Bridge in 1798 shows a vehicle which appears to be a long-bodied stage-coach or a very early omnibus. The driver wears a caped greatcoat and a wide-brimmed round hat.

Licensed cabs appeared in London in 1823, to be followed in 1829 by Shillibeer's omnibus. Charles Dickens in *Sketches by Boz* (1833–6) describes a cabman of that period:

175. Coachman, 1786.

He was a brown-whiskered, white-hatted, no-coated cabman; . . . his boots were of the Wellington form, pulled up to meet his corduroy knee-smalls . . . and his neck was usually garnished with a bright yellow handkerchief.

An illustration of 1827 shows a hackney coachman dressed in a long great-coat with four capes, a wide-brimmed slouch hat and a spotted handkerchief around his neck. He is in company with a "cad", who at that date was synonymous with the "waterman", and whose duties were to water the horses at the coach or cab stand and to look after them during the temporary absence of the driver. The cad wears a shirt, waistcoat, breeches, stockings and spats, a slouch hat and an apron. His neck is also encircled by a handker-chief, and from it hangs a numbered licence ticket. Dickens in *The Pickwick Papers* also describes a waterman of the same date:

a strange specimen of the human race, in a sackcloth coat, and apron of the same, who with a brass label and number round his neck, looked as if he were catalogued in some collection of human rarities.

(see Plate 33).

(Cabbies, watermen, and later bus and tram crews, were licensed by the authorities and all wore a metal licence label or ticket on their person.)

The term "cad" was also applied to the early bus conductors and it is

PLATE 31

PLATE 31

Parlourmaid serving at tea party. Black dress with fashionable
sleeves; starched bibbed apron; cap with streamers, like that
worn by ladies some 30 years earlier. 1893.

W. P. Frith. Photograph by courtesy of Messrs Newman Galleries, London, S.W.1.

PLATE 32

PLATE 32

(*a*) Engine driver, 1852.
   He is wearing a forage cap, jacket and
      trousers, probably canvas.

Print after H. Alken, published by Fores, 1852.

(*b*) L.N.W. Guard, wearing a heavy
   and elaborate shoulder belt.
      1852.

*Print after H. Alken, published by Fores,
      1852.*

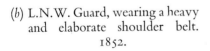

possible that it was transferred to the job with those watermen who took
employment on the new buses. *Sketches by Boz* refers to such a case:

> Mr Barker . . . seated in this capacity [assistant waterman on a hackney-coach
> stand] on a couple of tubs near the curb stone, with a brass plate and number
> suspended round his neck by a massive chain, and his ankles curiously
> enveloped by hay-bands

saw, with the onset of the buses, the necessity to

> adopt some more profitable profession

and ere long

> entered into a new suit of clothes and on a new sphere of action

as a bus conductor.

In one picture of Shillibeer's bus the driver wears a dark coat with a gold-
laced silk hat, like that of the coachman of a private family. The conductor
wears a short jacket and trousers. In another print the driver's coat is green,
with a cape, and he wears a peaked cap. The conductor also wears green.

Herring's picture "Hackney Cabriolet and Cabman", dated about 1830,
shows a depressed-looking individual wearing a battered top-hat, a greatcoat
with one cape and a large collar, turned down, and trousers strapped under
his boots.

During the middle decades of the nineteenth century the cabbie's costume
was generally a caped greatcoat, sometimes with as many as six capes,
trousers, and a top-hat or a "Bollinger" (a predecessor of the bowler). His
licence was generally attached to a coat button, although it could be suspended around the neck on a cord or strap. Sometimes he wore buttoned
cloth gaiters (Fig. 176).

It is noticeable that nearly all the contemporary descriptions and pictures
of the cabman show him in a greatcoat. A greatcoatless cabbie is rare. When
discovered he wears a short jacket, or a long-sleeved waistcoat, sometimes
with vertical stripes like a groom's. His legs are generally covered by a rug.

The driver of the four-wheeled cab, or growler, was often a ragged individual—his top-hat was battered and acquired at second hand. A cartoon by
John Leech (*Punch*, 1864) shows a maidservant carrying a rug and saying
to a cabbie:

> Missus says you're to cover yourself with this rug . . . because your gaiters
> and legs and things are really so very shocking.

176. Cab driver, wearing Bollinger hat, multi-caped overcoat and gaiters. 1851.

The hansom-cab drivers, however, had acquired a reputation for smartness by the latter half of the century. They were said to be dandy-like in their dress. A coloured lithograph of 1850 shows one wearing a brown coat and pale green striped trousers, with short boots and a top-hat. A writer of the 1880s states that "the cabman himself is a smart looking fellow". They often wore gloves, and sometimes a short cape in place of a greatcoat.

The bus driver of the same period, the 1840s to 1870s, had tastes in fashion akin to his counterpart of the cab. Two early pictures, one of 1845 and the other of 1852, show the drivers in top-hats. In one case he has a rug over his knees, in the other he wears a coat and light-coloured trousers. Conductors of the same period are also shown in top-hats. In the 1860s hats of the bowler type were largely worn by both drivers and conductors (see Plate 34). A variation is a flat wide-brimmed sailor hat with a ribbon having a bow with long ends at the back (Fig. 177). In 1866 leggings are shown on a conductor, who also has a bowler hat, dark coat buttoned on the top button only, and a waistcoat (Fig. 178). In 1877 a photo shows a smartly dressed conductor, whose light morning-coat and tall bowler contrast with the old-fashioned frockcoat, white tie, and tall silk hat of the driver. One conductor of the 1870s was photographed on his bus carrying a relic of the bus's stage-coach origin—a post-horn. This seems to have been an isolated instance.

PLATE 33

PLATE 33

Coach-stand waterman, or cad, 1805.

W. H. Pyne, Costume of Great Britain. *1808.*

PLATE 34

PLATE 34

Bus conductor, *c.* 1862. With passenger in crinoline.

Colour print. By courtesy of F. S. Read, London, W.C.1.

During this period, and indeed during the whole of the horse-bus era, uniforms were, with a few exceptions, never worn by the crews. An instance where they apparently were is recalled by Edmund Yates in 1865. He states that in his childhood the crews of Wilson's "Favourite" omnibus had "green liveries, renewed on . . . the Queen's birthday" (*Business of Pleasure*, Vol. I)—a splendid example of patriotism and publicity.

Why the bus-owners did not provide a uniform, as did the railways, is perhaps bound up with the complex system of payments and rewards made to the crews, who, apart from a small fixed daily wage, seemed to operate a primitive form of profit-sharing with the proprietors.

In 1861 a new feature was added to the London street scene—the tramcar. Introduced by an American of the appropriate name of Train, the tramcar was largely experimental during the 1860s, but was accepted and spread during the 1870s throughout London and the provinces. In a photograph of Train's Victoria Street tram in 1861 an official, presumably the conductor, seems to wear a uniform-type frockcoat with bright buttons and a flat peaked cap. Some time during the 1870s money satchels and bell punches

177. Bus Drivers, 1861. One wears bowler hat and leggings: the other has a "Sailor" hat.

178. Bus Conductor, 1866. ". . . nobody in Town, our 'Bus'
Conductor can take it easy!"

for tickets were introduced by the tramcar companies. In 1875 a Croydon
Tramways driver and conductor dressed in jacket, trousers, and bowler hat;
the driver's licence is fastened on a button and the conductor has a money
satchel slung over his left shoulder.

The last twenty years of the nineteenth century saw little change from the
previous decades in the dress of cabbies. By the middle 1880s the hansom
had outnumbered the growler, and what change is apparent in the dress of
drivers of both vehicles is for the better. Dark suits were mostly worn;
generally with a bowler hat, less often a top hat. In the 1890s, during the
summer, straw "boaters" occasionally appear. Grey toppers were also worn.
The rug seems less in evidence—possibly as contemporary photographs were
taken generally in sunny weather.

The bus crews in the 1880s and 1890s were still clad in plain clothes, an
exception being on the Metropolitan Railway buses, where the conductors
were given a uniform of frockcoat with metal buttons and peaked cap.
Another mark of the Metropolitan buses was the large red umbrella shelter-

ing the driver from the sun in the summer. Although this was fixed to the vehicle, it must really be included under the heading of "costume" (see Plate 35a).

During the 1880s money satchels seem to have been first used by the bus conductors, apparently introduced from the tramcars; later, in 1892, the London General Omnibus Company also imported the bell punch from the same source.

The normal headgear of the drivers was a top-hat or a bowler. Conductors are said to have preferred the bowler, as it was more convenient when putting their heads inside the door of the bus to collect fares or announce the stopping-places. An occasional Homburg was to be seen on the bus man's head when this type of hat became popular in about 1889.

The tramways were introducing uniform from 1880 on (see Plate 35b). A rather indistinct photo of this date shows an Ipswich tram, with five officials posed by it. Three wear short morning-coats, waistcoats and trousers, with bowler hats. One seems to carry a satchel and wears a licence tag—presumably the conductor. Two are clad in what are apparently dark blue uniforms, with metal buttons and badged peak caps. They wear whistle chains and are probably inspectors or time-keepers.

In many cases the "uniform" consisted of no more than a peaked cap with badge, worn with ordinary clothes, or in some cases a badge alone, worn on a bowler hat. Sometimes the bowler persisted when a full uniform was worn. A London County Council tram of about 1898/9 has a driver with a double-breasted overcoat with metal buttons, and leather cuffs, boots and leather leggings and a bowler with the letters L.C.C. in brass on the front. The conductor is similarly dressed, except that his hat does not aspire to the County Council's initials.

A mixture of uniformed and plain-clothes crews is common during this period.

The advent of the twentieth century saw the beginning of a revolution in public transport—the introduction of the internal-combustion engine to cabs and buses and the electrification of the tramways.

The driver of the early motor taxicab was influenced in his dress by that of the private chauffeur, who was generally clad by his employer in a livery of double-breasted coat with a high collar, breeches, boots and leather leggings and a peaked cap, with a linen dust-coat in fine weather. This style was employed, with variations, by the cabbie. To compensate for the loss of the many-caped greatcoat of his predecessors he took to the habit of wearing a selection of waistcoats simultaneously, and is reputed to have kept his change in the innermost pocket of the lowest layer. Like his ancestors of the horse era, he hung his licence tag, now an enamelled metal plate, from a button.

179. Bus Conductor, 1904, with ticket punch.

The motor-bus driver of pre-1914 also owed much to the chauffeur's livery. A "General" driver of 1911 wore a double-breasted jacket with leather cuffs, breeches, boots and leggings and a peaked cap. He had a white collar and a dark tie. In the same year long leather coats were also worn in the winter, and white or pale long dust-coats in the summer. On the Metropolitan buses white cap-tops were also worn.

Breeches and leggings were not always worn, and trousers were to be seen on both drivers and conductors. Inspectors wore jackets and trousers and peaked caps; in the winter they added a single-breasted overcoat with a velvet collar.

The smaller companies and some in the provinces still wore plain clothes, with the addition of licence tags, satchels, and bell punches.

The driver's rug, impractical when driving a mechanical vehicle, was superseded in wet weather by a waterproof coat.

Side by side with the new motor buses the horse bus survived in London until 1914 (the last L.G.O.C. horse bus ran in 1911), and the crews continued to be without uniform (Fig. 179). As the policeman held up the traffic the peaked-capped and legginged "engineer" of a General "B" type petrol bus would draw his throbbing and stinking contraption up beside a two-horse Tillings "garden seat", whose driver, adjusting the rug around his knees, would peer at the new-comer sideways from underneath his silk hat—and spit carefully into the gutter.

The trams, having gone into uniform at an earlier date, were not unduly influenced by electrification in the matter of clothes for their crews, but both they and their rivals the buses were about to suffer all the changes to personnel that the Great War was to bring about—including the advent of women as conductors: but this is another story, not within the scope of this book to tell.

CHAPTER IX

POSTAL SERVICES AND STAGE COACHES

"Of the many contributions of service to modern civilization which Britain can be proud to record, there can be few of such unassailable and universal benefit as the postal system" (G. Kay, *The Royal Mail*). The men employed in the system of communication have acquired an ever-increasing importance and with this a distinctive dress has gradually evolved. At first they were private servants, dressed in ordinary clothes.

In the fourteenth and fifteenth centuries letter-writing was in the hands of royalty and the upper classes. The sending of a letter depended on finding a *messenger* going in the right direction if one's own servant was not available.

> Item, gevyn to a messenger ffor berynge off a letter off the Kyngys iiis iiiid.
>
> 1463. *Expenses of Sir John Howard.*

In the *Taymouth Book of Hours* an early-fourteenth-century messenger is shown kneeling before Herod, who hands him a sealed letter (for the Magi). The messenger wears a long brown tunic (now often called a "cote"), the ordinary dress of the period, with a belt from which is suspended a shield-shaped letter-case. He carries a staff. He wears shoes and is bareheaded. (B.M. Landsdowne MS. 383, f. 93v) These letter-cases were often shield-shaped and bore the coat of arms of the employer.

Another early-fourteenth-century messenger is shown delivering a letter from which the seal dangles. He wears a short tunic horizontally striped in red and blue with a white line along the centre of each stripe. His hose are white, shoes black and a horn is suspended from his girdle. (B.M. MS. Roy. 10 E.iv., f. 3v). Short tunics were usual, as long ones would be likely to impair the pace of the letter-carrier.

Even at this early date speed was considered essential. A letter-carrier in the same manuscript, dressed in the usual short tunic, is depicted wearing a flowing veil streaming out behind his head, symbolizing speed. The veil was a scarf-like female headdress not worn by men (Fig. 180).

Some messengers, too, rode on horseback. Throughout the history of the postal service speed of delivery is always emphasized.

180. Letter carrier with a letter case attached to his belt,
early 14th century. See text.

Get posts and letters, and make friends with speed.

1596–7. *2 Henry IV*, I. i. 214.

He requires your haste-post-haste appearance, even on the instant.

1604. *Othello*, I. ii. 37.

In the reign of Henry VIII a definite postal system was set up. In 1516, Henry appointed Sir Brian Tuke as his "Master of the Posts". Letters were carried by *postboys* on horseback from London to outlying districts. The horses stood ready for service at inns called posthouses, which were conveniently spaced along the main roads.[1] The landlords of these inns, known as postmasters, had both to mount the postboys and then distribute the mail in their district by letter-carriers. Late in the sixteenth century local postmasters were ordered to reside at their posts, and apart from being ready with horses, to have "three good strong leather bags lined with baize or cotton" and three horns to blow by the way. No man was to proceed without a guide and the horn was to be blown "as often as he meeteth company, or passeth through any town, or at least thrice every mile".

The postal system was originally designed solely for Government service, but towards the end of the seventeenth century private letters were allowed

[1] The word "post" comes from the Latin "positus", meaning placed or fixed, and in time the fixed stations or posts of call for the mail gave the name to the whole system of letter-carrying.

(unofficially) to be included in the postmen's bags. Stage coaches for travel also frequently carried mail as well as passengers.

The postal delivery by postboy is symbolically illustrated in Fig. 182. He wears a doublet with the postbag suspended from a waist belt, a working man's hat and top-boots. (His boots are shown in Plate 58b.)

> Thence I went home and wrote a letter to Harpers and staid there till Tom carried it to the post boy at Whitehall.
>
>   *Pepys's Diary*, 10th January 1659–60.

> Behold this post boy with what haste and speed
> He travels on the road; and there is need
> That he so does, his Business calls for haste.
> For should he in his journey now be cast
> His life for that default might hap to go;
> Yea, and the Kingdom come to ruin too—
> Stages are for him fixt, his hour is set,
> He has a horn to sound, that none may let
> Him in his haste, or give him stop or stay—
> Then Post-boy blow thy horn, and go thy way.
>
>   1686. John Bunyan's *Book for Boys and Girls*.

181. A letter-carrier in doublet, short breeches unconfined at the knee, a "copotain hat" which went out of fashion in 1610; a stiff falling ruff and a post bag slung over his shoulder. 1613.

182. Postboy on horseback. 1647.

In 1660 Parliament passed an Act "for erecting and establishing a Post Office". In 1684 *The Complete Tradesman or the Exact Dealer's Dayly Companion* states: "The Post Office . . . is now kept in Lombard Street." Later, in 1710, the various postal systems were reorganized and put under the supreme control of a postmaster-general.

By-bags were introduced in the seventeenth century.

> With each Maile there goes a By bag which is carried by the Post Boy about his middle in which all the by letters are put, that is, such Letters as are sent from one Town to another upon the Roades and which did not reach London.

Letters crossed the seas in the reign of Charles II and mail was carried between Dover and Calais in vessels known as post-barques, later known as packet-boats because of the packet of State letters which they carried.

One of the earliest references to the wearing of distinctive clothing dates from 1590. "A livery of blue cloth with armorial bearings of the town (Aberdeen) worked in silver on his right sleeve" was ordered for the post.

As in medieval days, private messengers on foot were still employed for carrying parcels, goods or letters from one individual to another. In addition to this, in the City of London one could hire the services of a ticket porter, whose reliability was vouched for by his having a licence.

> The *Ticket-Porters* give good security for their Honesty, and Fidelity, so that no more need be done, but to take notice of his name, which is stampt on his Girdle, and repairing to their Governour, satisfaction may be had for any wrong or misbehaviour.
>
> 1684. *The Complete Tradesman. . .*

Ticket porters were very useful in the eighteenth century, and in the early part of the nineteenth century (Fig. 183). They were then largely employed

183. Ticket Porter with his licence of the City of London hung round his neck. He wears a rough coat and breeches. 1747.

in carrying messages and small parcels between members of Inns of Court, but anyone could avail himself of their services by paying according to the distance. In 1827 he was dressed in a rather colourful style. He is shown in a brown coat to mid-thigh, a yellow waistcoat, and breeches, pale grey stockings, dark grey spats and a white stock. He also wears a white apron reaching to just below his knees. His licence ticket was tied on round his waist or neck and had to hang in front. The ticket was about 3 in. × 4 in. and instead of bearing his name, as in the seventeenth century, bore the city arms.

It is supposed that the silver ticket bearing the City arms appended to their aprons, might have been the original distinguishing mark of their calling.

1827. W. H. Pyne, *The World in Miniature*.

A ticket porter when plying or working, is to wear his ticket so as to be plainly seen, under penalty of 2/6 for each offence.

1825–7. Wm. Hone's *Everyday Book*, Vol. I, p. 19.

POSTBOY OF THE EIGHTEENTH AND NINETEENTH CENTURIES

In the eighteenth century, in an official notice of 1728 the Secretary of the General Post Office ordered "that every letter carrier shall, as a badge of his employment, wear a brass ticket upon the most visible part of his clothing with the Kings Arms upon the same".

In spite of the blue livery chosen in Edinburgh in 1590, *Red* was the colour chosen for the British Postal Service. "Red had been from early times the royal colour of England and as the Post Office organization had its origin in the royal couriers, red was the natural choice. In course of time brilliance has given way to utility and scarlet piping alone remains, except for the scarlet frock coats of the door keepers at the Postmaster-General's Office." (P.O. Uniforms, Green Paper No. 27A).

> The post who came from Coventry
> > Riding in a red rocket,
> Did tidings tell how Timsford fell
> > A child's hand in his pocket.

1746. Sir Walter Scott, *Notes on Woodstock*.

The rocket (variously spelt "Roquelaure", "Rocklo"), common at this date, was a knee-length cloak with a single or double cape-collar and buttoned down the front, with a back vent for wearing on horseback.

"For more than two centuries the mounted post-boy was the most important link in the postal service and he continued well into the 19th century." His costume in the early days consisted of:

a cloak of heavy Norfolk russett, a good West of England serge;
a felt hat and heavy riding-boots.

A red jacket was adopted later as a distinguishing colour for the Post Office.

He carried a whip and a post-horn and the letter-bags on either side of the saddle (Fig. 184).

184. Post Boy in sleeved waistcoat, breeches and round hat but without the cloak. 1770's.

Figure 185 shows an early-nineteenth-century postboy in a blue, sleeved waistcoat with gold buttons, buff-coloured breeches, black top-boots and a brown top-hat.

MAIL-COACH

The first mail-coach service was inaugurated in 1784. The height of its fame which may be called the mail-coach era, was from 1785 to 1835, but by 1845 its career had ended.

Owing to the great improvement in the main roads after 1750, due to the two famous road engineers, Thomas Telford and John Macadam, speed was greatly increased. Speed with efficiency were still the hall-marks of the postal service. Mail coaches travelled by night, leaving London at eight o'clock, Sundays excepted, and were exempt from toll-gate charges; but they were liable to attacks by robbers. To safeguard from robbery, an armed guard had

PLATE 35

PLATE 35

(*a*) Metropolitan Railway omnibus, showing conductor in uniform, and driver's umbrella, 1888.

Detail from photograph. C. E. Lee, The Horse Bus as a Vehicle. *1962.*

(*b*) Horse-tram crew, 1897.

Photograph by courtesy of British Transport Commission.

PLATE 36

PLATE 36

(*a*) Mail Coach Driver. 1832.

After one of a pair of paintings by H. Alken, 1852, designed to contrast 1832 with 1852.

(*b*) Mail Coach picking up and dropping mail without stopping. Driver in white coat and top hat. 1838.

By courtesy of H.M. Postmaster General.

185. Post boy. 1805. See text.

to sit beside the coachman, and at first he was a soldier. Soon, however, *Post Office guards* were installed. Their duties were exacting; they not only had to protect the mail and passengers who were allowed to travel in the mail-coach, but they also had to see that no time in transit was wasted. The guard's weapons consisted of a cutlass in a sword-case at hand, a brace of pistols and a blunderbuss.

The success resulting from the arming of guards on mail-coaches led to the arming of horse mails, which were still in use on less-important roads. Young boys were replaced by grown men. Each was provided with a cutlass and a brace of pistols, also a strong cap for the head.

In order to keep to the timetable, the mail guard carried a time-bill in which were the precise times to the minute for the arrival and departure of the coach at each stage.

The mail-coach had the right of way over all other traffic on the roads, and the guard carried a long straight horn (sometimes a bugle), which he blew liberally to warn travellers to make way and toll-keepers to have the toll gates ready open. "TIME says the Post-Office (always personified on the roads) must be kept" (1841).

The first official issue of uniform clothing for London General Post carriers was made in 1793. The drivers and guards of the mail-coaches wore gold-braided scarlet uniforms, supplied by the mail contractors, who provided the coaches. At a later date the Post Office supplied the London mail guards with a scarlet cloth coat with blue lapels and blue linings, a blue waistcoat and a beaver hat with a gold lace hat band. The drivers had a similar outfit, but no gold lace on the coat. Uniforms other than those connected with the mail-coach will follow later.

The mail guard on the first mail-coach to Shrewsbury in 1793 was thus described by a contemporary:

> The Guard of the Mail-Coach is one of the grandest and most swaggering fellows I ever beheld, dressed in ruffles and nankeen breeches, and white stockings.
>
> 1793. Hon. John Byng, *The Torrington Diaries*, p. 236.

A print by Henry Alken (see Plate 36a), dated 1832, shows the mail-coach driver in a white coat lined with blue, white strapped trousers, two waistcoats green over brown, a white top-hat and a broad neck-tie, blue spotted with dots, and white gloves.

A cavalry officer in *The Whole Art of Dress* states:

> The Mail-Coach tie resembles a waterfall; immensely large cloth folded loosely round the neck and fastened with a common knot over which the folds are spread; Worn by professional drivers, generally.
>
> 1830.

The postboy when acting as postilion to the mail-coach and riding the nearside horse of a pair, wore an iron or stout leather guard strapped to his right leg to protect it from the offside horse and the shaft.

In order to maintain the speed of mail deliveries, the mail-coaches would pick up and drop mail without stopping (Plate 36b). The picture, painted in 1838 shows this being enacted. This was the forerunner of the railway travelling post office.

In 1832 George Eliot (in *Felix Holt*) wrote of the mail-coach that "still announced itself by the merry notes of the horn . . . for the glory had not yet departed from the old coach roads". But the "glory" was approaching its end, and although in some districts mail-coaches overlapped with railways until about 1845, the railways in 1838 began to take their place.

The first *travelling post office* with the Royal Arms on its central door was running in 1838, when railway companies were required by law to supply a special coach (van) for carrying and sorting letters. It had two compartments, one for the *guard* who supervised the changing of the bags *en route*, the other for the *clerk*, who stood at a table, sorting the letters into pigeon-holes on the wall (Fig. 186).

186. Travelling Post Office on the London and Birmingham Railway. Guard in overcoat and top hat. Clerk in tailcoat and trousers. 1838.

BELLMEN

Having dealt with the mounted and horse-drawn mail ending with rail travel, we must now turn to the mail distributed on foot in the eighteenth and nineteenth centuries.

The *bellmen* who began work early in the eighteenth century were in effect walking pillar-boxes. They paraded the streets of a town in the late afternoon, before the departure at night, of the mail-coaches. They rang a bell to announce their presence and carried a locked bag with a slit to receive letters not yet handed in at the suburban receiving post offices. Customers posted

187. Postman in red coat with grey collar and cuffs, blue breeches, white stockings, black shoes and grey top hat. He receives money from lady posting her letter. 1823.

their letters in this slit and paid the bellman (Fig. 187). In London and the provinces this arrangement was discontinued in 1846 and in 1852 the first road-side pillar-boxes were set up. Both Rowland Hill and Anthony Trollope claimed to be the originators of the idea. This service, together with Rowland Hill's introduction of the penny post in 1840, with the postage prepaid by affixing a penny stamp to the letter, ended the need for bellmen.

The dustman was first to forgo his brass clapper,
The Muffinboy speedily followed his shade,

PLATE 37

PLATE 37

(*a*) Country letter carrier in great coat, top hat and top boots. 1843.

Water colour. By courtesy of H.M. Post-master General.

(*b*) Country postman on a "penny-farthing." *c.* 1890.

By courtesy of H.M. Postmaster General.

PLATE 38

PLATE 38

(*a*) Telegraph messenger boy. 1904–1926.

By courtesy of H.M. Postmaster General.

(*b*) Stage coach post-boys (postilions).
1846.

*J. F. Herring, "Gretna Green" (Detail) 1846.
Walker Art Gallery, Liverpool.*

And now, 'tis the Postman that double-tongued rapper—
 Must give up his Bell for the eve's promenade.

Illustrated London News, June 1846.

On Rowland Hill's advice slits in house doors were coming into general use from about 1837 and this greatly improved the quick delivery of letters.

LETTER-CARRIERS

In 1772 the Post Office appointed a large number of letter-carriers to make a free house-to-house delivery within the area of the post town. These letter-carriers were the forerunners of the modern postman. As already stated, the first official issue of uniforms was made in 1793.

The Post Office Letter Carriers of London are to be provided with a uniform of red coats, faced with blue and to wear numbers.

The Times, 10th February 1793.

As their own clothes were generally very ragged, these letter-carriers needed to be smartened up. So they were supplied with scarlet cutaway (tail) coats with blue lapels and cuffs. Brass buttons on the coat were inscribed with the wearer's number. They also had blue cloth waistcoats and beaver hats with gold hat band and cockade. Apart from the colours, the styles were in the fashion of the day. The men, however, had to supply their own trousers. The early carriers sometimes carried a bell (Fig. 188).

In 1837 a curious reversal of colours was made for *district letter-carriers* of the suburbs, who were supplied with blue cutaway coats having scarlet collars; otherwise they had blue waistcoats and beaver hats with gold band and cockade.

In 1855, however, the London letter-carriers and district carriers were all dressed alike. The cutaway coat was replaced by a short scarlet frockcoat and the wearer's number transferred from his coat buttons to the collar of his coat, while the beaver hat was replaced by a glazed top-hat without a gold hat band. In London a pair of trousers was supplied instead of a waistcoat, which the men had to provide for themselves (see frontispiece).

As it was found that the scarlet uniforms of the letter-carriers very quickly became soiled, in 1861 scarlet was replaced by blue. The uniform then issued was a blue coat with scarlet collar and cuffs and scarlet piping, and the letters

188. Letter Carrier and Bellman in red cutaway coat with blue collar, black top hat with gold band and cockade, grey waistcoat and trousers. *c.* 1830.

189. A district letter carrier in blue coat, lapels blue but collar red, brass buttons. Trousers pale fawn. Top hat black with gold band. 1837–55.

G.P.O. above the wearer's number was embroidered in white on each side of the collar. The blue waistcoat was piped with scarlet and the blue winter trousers had a broad red stripe down each leg. The summer trousers, in grey, had a scarlet cord stripe. In later years the scarlet collar and cuffs were abolished. In 1862 the single-peaked shako, deep behind, was introduced instead of the tall hat (Fig. 190).

190. Postman wearing the single-peaked shako. 1885.

Then in 1896 the shako of the London postmen was provided with a cloth-covered peak at the back as a protection against rain, with a drop front peak of glazed leather. A lighter-weight shako was introduced for summer wear, and in 1909 to 1910 this became the standard hat for London and provincial postmen (Fig. 191). This hat for twenty-five years was peculiar to the Post Office Service. "The shako has disappeared in favour of the modern style military cap, but the blue cloth and red piping remain as a reminder of the original uniform."

191. London Postman wearing a double peaked shako. 1904.

Provincial and country postmen (see Plate 37a) did not go into uniform until about 1879. Even after this date some slight divergence from the rule might be seen, as in the photograph of the postman on a "penny-farthing" who wears a boater hat (see Plate 37b).

Though postmen used to carry bells, few could have carried umbrellas. The *Morning Post* of 1844, however, gives a delightful account of an old postman of East Cowes who always carried an umbrella and unknowingly lent it to the Queen and Prince Albert, who were out walking and caught in the rain. ". . . the old postman tendered his gingham, but perfectly water-proof umbrella." At Osborne House the umbrella was returned with a five-pound note. "The old letter-carrier who for more than twenty years has never had a day absent from his duty . . . expresses his intention of never more using the umbrella, but preserving it as an heirloom" (1844).

Postwomen were not usually employed until after 1914, but their services were sometimes required in remote country districts.

> From the Village Post Office, letters were distributed by a male postman, and for the more outlying houses and farms, by two women letter-carrier carriers. The elder woman Mrs Gubbins, was an old country woman who wore for her round a lilac sunbonnet, apron and shawl.
>
> Flora Thompson, *Candleford Green*. (Reminiscences of her adolescence in rural Oxfordshire, in the 1890s.)

The term *postman* became official in 1883, replacing "letter-carrier", be-cause the postmen began to take parcels as well as letters. Postcards were

192. The only postman in Newcastle; wearing a loose overcoat, double-breasted waistcoat, breeches and a top hat. 1821.

introduced in 1870 and telegraphs were taken over by the Post Office in the same year.

A *telegraph messenger boy's* uniform is shown in a photograph of 1904. He wears a short coat with a belt and stand collar with his number, a peaked cap, trousers covered below by leggings; also boots. In cold weather he has a long belted overcoat with a turn-down collar (see Plate 38a).

About 1910 postmen and boy messengers engaged on cycling duties were given knickerbockers and puttees as part of the standard uniform, but they were unpopular and discarded some fifteen years later.

The Post Office and its uniforms have been dealt with fairly fully, since the Post Office touches the lives of so many people. In fact, "it is from the rudimentary beginnings in Sixteenth Century England that there has evolved the International Postage System of today, with the peoples of the World held together by a postage stamp" (F. G. Kay, *Royal Mail*).

STAGE-COACHES

The stage-coach is defined as "a coach that runs regularly every day or on stated days between two places for the conveyance of passengers". These began to function at the end of the seventeenth century. In the eighteenth century their journeys were often similar to those of the mail-coaches, stopping at fixed posts to change horses. The garb of the driver varied considerably. In the eighteenth century he wore a wig.

> The coachman's cauliflower built tiers to tiers
> Differ not more from bags and brigadiers
> Than great St George's or St James's styles
> From the broad dialect of Broad St Giles.
>
> 1775. Prologue by G. Colman to *Bon Ton* by David Garrick.

The bag wig, often shortened to bag, had its queue enclosed in a black silk bag at the back of the neck. The brigadier was a military style of wig with a double queue. The cauliflower was a mass of close curls.

In 1836 a coachman wore:

> An embroidered coat reaching down to his heels and a waistcoat of the same.
>
> C. Dickens, *The Pickwick Papers*.

In 1876 we have this description:

> The swell dragsman was a well dressed neatly looking fellow decked out in a neat brown coat, white hat, corduroy breeches, well polished boots, cloth leggings and a splendid pair of double sewn buckskin gloves.
>
> Lord William Lennox, *Coaching*.

In 1841 the following comment by a cockney was recorded about a London stage-coach driver:

I thinks some of these Lunnen coachmen are a little above their situation.
. . . I could not help saying to our guard t'other day when he told me he met
one of what they calls the "swell dragsmen" out of Lunnen, at work in *kid
gloves* and with a bunch of curls sticking out on the off-side of his hat, that
I should like to put a twitch on his nose and trim him about the head, as
we do a horse. I'd put the dogskins on him too; what real Coachman ever
druv in anything but dog-skin gloves?

> 1841. Nimrod, *The Coachman and the Guard*, p. 233.

The ordinary stage-coachman was not so smart, especially when dressed
like Tony Weller:

Round his neck he wore a crimson travelling shawl . . . over this he mounted
a long waistcoat of a broad pink striped pattern, and over that again a wide-
skirted green coat, ornamented with large brass buttons. . . . His hair, which
was short, sleek and black, was first visible beneath the capacious brim of a
low-crowned brown hat. His legs were incased in knee-cord breeches and
painted top boots and a copper watch-chain, terminating in one seal, and a
key of the same material, dangled from his capacious waistband.

When stage-coaches travelled long distances they were usually supplied
with postilions who were known as postboys, as their duty was to be ready to
change horses at the "posts" or inns where the horses were in readiness. The
postboy in this sense had no connection with the mail or postal service.

A smart postilion in the eighteenth century is described by Smollett:

In the afternoon, as our aunt stept into the coach, she observed, with some
marks of satisfaction, that the postillion, who rode next to her, was not a
wretch like the ragamuffin who had drove them into Marlborough. Indeed,
the difference was very conspicuous. This was a smart fellow, with a narrow-
brimmed hat, with gold cording, a cut bob, a decent blue jacket, leather
breeches, and a clean linen shirt, puffed above the waistband.

> 1771. T. Smollett, *Humphry Clinker.*

The small hat and the cut bob which was a short wig would have been convenient on horseback.

The postboy in the early nineteenth century is shown in Plate 38b and is
described by a contemporary as follows:

Our own horses took us to Woodford . . . and there four posters were
"clapped on" in a very few minutes at the sound of "Horses on" from the

ostler of the inn. Then the two post boys, in high white beaver hats, blue jackets, red waistcoats, white neckcloths, short white corduroy breeches, and bright top boots, started off at a smart trot, which was continued the whole stage up and down hill, often stopping for a moment for a post boy to dismount and put on a drag.

1822. Journey from London to Earlham, described by Augustus Hare, in *The Gurneys of Earlham*, 2 vols.

CHAPTER **X**

POLICE

CHARLEYS AND BOBBIES

1. Charleys

> Watchman, what of the night?
>
> Isaiah xxi. 11.

It is difficult to say how old the office of watchman is: certainly the Royal Writs of Watch and Ward issued by Henry III in 1252/3 make specific reference to men to be chosen in every township "to follow the hue and cry . . . with bows and arrows and other light arms . . . provided at the common cost of the township". These forces of law and order were strengthened under Henry VII by the introduction of high constables and petty constables, and such a watch is described by Shakespeare in *Much Ado About Nothing*, III. iii. Here Dogberry and Verges, the constables, are clad in gowns and the men of their watch are armed with bills and carry lanterns (see Plate 39).

Burghley describes the watch in 1586 when looking for the Babington conspirators as armed with staves only (S.P. 12/192/22, quoted by A. L. Rowse, *The England of Elizabeth*).

In the seventeenth century the constables' watch in London is mentioned by Pepys, who also speaks of the bellman.

> I staid up until the bell-man came by . . . and cried "Past one of the clock and a cold, frosty, windy morning".

> Met with the bellman, who struck upon a clapper, which I took in my hand, and it is just like the clappers that our boys frighten the birds away from the corn with.

> *Diary*, 1660.

The bellman seems to have been complementary to the watchman, who also called the hours, and the precise distinction between the two, if any, is difficult to make. In an early-seventeenth-century print he is shown as clad in doublet, hose and gown, a round hat with a turned-up brim, and carrying a lantern and staff in addition to his bell (Fig. 193).

193. A London Bellman. Early 17th century.

The watch as represented in the sixteenth and seventeenth centuries is clothed in much the same way, sometimes with a spear or pike instead of a staff, and with a bell or "clapper". This latter is more generally known as a rattle, and survived in the Metropolitan Police as the means of raising an alarm until 1884. Today its use is confined to encouraging footballers.

Both Charles I and Charles II took an interest in the efficiency of the London watchmen, and to both of these monarchs has been ascribed the origin of the nickname "Charley" for a watchman. Whoever the proper Charley may have been originally, this was certainly the cant term for one during the eighteenth and nineteenth centuries. In 1749 Henry Fielding, then the Bow Street Magistrate, unofficially established a watch which developed during the years 1760–70 into the famous Bow Street Horse and Foot Patroles. These Patroles did not wear uniform until 1805, when the Horse Patrole, which had been discontinued for a number of years, was revived with blue coats and red waistcoats. In 1822 the Foot Patrole was put into a similar uniform of blue coat and trousers. This uniform no doubt had some influence on the subsequent costume of Peel's New Police seven years later. The red waistcoat gained the Patroles the popular description of "Robin Redbreast", which later came erroneously to be applied to the Bow Street Runners—a plain-clothes detective force.

The great majority of illustrations of watchmen surviving are of the early nineteenth century, and they are generally in agreement that the Charley of this period was clad in a long greatcoat, with a cape, breeches with stockings or gaiters, black shoes or boots, topped with a low-crowned, wide-brimmed slouch hat. He carried a staff or cudgel, and a lantern. His rattle was carried suspended from his clothing (Fig. 194). Busby, in *Costume of the Lower Orders*

194. A London Watchman. 1835.

of London, (1820), states, "They carry a lantern and thick stick, and have concealed a rattle." In one instance the greatcoat is shown as grey, but shades of brown or fawn seem the most popular colours; although *The Times* refers to white coats. The passage, quoted by Hone in the *Table Book,* is dated October 1827 and reads:

> Had a council of thieves been consulted, the regulations of the Watch could not have been better contrived for their accommodation. The coats of the Watchmen are made as large and of as white cloth as possible, to enable the thieves to discern their approach at the greatest distance; and that there may be no mistake, the lantern is added.

This passage would indicate that the coats of the Charleys were provided by the authorities, which is also borne out by the appearance on the back of a watchman (see Plate 40a) illustrated in Pierce Egan's *Life In and Out of London* (1828) of an identifying number. The number—"SW No: 9"—is marked in letters about six inches high on the back of the greatcoat, in two lines below the waist.

A similar method of identification was used in Glasgow according to Howard in *Guardians of the Queen's Peace*, who illustrates a watchman of that city in 1800 bearing a large figure 6 on his back, but in this case above the waist.

One feature shown in many of the illustrations is a night-cap or muffler worn on the head underneath the hat; a habit that was noted by Charles Dickens. Mr Pickwick, surprised in the Middle Aged Lady's bedroom in the Great White Horse at Ipswich, "put on his hat over his night cap, after the manner of the old patrol". This additional headwear is presumably a protection against that "cold, frosty, windy morning" remarked upon by Mr Pepys's bellman and underlines the fact that most of the Charleys were old and decrepit—as an extract from the *Morning Herald* of 30th October 1802 also shows. As quoted by Ashton (*England a Hundred Years Ago*), the report states that a man applying for the job of watchman was turned down on the grounds that the Vestry was "astonished at the impudence of such a great sturdy, strong fellow as you being so idle as to apply for a watchman's situation when you are capable of labour".

2. Bobbies

> There goes the Bobby in his black shiny hat
> And his belly full of fat.
>
> Child's Rhyme, nineteenth century.

The British Police Forces as we know them today are the result of Sir Robert Peel's Police Act of 1829, which set up the Metropolitan Force and also added the words "peeler" and "bobbie" to the language. This Act was followed in 1835 and 1839 with two others, under which the Provincial Forces were raised.

The need for a well-organized and disciplined body in the Metropolis was made evident by the inability of the existing system of parish constables and watchmen to cope with the increasing crime and public disorder of the early nineteenth century. The success of the small Bow Street Horse Patrole, recognizable in their blue coats and red waistcoats, showed the value of a well-directed, uniformed body, although public opinion was not in favour of any kind of uniformed police. So opposed was the mood of the nation to any suggestion that the new Metropolitan Force, backed as it was by the Government, could in any way be regarded as a para-military corps, that it

PLATE 39

PLATE 39

Watchman, 16th century. A carved bench-end.

Bishop's Hull, Somerset. National Monuments Record. Photograph by
F. H. Crossley.

PLATE 40

PLATE 40

(a) A watchman showing night-cap worn under the hat, and rattle attached to belt. The greatcoat bears an identification number. 1828.

Caricature by R. Cruikshank in Life in and out of London *by Pierce Egan. 1828.*

(b) A provincial policeman carrying a short truncheon. His collar-badge and horizontally striped armlet indicate he belongs to a provincial force. 1855.

Lithograph by Day. Published by Ackermann.

was for a time seriously suggested that its members should be dressed only in plain clothes.

However, it was finally decided that the advantages of a uniform as an aid to discipline, and possibly, at least in the eyes of Colonel Rowan[1], as a means of fostering an *esprit de corps*, outweighed the arguments for plain clothes.

The uniform eventually approved and worn by the first members of the "New" Police in London in 1829 was a fine example of British compromise. Uniform it was—military it was not (Fig. 195).

195. One of the "New Police". 1829.

Colonel Rowan had said that it should be quiet, and the blue coat, blue or white trousers according to the season, and black tall hat were almost indistinguishable from those of the man-in-the-street of the day.

The dark blue swallow-tail coat had metal buttons down the front and at the cuffs. A white letter and number were embroidered on the stand-up collar; the letter indicated the Division to which the constable belonged and his own identity was established by the numerals.

In the Museum at Scotland Yard is a very early uniform—thought to be about 1830. The cloth of the coat is of good quality, superior to that used in

---

[1] One of the two Joint Commissioners who originally headed the Metropolitan Police.

contemporary soldiers' uniforms; with seven metal buttons embossed with a crown and the words "Metropolitan Police". The white duck trousers, with small falls (a horizontal buttoned flap in place of a fly fastening) and with an adjusting lace at the back, seem shoddy in comparison with the coat. It is interesting to note that as late as 1890 the Commissioner was complaining about the poor quality of the "wretched trousers".

The tall hat was the normal top-hat of the early nineteenth century, re-inforced with cane strips and with a leather top. For winter wear a dark brown overcoat was issued, as also was a cape for bad weather.

In the early days officers of the rank of inspector and above in the Metropolitan Force had to buy their own uniforms; later these were provided as for the lower ranks.

In the provinces we find that in 1854, Bury St Edmunds was advertising for a Superintendent of the Borough Police at a salary of 25s. per week and a suit of police clothing every year.

In 1830 the duty armlet was introduced into the Metropolitan Force to enable the public to distinguish men who were on duty (see Plate 40b). The armlet was "a piece of striped list [encircling] the cuff of his coat"; the stripes were blue and white, vertical, and the armlet worn on the left cuff of con-stables only. In 1855 a similar armlet was introduced for sergeants, but on the right cuff.

From 1829 until 1897 the sergeants and constables were issued with two pairs of boots annually, but in the latter year a cash allowance replaced the issue in kind. Leggings or gaiters were tried out for winter wear in the mid-century, and some time before 1859 the cloth cape was replaced by oilskin. A "vegetable leather" pattern was tried out unsuccessfully in 1860.

A new look was introduced in 1864, when the first helmets and tunics replaced the top-hat and swallow tail (see Plate 41a), and a new-pattern greatcoat superseded the original double-breasted frock type. A generation had passed since the advent of the New Police and the replacement of the civilian top-hat by the quasi-military continental style helmet met with little or no opposition. In fact, approval of its introduction was expressed in a music-hall song of the day:

> Instead of the old flower pot tile
> The helmet is a better style.
> It has more room and cap-ac-i-tye
> To hold cold mutton or rabbit pie.

With the new uniform came the addition of rank chevrons for the sergeants and the shifting of their duty armlet to the left arm.

Unshakeably linked with the policeman in these days is his whistle, but this did not appear in London until 1884—when it replaced the time-honoured rattle.

With minor exceptions and modifications the Metropolitan uniform established in 1864–5 remained unaltered for the next seventy years, and in many items is unaltered to this day.

In general the other forces of the New Police established after the Acts of 1835 and 1839 copied the Metropolitan uniform, with local variations, and as the Metropolis introduced reforms, so did the Provinces (see Plate 41b). The City of London, jealous of its ancient privileges, did not accept the Metropolitan Force within its boundaries and established its own force. The City Police adopted a different style of helmet and a red-and-white duty armlet to distinguish themselves from their bigger neighbour.

Birmingham City Police chose a blue-and-white horizontally striped armlet which they wore on the opposite cuff to the Metropolitan; the Manchester Force appear never to have worn an armlet at all (see Plate 42a). In Colchester in 1868, during the Fenian Riots, red horizontally striped armlets were issued to the Special Constables. Two years earlier Colchester purchased "clothes", boots, hats, and leggings from local tradesmen for the Borough Police, and also, a separate item, "trousers for the Head Constable".

Most forces seem to have worn at one time or another arm badges showing proficiency in First Aid, and Manchester City Police Horse Ambulance Section was distinguished in the early twentieth century by wearing peaked caps instead of helmets (see Plate 42b).

In addition to ambulances, the provincial Police in many cases also provided the fire brigades, and a distinctive uniform and protective clothing were issued to these firemen/policemen.

To summarize, a table of significant dates in the history of the Metropolitan Police uniform is given below.

1805   The Horse Patrol re-established at Bow Street. Black leather hat; blue greatcoat, coat and trousers. White gloves, Wellington boots and spurs. Scarlet waistcoat, giving them the name "Robin Redbreasts".

1829   Establishment of Metropolitan Police with issue of first uniforms.

Lanterns, swords and belts, pistols and handcuffs were kept in the stations. Rattles to be carried in greatcoat pocket when worn.

1830   Annual uniform issue to each officer laid down as

Greatcoat and badge	Cape
Coat	2 pairs of trousers
2 pairs of boots	1 hat and 2 covers
1 stock	1 button brush and stick
1 20 in. stave, rattle, and book of instructions	

Subsequently each year a replacement issue of

1 coat	2 pairs of trousers
2 pairs of boots	and 1 hat

In 1830 the duty armlet was introduced.

196. Constable in single breasted greatcoat and carrying a bull's-eye lantern. He appears to be a City policeman from the crest on the helmet. 1869.

197. Constable, showing truncheon case suspended from belt. He has the crested helmet adopted by the City Police. 1869.

1831   Firearms only to be carried by express permission of the Commissioners.

1836   The issue of button brush and stick appears to have ceased.
        Swords supplied to the Horsed Police.

1856   20 in. stave replaced by 17 in. truncheon.

1859   Oilskin capes known to be in use.

1862   Hats supplied free to inspectors.
        Chin straps unsuccessfully tried out.

1864   The New Pattern Uniform. Helmets introduced, with helmet plate bearing Divisional letter and number. New-style greatcoat (Fig. 196). Tunics with metal numerals replaced coats with embroidered numbers. Belts a general issue to hold a truncheon case (Fig. 197) and lantern. Mounted Police supplied with leather gloves.

1880   Two greatcoats allowed to be kept in wear.

1884   Police whistle adopted in place of rattle.

1885   Cutlasses and swords generally withdrawn from stations (but not from Mounted Branch until 1925).

1886   Provision of white gloves by individuals no longer necessary.

1887   Present pattern of truncheons introduced and truncheon pockets provided in trousers and greatcoats.
Truncheon cases withdrawn.

1889   Jack-boots supplied to Mounted Branch.

1897   Cash allowance in lieu of boot issue.

1910   Black gloves first issued.

1911   White cotton gloves first issued.

1912   20 in. truncheon issued to Mounted Branch.

THE RIVER POLICE

The present Thames Division of the Metropolitan Police dates back to 1798, and was not incorporated into the Metropolitan Force until 1839. Their leader in the beginning was a magistrate, who had under him two assistants and seven constables. Their dress would appear to be that of the rivermen and seamen of the day. When the police uniform appeared it had in the Thames Division a nautical flavour. In the 1890s "they have a glazed hat and seaman's cap and jersey and double-breasted jacket"—in addition to a double-breasted greatcoat. The inspectors wore peaked caps. In the Museum at Scotland Yard is a River Police hat of 1883; it is of black varnished leather, "boater" shaped, with wide ribbon and a large bow.

PLATE 41

PLATE 41

(a) Metropolitan Police Constables at Devonport Dockyard.
The man on the left is in the new uniform and the one in the background extreme right wears the old pattern with duty armlet and top hat.
c. 1864–5.

By courtesy of Messrs. Merryweather & Sons Ltd.

(b) A Manchester City Police Sergeant wearing an overcoat. 1860s.

By courtesy of the Chief Constable, Manchester City Police.

PLATE 42

PLATE 42

(*a*) Manchester City Constable. *c.* 1910.

By courtesy of the Chief Constable, Manchester City Police.

(*b*) Sergeant and Constables of Manchester City Police Horse Ambulances. *c.* 1910.

By courtesy of the Chief Constable, Manchester City Police.

CHAPTER XI

FIREMEN

And now my doubts to rest are laid
It is, it is, the Fire Brigade.

Anon, *c.* 1883.

The English Parish vestries had for centuries been charged with the provision of fire-fighting equipment and the raising of temporary firemen as need arose, but the system was inefficient and the equipment and men generally inadequate.

The losses occasioned by the Great Fire of London in 1666 are generally regarded as the immediate occasion of the inception of fire insurance in Britain, and from the very beginning the fire insurance offices maintained their own firemen—originally part-time, but later as a whole-time employment. These Insurance Brigades supplemented (or supplanted) the parochial organizations and were the principal source of fire protection in the country for some two centuries. During the nineteenth century, starting with Edinburgh in 1824, many of the provincial insurance brigades passed to centralized control, and in 1866 the Metropolitan Board of Works assumed the responsibility for the London Fire Engine Establishment, founded in 1833 by the Metropolitan offices pooling their services. During that century, heyday of private enterprise and philanthropy, many volunteer brigades were formed, some by works and factories, who gladly deployed them in defence of their neighbour's property when required.

Up to the end of the seventeenth century no particular form of clothing seems to have been worn by the men called upon to fight fires—they were no doubt *ad hoc* teams organized at the time, and clad in their everyday garments.

When the insurance companies inaugurated their own fire services they, like the railway companies later, realized the value of a distinctive uniform, both to *esprit de corps* and to publicity. Thus the Friendly Society in 1683 kept "in livery, with silver badges, about twenty men"; and in 1696 the Hand-in-Hand started business employing eight watermen provided with caps, coats, and breeches . . . blew lined with red, a red edging being put upon the same.

The Thames watermen (Fig. 198), whose main employment was manning the numerous boats engaged in the Thames passenger traffic, were favoured by the companies as part-time firemen for a number of reasons—e.g. they

198. Thames Waterman, 1824.

were their own masters, they were centred around the City river-side stairs, close by the companies' offices, and their river training, and in some cases sea-going experience, was adaptable to the business of fire-fighting and the use of ladders and ropes. In the late eighteenth century and early nineteenth century discharged sailors were also favoured as firemen in both London and the provinces. This preference for river and seamen had a noticeable influence on the design of the fireman's uniform. The cut of the coat often followed that of the waterman's, and the badge, generally worn on the left arm, was similar to the arm badge of the licensed waterman. In some cases, however, a fireman's badge was worn around the neck, either in addition to or in place of the arm badge. In the nineteenth century a pronounced nautical flavour was evident in some of the uniforms and headgear adopted by the brigades then being started by local authorities.

In addition to firemen proper the companies also recruited porters whose job it was to salvage goods and remove them out of danger. These porters likewise wore the company's badge around the neck or on the left arm, but during the seventeenth and eighteenth centuries do not appear to have been given a uniform.

In 1707 the fire insurance companies' efforts were acknowledged by Parliament in the Fire Act, and specific mention is made of "coats and badges" given "unto Watermen for service and assistance in extinguishing of fires".

The fireman's badge was from the very beginning regarded as a sign of integrity, both of the individual and of the company, and it was to be surrendered when an employee left the service. Stringent rules were laid down regarding the wearing of it. In 1725 the London Assurance Company minutes record that

> Firemen or Porters appearing without their Badges to forfeit for the first offence 2/6 each to the use of the poor to be paid to the Secretary.

For a second offence suspension, and for a third dismissal, were the penalties.

Until the early years of the nineteenth century badges were of silver; the foremen's silver-gilt. In 1721 the Royal Exchange Assurance ordered thirty-five fireman's badges and twenty-one for the porters. The foremen's "to be made larger than the others and gilt". The contemporary value of their silver badges was quite considerable, and instances appear of men pawning them, with consequent dismissal. They also got lost, and in 1753 the London Assurance offered a reward of two guineas for the recovery of one, the waterman concerned having overset his boat and lost his coat and badge overboard. This shows that the fireman-waterman wore his office uniform at all times; a requirement laid down by the London Assurance in 1722.

In the late eighteenth century batons were sometimes carried by the foremen as a sign of their authority. These batons were like the constables' or tipstaffs', either of metal or wood suitably decorated with the company's insignia.

After the end of the Napoleonic Wars the badges were made of copper or brass, and later of white metal; late in the nineteenth century embroidered cloth badges were worn by the surviving company brigades.

The design of the badges, whatever their material, was similar to that of the company's fire mark fixed to the properties that they insured (Fig. 199),

199. Fireman and Porter of Sun Fire Office, 1727. From a Sun Insurance Policy.

except in some cases after about 1815 when the company's initials or cipher were shown.

In the early days coats and headwear alone seem to have been the usual provision, and in some cases this lasted up to the end of the nineteenth century. The Hand-in-Hand's breeches mentioned above were an exception.

In 1709 or 1710 the "Sun" dressed its firemen in "blue liveries with silver badges", and the earliest illustration of a company fireman is a woodcut which appeared on "Sun" policies in the 1720s (Fig. 199). This shows a fireman and porter. The fireman wears what may be a buff jerkin with a deep skirt, with a waist belt in which is an axe. He wears a leather cap or helmet with a crest and neck-flap. Breeches, stockings and shoes complete his costume. The Company badge is on the left arm. The porter is dressed in a common coat with round cuffs, breeches with roll-up stockings and shoes. His badge is around the neck on a chain or cord and he wears a three-cornered cocked hat.

Of about the same date is a description of the Royal Exchange Assurance livery worn by the firemen and porters; "all cloathed in yellow, and have everyone Badges on which is impressed the Royal Exchange and Crown, to distinguish them from servants belonging to others". In 1776 the colour was changed to green.

Another cut illustrating a fireman and a porter appears on the Bristol Crown Fire Office policies in the mid-1730s. It is reminiscent of the "Sun" design of a decade earlier, but differs chiefly in the costume of the porter, who is shown as a much less elegant figure than his "Sun" counterpart, and he wears a coarse apron (Fig. 200).

200. Fireman and Porter of Bristol Crown Fire Office, *c.* 1735. From an Insurance Policy.

In 1750 the "Sun" produced a new version of the fireman and porter for their policy heading. The fireman's coat has buttons to the waist only (a feature of the second half of the century) and reveals a single-breasted waistcoat beneath. The breeches are buttoned over the stockings. The helmet is of leather, with a crest and a wide brim, extending to a neck-flap at the back. He has round-toed shoes with large buckles. His badge is on the arm.

In 1782 the Phoenix Fire Office was founded and its "Engineers, firemen and porters" are described in a contemporary leaflet as wearing

> a uniform of crimson cloth with a silver badge, the emblem A PHOENIX rising from the Flames—which is also the Office Mark; each Man bears a number on his Badge, and should any of them misbehave or be negligent on Duty the Office will be much obliged for Information. . . .

Like the schoolboy's house cap of later days, the distinctive means of identification could at times be a disadvantage to the wearer. This early Phoenix uniform has been reconstructed and shows a coat with a standing collar, narrow buttoned revers from neck to waist of a military style and mariner cuffs (that is with a vertical buttoned flap); a crimson single-breasted waistcoat and crimson breeches, grey stockings and yellow garters. Buckled round-toed shoes and a broad-brimmed round hat completed the costume. This appears to have been the "full dress" livery of the company, as a very much less ornate version dating from perhaps the late 1790s has been preserved. It is also crimson, but much plainer, and a black leather helmet is preserved with it.

Generally during the eighteenth century the firemen's liveries followed the fashion of everyday clothing, with a leaning towards the military at the end of the century, the distinction between the companies' brigades being shown by the colour and the arm badges.

In the early nineteenth century it seems that the ceremonial or full dress became quite different from the working uniform, with a tendency towards shorter coats for working in, and after 1840 the shifting of the badge from arm to chest.

In 1804 the Kent Fire Insurance Company adopted a grey linen uniform, with sealskin helmet; this was changed to grey worsted in 1809.

William Pyne's coloured engraving of 1805 (see Plate 43b) shows a "Sun" man in the foreground and men from other brigades in the background. The "Sun" fireman is clad in a blue coat and double-breasted waistcoat. The coat, worn open, has twelve buttons from neck to waist and a further button on the stand collar. He wears striped stockings rolled up over the breeches (also blue) and fastened above the knee with tied garters, and buff-top boots. In addition to a large badge on the left arm (see Plate 43a), he wears another on his heavy leather helmet. The men working the engine are in similar uniforms, but green in colour, with round hats. As Pyne depicts the men in action, these are presumably working clothes. An extant Hand-in-Hand uniform of about 1810 may be ceremonial: dark blue coat, stand collar, all piped in red, red-laced wings (a stiffened decorative band projecting from the shoulder over the sleeve after the fashion of an epaulette) and cuffs; the breeches are of orange plush with grey stockings. Black shoes and a silk top-hat complete the outfit.

Plush breeches were worn for work also: Horace Smith wrote in 1809:

> The summoned firemen woke at call
> And hied them to their stations all:
> Starting from short and broken snooze
> Each sought his pondrous hob-nailed shoes:
> But first his worsted hosen plied,
> Plush breeches next in crimson dyed
>   His nether bulk embraced.
> Then jacket thick of red or blue
> Whose massy shoulder gave to view
> The badge of each respective crew.

In 1820 T. L. Busby drew the foreman of the Hope Insurance Company in his uniform of red short-skirted frockcoat and waistcoat, blue breeches with top-boots and black hat (Fig. 201); a uniform very similar to other companies' of that date, except for the colours. In all the coats of this period the "skirt" is very pronounced—a feature persisting into the 1830s, and to be seen also in the coats of the Thames watermen at this time.

A significant event took place in 1824 when the Edinburgh insurance offices combined their brigades to make the Edinburgh Fire Engine Establishment under the superintendence of James Braidwood. Braidwood had studied the continental fire brigades and he introduced a practical and up-to-date uniform for the Establishment (see Plate 44a). Let him describe it for himself:

> The whole are dressed in blue jackets, canvas trousers, and hardened leather

201. Insurance Brigade Fireman, 1820.
(William Mead, foreman of the Hope Insurance Co.)

helmets, having hollow leather crests over the crown to ward off falling materials. The form of this helmet was taken from the war helmet of the New Zealanders, with the addition of the hind flap of leather to prevent burning matter, melted lead, water, or rubbish getting into the neck of the wearer.

Trousers had become more popular in civil life from about 1807 and by the 1820s were well established.

A picture of *c.* 1830 of a full dress of the Royal Exchange Company shows the final flowering of the insurance brigades' glory: the full-skirted frockcoat has small wings, buttoned slit cuffs, and twelve buttons as large as a crown piece. The breeches are buttoned at the knee and like the coat are green. Neckwear is a cravat, or stock; and the hat is a tall silk, wider at the top than at the brim, encircled with a gold band. A large badge is worn on the arm, white stockings and neat shoes fastened with laces adorn legs and feet (see Plate 44b).

In the 1820s a full-dress uniform in colours distinctive for each company had been established for the following fourteen insurance companies:

PLATE 43

PLATE 43

(*a*) Silver arm badge of Sun Fire Office Fireman (now Sun Alliance Insurance Group).

By courtesy of Sun Alliance Insurance Group.

(*b*) "Sun" Fireman of 1805. Men of other brigades in background.

W. H. Pyne, Costume of Great Britain. *1808.*

PLATE 44

PLATE 44

(a) Edinburgh Fire Engine Establishment, 1850. In uniforms introduced
by J. Braidwood in 1824.

By courtesy of The Fire Protection Association.

(b) Fireman of Royal Exchange Insurance Brigade, in full dress. *c.* 1830.

By courtesy of The Fire Protection Association.

Company	Coat and Waistcoat	Breeches	Facings	Lace (braiding)
1820 Hope	Red lined blue	Blue	—	Yellow
1825 Atlas	Green Waistcoat saffron	Saffron	Saffron	
1825 Caledonian	Blue	Blue	Orange	Orange
1825 County	Buff	Blue	Yellow	Yellow
1825 Guardian	Brown Waistcoat red and yellow striped	Brown	Red	Yellow
1825 Hand-in-Hand	Blue	Orange	Red	Red
1825 Kent	Brown or Black	Brown or Black		
1825 Norwich Union	Blue	Blue	Red	
1825 Phoenix	Crimson	Buff	Green	Yellow
1825 Royal Exchange	Green	Green	Green	
1825 Sun	Blue	Blue	Blue	
1825 Union	Dark brown	Dark brown	?	?
1825 West of England	Dark blue	Dark blue	Dark red	Red
1825 Westminster	Royal blue Lined yellow	Black	Yellow	Yellow

In 1833, copying the example of Edinburgh, the principal Metropolitan insurance companies pooled their brigades to form the London Fire Engine Establishment. The individual company uniforms disappeared and those men not employed in the new Establishment were, by one company at least, allowed to retain their own uniforms, but the badges were withdrawn. The Establishment dressed all its crews in a plain uniform of grey coats and trousers and black leather helmets. (Fig. 202). Wellington type boots were sometimes worn.

The Royal Society for the Protection of Life from Fire was founded in 1836

202. Fireman of the London Fire Engine
Establishment, 1834.

to provide fire escapes in various parts of London, which were manned at night by crews which in 1843 were described as dressed in tarpaulin coat and trousers, and a cap with the initials of the Society. They also had a helmet, lamp and rattle.

The various volunteer fire brigades founded during the nineteenth century tended to follow the lead of the Fire Engine Establishments, with variations and additions of their own. The leader of one such brigade—Frederick Hodges—active from 1851 to 1865, was photographed in a splendid attire of double-breasted jacket, with wings and brass buttons, the collar and cuffs faced with a different colour; a leather belt with elaborate belt plate; lanyard and whistle. He wears a plumed helmet and round his neck hangs a brass gorget piece. Volunteer uniforms were either provided by the men themselves or by public subscription.

In 1866 the London Fire Engine Establishment became the Metropolitan Fire Brigade, and Massey Shaw, its leader, introduced from Paris the brass helmet of the Sapeurs-Pompiers. The Proceedings of the Metropolitan Board of Works for that year refer to the acceptance of "Mr Almond's tender for helmets", but does not state their material. Also at this date it is probable that the grey uniform was changed to navy blue.

Insurance brigades in the provinces also adopted more up-to-date uniforms as the nineteenth century progressed. In 1842 the Essex and Suffolk Fire Office provided its brigade in Colchester with hats bearing the company's name; in the same year this company's Chelmsford brigade still had an arm badge.

The provincial brigades soon copied the London Fire Brigade brass helmet, much, it is recorded, to the annoyance of Captain Shaw, and by 1881 the *Fireman* magazine recommends "a well made brass helmet, symmetrical and light, with fittings firmly and neatly fixed . . ." These brass helmets were crested, peaked back and front, and ornamented with repoussée designs of crossed torches, dragons, crossed axes and hosepipes. They had brass chin chains and the whole was leather lined.

Off duty and when waiting "on watch" the London Fire Brigade wore flat sailor hats (Fig. 203), as we see from the frontispiece to J. M. Ballentyne's *Fighting the Flames*, published in 1867, which shows the scene in a watch-room: the men's belts and axes and helmets hang on the wall.

203. Fireman in sailor hat, waiting "on watch". 1855.

The sailor hat was popular with many of the provincial brigades, some of whom adopted a very naval-like uniform. At Weston-super-Mare in 1881 the men wore reefer jackets and sailor hats with a ribbon tied in a bow with flowing ends at the back. In 1900 the Sheffield Brigade introduced an exact replica of the Royal Navy's uniform, except that the hat tally (or cap ribbon) read "Sheffield Fire Brigade" in place of a ship's name. This undress uniform was worn only for a short time; was this due, perhaps, to jealousy on the part of the Lords of the Admiralty?

By the 1880s dark blue had become the most common colour for uniforms. J. C. Merryweather wrote in *The Fire Brigade Handbook* in 1888:

> The tunic usually recommended for volunteers is very similar to the London Brigade pattern tunic, and is made of stout blue, waterproof cloth.

In addition, Merryweather lists helmets, cloth trousers, belt, axe and pouch, undress cap and boots as desiderata. The buttons of the tunic were commonly ornamented with crossed hatchets and a helmet, or torch, but some brigades had their initials or a special design made for them.

A few years before the above was written outfitters offered, *inter alia*, "belts and pouches in patent and leather"; and Napoleon and Wellington boots.

In London the voluntary principle gave rise to the London Auxiliary Fire Brigade in 1875, whose uniform was similar to the Regular brigade, but with black buttons instead of brass, and with the brass helmet painted black.

The dress of brigades in the latter part of the century presented a wide variety of single- and double-breasted tunics and coats, side hats, glengarries, forage caps, cheesecutters, and ceremonial helmets, in addition to the workaday attire of officers and firemen. A typical volunteer working uniform of 1881 is that of the Uxbridge Brigade (Fig. 204), where the officers wear the double-breasted tunic open at the neck with a collar and tie.

In 1894 Messrs Merryweather were advertising "helmets of all designs and shapes in leather, brass, cork, felt, and plated. Undress caps of all patterns for Officers and men" (see Plate 45a). Fancy buckles and shoulder-knots were also on sale, as well as humdrum items such as boots and overalls.

In many instances in the provinces the local authorities imposed the task of fire-fighting on their police forces. In some cases firemen were enrolled into the brigade, which was administered by the Chief Constable—in other cases some of the police themselves were either detailed for fire-fighting or were taken from other duties as the occasion demanded to act as firemen. Some forces adopted firemen's uniform *in toto* for their men so employed; in others the policemen wore their normal uniforms with appropriate variations. A photo of the Chief Constable and Chief Fireman of Blackburn in 1914 shows him wearing a forage cap with gold-braided peak and a laced and frogged coat with no badges or visible buttons. An inspector of the Sheffield Police Fire Brigade of the same date wears a similar uniform.

The fireman's uniform at the beginning of this century did not differ significantly from that at the end of the nineteenth (see Plates 45b and 46). Generally it was dark blue, with a double-breasted tunic, trousers and leather Wellington boots, and an elaborate crested brass helmet. A broad leather waist belt with a plain square brass buckle supported an axe and in some cases a hank of light rope. On the left breast was an embroidered badge with the fireman's number. Officers were distinguished by having no badge and by various ornamentations to the collar and cuffs. Sometimes metal shoulder straps and wings were also worn by officers (see Plate 46).

204. Volunteer Brigade Uniforms, 1881. Members of the Uxbridge Volunteer Brigade.

However, this modern and workmanlike outfit did not, apparently, meet with universal esteem and approval, with consequent effect on the morale of the wearers, for we read in the *Fireman* of December 1909 that "Alfreton Fire Brigade resigned owing to the fact that their appearance in uniform excited the hilarity of the vulgar". Perhaps the authorities responsible for the Alfreton Brigade had not read the words of the *Fireman's Herald* of 1885, which said, with particular reference to the insurance companies,

> . . . the generality of mankind shews its character in its clothing and this instance of the fireman, as anybody else, being true it behoves fire companies

to spend considerable thought on the subject before they select a uniform, for they certainly want a uniform which adds to their importance rather than one which belittles them.

Protective Clothing

The earliest item of protective clothing for the fireman was, of course, the helmet. First of leather, then of metal, and latterly, on account of the danger

205. Sun Fire Office smoke helmet. 18th century.

from live electric cables, etc., of a variety of non-conducting materials. When the helmet was introduced is not known, but a print attributed to 1569 shows a man filling a large fire-squirt. He is wearing what may be a

206. The "Pauline" Apparel. 1830.

round leather helmet. Similar helmets are reputed to have been used during the Great Fire of 1666.

One of the greatest hazards in fire-fighting is the danger of suffocation by smoke and "smoke maskes" were in use in the eighteenth century (Fig. 205). To the snout a pipe was connected to reach out to pure air. In 1830 the "Pauline apparel" was introduced from France. This was a one-piece upper garment of a pullover type incorporating a hood with eyepieces. It was thigh length and pulled tightly around the waist by a belt. At one side, above the belt, an air hose led to a bellows situated in the open air (Fig. 206).

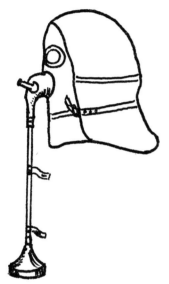

207. The "Roberts" hood and mouthpiece. Early 19th century.

Later a self-contained breathing apparatus was introduced. As described in the *Engineer's and Mechanic's Encyclopaedia* (1841 edition), it was a leather hood, the lower part padded with cotton, secured by a strap around the neck. A pipe about $2\frac{1}{2}$ feet long came from a nosepiece and ended in a trumpet-mouthed container which held a sponge soaked in water. The pipe was secured to the uniform buttons by straps with button-holes in them. This was known as the "Roberts" hood and mouthpiece (Fig. 207).

Various types of breathing-mask similar to those described above were produced during the nineteenth century; leather "smoke jackets" were in use in 1881. At the beginning of the 1900s the modern oxygen-cylinder self-breathing apparatus was introduced.

During the nineteenth century a variety of waterproof material was used for uniforms—tarpaulin jackets and later proofed cloth for tunics. Waterproof leggings are mentioned in the 1880s; and rubber boots were advertised in the 1890s.

Numerous experiments to fire- or flameproof cloth were carried out, but no evidence of their successful use for firemen's clothing has as yet come to light.

PLATE 45

PLATE 45

(*a*) Two Firemen on Merryweather
Tricycle Fire Apparatus. *c.* 1890.

*By courtesy of Merryweather & Sons, Ltd.
London.*

(*b*) Fashion Plate, from "Tailor and
Cutter", Fireman's Uniform, early
20th century.

By courtesy of the Tailor and Cutter.

PLATE 46

PLATE 46

Chelmsford Fire Brigade, early 20th century, showing rope
carried on belt; cloth, numbered badge on left breast.

By courtesy of the Essex Record Office.

CHAPTER XII

MISCELLANEOUS SERVANTS OF THE PUBLIC

DUSTMEN

Dustmen were the men employed in the removal of dust, rubbish or garbage. In 1670 an Act of Parliament ordered that

> "dirt, ashes or soil of their houses should be in readiness for the carmen, by setting out the same over night in tubs, boxes, baskets or other vessels, near and contiguous to their houses". The dustmen then gave notice of their being in the streets with their tumbrils or carts, by loudly knocking a wooden clapper.
>
> 1808. W. H. Pyne, *The Costume of Great Britain.*

By the early nineteenth century, however, the dustmen announced their presence by ringing a bell.

Although dustmen were invaluable public servants, they were not paid by the inhabitants of the town they served, but by the owner of the dustcart, who had "a profitable" concern thereby. In the dust-yards the refuse was often sorted by women and the ashes, cinders, metal, leather and bones sold for their respective uses. A running or flying dustman was a man who removed rubbish from these dust-holes without licence, for the sake of what he could pick out of it. These men obtained their cognomen from their habit of flying from one district to another (see Plate 48a).

> At Marlborough Street one day, early in November 1837, two of the once celebrated fraternity known as "flying dustmen", were charged with having emptied a dust-hole in Frith Street without leave or licence of the contractor.
>
> Quoted in *First Year of a Silken Reign,*
> by A. Tuer and C. Fagan. 1887.

The clothes of the early dustmen were probably undistinctive, but all through the nineteenth century they seem to have followed a definite pattern.

In the early nineteenth century a dustman is shown wearing a short white jacket, brown breeches, a blue apron, buff stockings, grey spats and a fan-tail hat. The spats, and more especially the fan-tail hats, were usual for the dust-men all through the nineteenth century (see Plate 47a). Mayhew in 1851, however, depicts a dustman in a top-hat and wearing a smock.

"Dusty Bob" the "Parish Dustman" in 1829 is a magnificent figure with his bell and his tools and his spreading fan-tail hat (Fig. 208). His coat is brown, waistcoat blue, breeches red, stockings striped blue and white, shirt criss-cross in blue, spats brown, apron white and the cap worn under his fan-tail hat is red.

By the 1830s some dustmen wore smocks, as being more protective than aprons. This is shown in Plate 47b, where the dustman rings his bell and shouts "Dust Ho!" as he leads his dustcart through the town, whilst working

208. "Dusty Bob". In spite of his gay colours (see text) he remarks:
"I don't vonder I looks black
    I has all the dirty work in the Parish to do." 1829.

for Thos. Salisbury, a London contractor and owner of the cart. The dust-collecting contractors were appointed by the Court of Sewers of the City and in outer London areas by the respective parish vestries.

By the 1850s smocks were coming into general use and many dustmen wore trousers instead of breeches. The men shovelling in the dust-yards now wore wide top-boots.

By the end of the nineteenth century trousers hitched up by a string under the knee were usual and some men wore their shirts hanging out over their trousers in place of a smock. The fan-tail hat, however, persisted till the twentieth century, though often replaced by a soft hat or cap (see Plate 48a).

CHIMNEY-SWEEPS

Golden lads and girls all must,
As chimney-sweepers, come to dust.

1610–12. Shakespeare, *Cymbeline*, IV. ii. 262.

In past centuries the all-important task of keeping chimneys swept devolved largely on small men, and particularly on small boys. Chimneys were large and could be climbed by boys, who had to scrape away the soot. As they emerged black all over one could almost say that their occupational costume was soot. The following quotation shows the number of chimneys for one residence that required sweeping in 1589.

Paid to Michael Muns of Fryerning for sweeping of 7 chimneys at West Horndon, viz. the nursery chimney, one of the kitchen ranges, the bakehouse, the dairy, the porter's chimney, the great room in the gatehouse and my chimney in the outer gatehouse after 2d. the piece, one with another 14d.

Petre Archives E.R.O. (D/DPA 10 A).

Pictures of sweeps in the seventeenth century show them in ragged dirty clothes of their period. One man in 1640 is depicted wearing a long loose coat hitched up at the waist and a slouch hat turned up (Fig. 209).

The man that sweeps the chimneys,
With the bush of thornes:
And one his neck a truss of poles,
tipped al with hornes.

209. (*a*) Small boy in tight, short sleeved waistcoat, torn breeches and
mules on feet. (*b*) Man in belted jacket or "jump", breeches, short
spats, square-toed shoes and a broad-brimmed hat. 1689.

> With care he is not cumbred,
>   he liueth not in dread:
> For though he wears them on his pole,
>   Some weare them on there head.

Ballad, 1612 in *The Pepysian Garland*.
Edited by G. H. E. Rollins.

In the eighteenth century the usual clothes worn by these climbing boys
were a belted jacket, breeches, stockings and shoes, and a soft cap. These
garments were ragged and, of course, black; but in spite of their miserable
condition the boys could play pranks with the soot.

A gentlewoman, unluckily stooping to buckle her shoe at a linen-drapers
shop, her Hoop Petticoat of a more than ordinary circumference, flew up,
and an arch little chimney sweeper, passing by at that instant, conveyed him-

self underneath the machine and, with a loud voice cry'd out "Sweep! Sweep!" The gentlewoman being affrighted, leap'd back, the boy struggling to get out threw madam in the dirt . . . and left the lady in no small confusion.

> 1718. Wm. Lee, *David Defoe, his life and recently discovered works* (from 1716–1729) (J. C. Hooton, London, 1869).

Men, too, could play their jokes.

> Chimney-sweepers have no right by Charter to rub against a person well-dressed, and then offer him satisfaction by single combat.
>
> Eighteenth-century pamphlet quoted in T. Burke's *The Streets of London*, 1940.

The boys were usually employed by hard taskmasters who had frequently kidnapped or stolen these children. Their plight was at last recognized by philanthropists, the chief one being Jonas Hanway (of umbrella fame!). He introduced an Act of Parliament in the 1780s

> that every chimney sweeper's apprentice shall wear a brass plate in front of his cap, with the name and abode of his master engraved on it, thus enabling any humane person to take immediate cognizance of their treatment.

After this date, all pictures of sweeps show them wearing this badge on their caps (Fig. 210). (See Mr and Master Soot in *Happy Families*, 1850.)

Their cruel occupation, however, was gradually coming to an end. Recommendations in 1832 were made by the House of Commons to prevent the further use of climbing boys in sweeping chimneys, but it was not until 1842 that Parliamentary enactment prohibited the employment of boys for the purpose of sweeping chimneys. This law, however, was violated on many occasions, even into the twentieth century. House-proud gentlewomen and those who lived in houses with large old-fashioned chimneys thought the boys left the room cleaner than the man with the long brush. Adult sweeps, however, were largely replacing the boys from the second half of the nineteenth century. By 1851 the costume was usually a jacket, waistcoat and trousers of dark-coloured corduroy; or instead of a jacket a waistcoat with sleeves. Over this, when at work, the sweeper often wore a loose sort of blouse or a short smock of strong calico or canvas. A shabby top-hat replaced the cap with the brass plate. At the end of the century this was replaced by a

210. Chimney sweeper in ragged soot-begrimed clothes, wearing cap with brass plate for identification. He holds a brush in one hand and a scraper in the other; has a sack over his shoulders for the soot. 1820.

shabby bowler hat or peaked cap and the sweep carried the extendible sweep's brush, invented as early as 1802 (Fig. 211).

> I reverence these young Africans of our own growth—these almost clergy imps, who sport their cloth without assumption; and from their pulpits (the tops of chimneys), in the nipping air of a December morning, preach a lesson of patience to mankind.
>
> 1823. C. Lamb, *Essays of Elia.*

LINKBOYS

A linkboy or linkman was one who carried a link or torch to light passengers in the streets of a city by night. Before street lighting by lamps was effectively established the linkboys could perform a valuable service to the public.

> So with a linkboy to Scott's.
>
> 4th February 1659–60. Pepys's *Diary.*

Seventeenth-century linkboys appear to have worn short doublets, breeches and round hats (Fig. 212).

211. Sweep wearing jacket and trousers and holding a sack and an extendible sweep's brush. 1884.

212. Linkboys patrolling the streets with lighted links, i.e. torches.
c. 1760–80.

Eighteenth-century linkboys were among the very poorest of lads and men and are always depicted in very ragged clothes. They would crowd round theatre doors to show you to your chair or carriage or run by your side to your home for a halfpenny. As a result of their poverty they were often thieves. Gay, in his *Trivia*, does not give them a good character:

> Though thou art tempted by the linkman's call,
> Yet trust him not along the lonely wall.
> In the midway he'll quench the flaming brand
> And share the booty with the pilfering band.
>
> 1716.

In an illustration of 1747 (Fig. 213) a linkboy is depicted in a shirt, with a cloth or possibly an apron rolled up round his waist, ragged breeches, stockings, shoes and a crumpled tricorne hat worn sideways. In his hand is the usual torch. Linkboys' clothes always appeared dark or black, especially when the torches were poor.

> Then shall't thou walk unharm'd the dangerous night
> Nor need th' officious link-boy's smoky light.
>
> 1716. John Gay's *Trivia*.

213. Linkboy in shirt and ragged breeches. 1747.

PLATE 47

PLATE 47

(a) Dustman in white jacket, brown breeches, blue apron,
buff stockings, grey spats and fan-tail hat. 1808.

W. H. Pyne, Costume of Great Britain. *1808.*

(b) London dustman wearing
smock, fan-tail hat and boots.
1834.

G. Scharf I. Drawing (detail). British
Museum.

PLATE 48

PLATE 48

(*a*) "Flying dustman" in dirt
white jacket, trousers an[d]
hat. 1878.

Photograph in Street Life i[n]
London, *edited by J. Thomson an[d]
Adolphe Smith, 1st January, 187*[8]

(*b*) Linkboy on left under the table.
Lighted candles in the window
(see page 286 under Lamp-
lighter). Also barber-surgeon
inside with sign over window
"Shaving, Bleeding and teeth
drawn with a touch." Freemason returning home; badge
and apron. 1738.

*Detail from Hogarth's "Night" from "Four
Times of Day". 1738.*

In Hogarth's "Night" from "Four Times of Day" there is a linkboy under the table in ragged clothes, his stockings slipping down, and he wears an unfashionable small hat (see Plate 48b).

Yet, in spite of street lamps, linkboys continued to work through the nineteenth century. In W. H. Pyne's "The World in Miniature" a linkman is shown guiding a fashionable lady and gentleman out of the theatre. The linkman wears a brown cut-away tailcoat, fawn breeches, high-lows (i.e. boots reaching only to the calf) and a short apron, fawn with black stripes. He shades his torch with his black beaver hat. His licence to trade is slung round his neck.

By the end of the nineteenth century linkboys were rarely needed, but even as late as 1890 this statement was made:

> Improved street lighting has made the employment of linkboys generally unnecessary, but they are still required in London during dense fogs frequently occurring there.
>
> 1890. *The Century Dictionary.*

In the absence of linkboys or street lamps in the country, an unexpected way of guiding ladies in the dark is described by Parson Kilvert in 1873:

> My Mother says that at Dursley in Gloucestershire, when ladies and gentlemen used to go out to dinner together on dark nights, the gentlemen pulled out the tails of their shirts and walked before to show the way and light the ladies. These were called "Dursley Lanterns".

LAMPLIGHTERS

(Street Lighting)

In the reign of Henry V (1413–22) the Mayor of London

> ordained lanthorns with lights to be hanged out on the winter evenings between Hallontide [Nov. 1st] and Candlemasse.

In 1512, upon rebuilding the steeple of Bow Church, arches or bows were erected for bearing lights nightly in the winter,

> whereby travellers to the cittie might have the better sight thereof; and not misse their ways.

In 1588, under the fear of the approaching Armada, every householder in

London was ordered to hang a light outside his door. Citizens in York, too, were compelled to place lighted candles in their windows. This method of street lighting was obviously unsatisfactory.

> There happened this week so thick a Mist and Fog that people lost their way in the streetes . . . robberys were committed betweene the very lights which were fixt between London and Kensington on both sides.
>
> 1699. *Diary of John Evelyn.*

Even as late as 1738 candles in windows were displayed (see Plate 48b), Hogarth's "Four Times of Day"—"Night".) However, by the Act of 1736, the streets of London were regularly lighted by lamps, from sunset to midnight only, at first. To begin with 1,000 lamps were lighted, soon to be increased to 5,000 in the "City and liberties alone", but including Westminster and the suburbs the number amounted to 15,000.

Lamplighters were employed in the forenoon in trimming and cleaning the lamps; in the evening in lighting them, and they had to take turns at midnight to replenish such as were burning out. From 1736 to the second decade of the nineteenth century oil lamps were used. Gas was then introduced, but oil lamps continued, especially after an improved oil lamp made its appearance in 1803. Finally towards the end of the nineteenth century electric lighting gave a better standard for the lighting of the whole of London.

The costume of lamplighters was not distinctive. A mid-eighteenth-century man is depicted wearing a dark waistcoat, but no coat, light breeches, stockings, shoes and an apron swathed round the waist, with a pair of scissors for trimming the wick. He wears a wide-awake hat (Fig. 214).

Another of about 1780 wears a striped jacket, open over a double-breasted waistcoat, light breeches, horizontally striped stockings and black shoes. His apron is also tucked up round his waist and holds the scissors. He wears a "round hat" of the period (see Plate 49a opp. p. 308).

Another in 1805 is somewhat similarly clad (though less fanciful). A ladder, as well as the scissors and oil-can, is common to them all (see Plate 49b). The lamplighter in the picture of 1780 (see Plate 49a) sings:

> I'm jolly Dick the Lamplighter
> They say the Sun's my dad,
> And truly I believe it, Sir,
> For I'm a pretty lad.

Father and I, the world delight
And make it look so gay:
The difference is, I lights by night
And Father lights by day.

C. Dibdin.

214. Lamplighter, carrying his ladder and oil
can. *c.* 1770.

DISTRICT MESSENGERS

These messenger boys, whose motto was "Swift and Sure", are best remembered by their saucy little pill-box caps, worn at a sharp tilt to the right with a leather strap under the chin.

Their days of activity started in 1890 and ended in 1959, well after the period covered by this book. Their uniform remained unaltered throughout and was supplied by the firm that employed them.[1] The uniform consisted of a blue serge military style tunic with Prussian collar, a belt and white-metal buttons. Crossing the tunic was a Cambridge blue shoulder belt. Trousers were of blue serge.

The pill-box cap encircled with two lines of white braid had a white-metal cap badge stamped with the boy's number and the name of his firm (Fig. 215).

[1] Ashton and Mitchell Ltd.

215. William Thomas Jagger. 1899. See text.

Lord Manners, who was associated with the start of the company that employed these boys, provided them with a peacock badge in white metal for good behaviour. This badge was attached to their caps and the boys became known as "peacock boys". Silver badges of merit worn on the breast were also supplied by the firm.

A boy named Jaggers was a star turn. He was sent to America in 1900. The account of his journey states that:

> He is now speeding across the American Continent to deliver a letter in Hanford, California, having left London just in time to catch a Cunard liner on April 1st, 1899.

District messenger boys were subsequently known as "Jaggers".

BARBERS

A barber is defined as "one whose occupation it is to shave or trim beards, a hairdresser". By the nineteenth century the term hairdresser was always used for women in this occupation and also for men serving ladies.

In 1461 Edward IV granted a Royal Charter to the Barbers' Company. Many barbers undertook minor surgery; indeed, the barber's pole, which became the sign of the barber's hairdressing shop, dates from the time of the barber-surgeons, when the patient who was being bled had to grip a pole in his right hand to keep him steady and assist the flow of blood. (See illustration under barber-surgeons in 1340.) This section deals simply with barbers who were solely hairdressers.

In spite of their hairy occupation barbers do not appear to have worn protective clothing, except as a rule an apron. In the sixteenth and early seventeenth centuries barbers wore long checkered aprons (without bibs) and became known as "checkered-apron men" (Fig. 216).

> A barber is always known by his cheque particoloured Apron; it needs not mentioning; neither can he be termed Barber (a Poller or Shaver as anciently they were called) till his apron be about him.
>
> 1688. Randle Holme, *Academy of Armory*.

216. Barber or "Checkered Apron Man". His apron covers his long-skirted doublet and he brandishes his scissors ready for work. Second half of 17th century.

217. Fashionable barber aping his master's attire but wearing a
striped apron instead of a chequered apron, over a white one. 1696.

An ultra-fashionable barber in Fig. 217 is shown dusting powder from his
master's back with the remains of an old wig. Of the dissolute master we read:

> This vain gay thing sets up for man,
> But see, not fate attends him:
> The powd'ring Barber first began,
> The Barber-Surgeon ends him.
>
> 1696.

In the eighteenth century the almost universal adoption of wigs and powder
necessitated larger aprons with bibs, though even then the fashionable barber
might work without one (Fig. 218).

Strange to say, the eighteenth century produced some female barbers.

We rise; our beards demand the barber's art
A female enters and performs the part
The weighty golden chain adorns her neck
And three gold rings her skilful hands bedeck
Smooth o'er our chins her easy fingers move
Soft as when Venus stroked the beard of Jove.

1767–93. John Gay, *Journey to Exeter*.

A curious illustration of a female barber, shaving a customer, is shown in a satirical print of 1776. She wears an old-fashioned hooded cape and a small mob-cap, but no apron. Protective clothing is confined to her customer, who has a towel draped round his neck (Fig. 219).

218. Barber in fashionable coat, waistcoat and breeches, wearing a bag wig, sometimes confusingly shortened to "bag", but no apron. 1776.

219. Female barber.

> "Is that a soldier? Sure the painter lies
> At most he's but a soldier in disguise.
> For who can think that he who guards our Land
> Should thus be nose led by a Female hand." 1776.

In a coloured lithograph by John Jones, after a drawing by H. Bunbury, two barbers are depicted, both wearing large white aprons reaching to their feet. The aprons have large pockets for their implements, but no bibs. One of the barbers wears a physical wig [physician's] similar to that worn by his customer. In the eighteenth century wigs were costly and valuable to barbers. A strange method of stealing wigs was undertaken by a man who paraded the streets with a small child perched up on his shoulders. The child was instructed to seize a gentleman's wig as he passed by.

During the early part of the nineteenth century wigs still played an important part in the barber's occupation.

> He usually wears powder, for it looks respectable, and is professional withal. The last of the almost forgotten and quite despised race of pigtails, once proudly cherished by all ranks—now proscribed, banished, or if at all seen, diminished in stateliness and bulk—"shorn of its fair proportions"—lingers

proudly with its former nurturer. The neat-combed, even-clipped hairs, encased in their tight swathe of black ribbon, topped by an airy bow, nestle in the well-clothed neck of the modern barber . . . As he sits, patiently renovating some dilapidated peruke, or perseveringly presides over the development of grace in some intractable bush of hair, or stands at his own threshold, in the cleanly pride of white apron and hose, lustrous shoes and exemplary jacket, with that studied yet seeming disarrangement of hair . . . He dwells in an area of peace—a magic circle whose area might be described by his obsolete sign-pole.

1825–7. Hone's *Everyday Book*, Vol. 1.

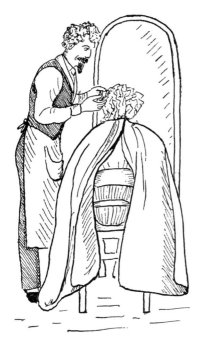

220. Barber working in shirt sleeves and wearing an apron with pocket. 1869.

By now the term hairdresser was coming into general use and barber was generally confined to those tending male customers. In the 1820s the suit was still a tailcoat or jacket with breeches, and over this barbers wore long aprons, sometimes bibbed and often with double pockets in front containing scissors and comb. In the 1860s, under his apron, the fashionable barber wore a frockcoat and trousers, though when at work the coat was usually discarded and the barber worked in shirt sleeves and waistcoat (Fig. 220). It was not until about the turn of the century that he adopted a white coat or over-all. But, for the sake of dignity, when attending a lady client in her home he wore the frockcoat unprotected, even by an apron. A good example of the protective apron is shown in Plate 62, where it denotes "barbery" as one of the functions of Dicky Gossip, the Jack of all Trades.

CHAPTER XIII

MEDICAL PROFESSION

BARBER-SURGEONS

Until the twelfth century the practice of surgery and medicine was almost entirely confined to the clergy. The barbers, however, frequently assisted the monks in their surgical operations and so gained enough knowledge to practise individually.

When, in 1163, the Pope forbade monks to practise surgery, many of the barbers who had assisted them carried on, on their own as barber-surgeons, alongside the secular medical profession. They performed minor operations such as bleeding a patient, tooth-drawing and cauterization. These barber-surgeons did not wear any distinctive clothing, but dressed in the style of their period (Fig. 221).

The respective functions of barber-surgeons and surgeons became clearly defined when the Barbers' Guild was united by Royal Charter under Henry VIII with the Company of Surgeons, it being enacted that the barbers should continue with such minor surgery as described, while the surgeons were forbidden to undertake "barbery and shaving".

A painting by Holbein in 1541 shows Henry VIII conferring a Charter upon the Surgeons Company.[1] On this ceremonial occasion formal attire had to be worn. It was not specifically the garb of their calling. The style was such as would be worn by any of the learned professions; the colours, however, were distinctive. The livery hoods worn suspended over the shoulder were of red and black. The wearers, known as livery men, as in other guilds, comprised only the more important members (Fig. 222).

Much of the clothing worn by the master barber-surgeons could be very costly and consequently was frequently mentioned in their wills; for example in 1561:

> I will that the masters of the livery of my companie be at my buriall . . . I give and bequeath to . . . my best gowne garded [bordered] with velvet,

[1] Probably represents the union of the Barbers and Surgeons by Act of Parliament in 1540.

221. Barber-Surgeon in a blue cote-hardie (the 14th century supertunic). It was belted and the elbow sleeves ended with a hanging flap.
Patient in long tunic and gripping what came to be the "barber's
pole". 1340. Luttrell Psalter.

furred and faced with sables, my cote of braunched velvet [figured velvet]
. . . also . . . my gowne of browne, blue lyned and faced with blacke budge
[lamb-skin with the wool dressed outwards] my cassocke [a long loose over-
coat] of black satten furred and garded with velvet . . . I bequeathe . . . my
best single [unlined] gowne faced with blacke satten . . . my doblet of
crimson satten.

Another will dated 1566 states:

I bequeath . . . my gowne furred with ffox which I commonlie ride in.

If an apprentice misbehaved himself he might be threatened with a whip-
ping by being shown a "bullbeggar".

. . . he had the bullbeggar showed him, whoe upon his humble submission
. . . was spared in hoape of his better service . . . hereafter.

1627.

The bullbeggar was a sack-like garment with apertures for the eyes and arms and was put on over the head and body of the person appointed to flog the apprentice, who was thus prevented from identifying his castigator.

Barber-surgeons rode on horseback to visit their patients and consequently spurs figure in their inventories. A barber-surgeon of Writtle in 1721 had "a pair of silver spurs worth one pound". (F. Steer, *Farm and Cottage Inventories of Mid Essex 1635–1749*.)

In Hogarth's picture "Four Times of Day"—"Night", 1738, a barber's shop is shown. Under the sign of the barber's pole hangs a drawing of a man having a tooth extraction and beneath this is the inscription: "Shaving, Bleeding, and Teeth drawn with a touch—Ecce Signum." (See Plate 48b.)

(a)   (b)   (c)

222. (a) Royal Physician, in furred gown and round bonnet. (b) Surgeon to the King; gown of brocaded damask doublet sleeves emerging and doublet skirt and hose visible in front. Black coif on head. (c) Ditto but bare-headed. Both (b) and (c) have livery hoods of red and black, hanging behind held in front by the long liripipes (i.e. extensions from the pointed cowl). 1541.

In 1745 the union of surgeons and barber-surgeons was ended by an Act of Parliament. In this connection the Minutes of a Meeting of the Governors of St Bartholomew's Hospital, April 2, 1747, are interesting.

> The surgeons have asked permission to have the arms of the company of Barber-surgeons—now dissolved—removed from the scarves and replaced by the arms of the company of surgeons, the alteration being already ordered by the governors of St Thomas's Hospital. It is decided to give this permission but not at the expense of the hospital.

In spite of this, the barber-surgeons continued to call themselves surgeons and in 1797 there was an outcry among surgeons protesting against this designation. Why should the "pitiful paltry, shaving, soaping, Beggarly Barbers go under the denomination of Barber Surgeons"?

The next illustration (Fig. 223) shows a surgeon attacking a barber-surgeon with the caption: "I'll teach you beggarly scoundrel to call yourself *Barber*." The barber-surgeon wears an apron with pocket for his instruments.

A barber-surgeon of 1804 in the next illustration is shown bleeding his patient. The barber wears a brown coat, red waistcoat, buff-coloured

223. "I'll teach you beggarly scoundrel to call yourself *Barber*." (*a*) Surgeon in mauve coat, pale breeches and wearing a wig known as a "long bob". (*b*) Barber-Surgeon in blue coat, yellow breeches and wearing a wig known as a "short bob". 1797.

breeches, white stockings and top-boots with rust-coloured tops, also spurs. His hair simulates a wig. These are the clothes of his period, though rather bright (Fig. 224). It is remarkable that he has no protective clothing of any kind.

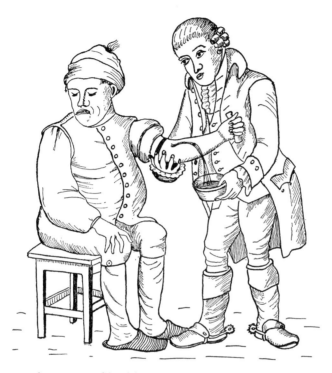

224. Barber-Surgeon blood-letting. See text. Compare with Fig. 221. 1804.

Despite all protests barber-surgeons continued with their surgery until 1821, when the last barber-surgeon of London died.

PHYSICIANS

As with the other learned professions, medicine and surgery in early medieval days partook of a religious character and was practised and taught by monks. They did, however, train secular doctors, and after 1163, when the Pope forbade monks to practise surgery, doctors no longer wore a monk's habit.

225. Physician and Laboratory Assistant. *c.* 1160. See text.

226. Anglo-Norman Physicians. 13th century. See text.

Later, training became concentrated in the universities and degrees were given in surgery and medicine.

As early as the sixteenth century the terms "physician" and "doctor" meant a general practitioner and were understood to be synonymous; but the word surgeon, though sometimes used vaguely for any medical man, had come to be generally confined to the surgical specialist.

Except in formal academic dress, there has not been any distinction in attire between physicians and surgeons, apart from the protective clothing of surgeons and anatomists, described later.

The medieval lay doctors wore the clothes fashionable at their time, but usually of a fine texture and often the headgear was distinctive. In the drawing of 1160 (Fig. 225) the doctor (giving instructions to his assistant, using a pestle and mortar) wears a long embroidered supertunic with an embroidered belt and a "Phrygian" bonnet. A dignified mantle is fastened by a brooch on his right shoulder.

227. Dr Gilberd with fur-edged gown over doublet and trunk hose. 1570.

The physicians of the thirteenth century (Fig. 226) are shown wearing gowns typical of the period, with hanging sleeves, and hoods thrown back over the shoulder. The doctor on horseback has a shorter gown, ending well above his tunic, or cote as it was now usually called. Both men wear a headgear that tended to be confined to the learned professions and known as a "pileus".

Bright colours were worn by Chaucer's

> perfect practising physician . . . In blood-red garments, slashed with bluish-grey and lined with taffeta, he rode his way.
>
>   *c.* 1387. Translation by Nevil Coghill—Penguin Series, 1951.

In the sixteenth century, over the doublet and trunk hose, or later breeches, fashionable in their day, doctors still wore the long medieval gown (Fig. 227). Length conferred dignity, and some form of headgear was usually worn indoors as well as out of doors (Fig. 228).

In a picture showing a physician and surgeon walking in the funeral procession of Sir Phillip Sidney in 1588 (Fig. 229), they both wear ankle-length overcoats, known as gabardines, and tall hats. Their ceremonial hoods hang

228. Physician out walking, in an overcoat known as a gabardine and a flat cap worn over a coif. On his feet he wears "mules". 1562.

229. Physician and surgeon dressed alike. 1588.

behind and are prevented from slipping down by the long streamers held by hand in front. These streamers are the vestigial remains of the fifteenth-century liripipe, a pendant tail extending from the pointed cowl of the medieval hood, which was now reduced to a symbol of learning. There is nothing here to distinguish the physician from the surgeon, but both doctors resemble the knights in wearing ruffs, whereas the esquires wear falling bands, i.e. turn-down collars.

The following is the will of a surgeon to Edward VI, showing the garments he prized most.

> I bequeth . . . my newe coloured gown guarded [bordered] with velvett and faced with foynes [the fur of the polecat] and my best rydinge cote guarded with velvett, and my dublett of redde taffeta . . . Also I bequeth my foxe

furred gowne and a dublett with blewe taffeta sleves and my blacke
mornynge cote.

1549–50.

Portraits of doctors in the sixteenth and seventeenth centuries still show
them in the fashion of the day, with the addition of the all-important gown
and always some form of headgear (Fig. 230).

230, Physician and Mathematician wearing
fur-edged gown and flat pleated "bonnet"
worn with the fashionable tilt over a coif.
1559.

In about 1650, John Aubrey made the following remarks about the famous
physician William Harvey (b. 1578, d. 1657):

> He was very Cholerique and in his young days wore a dagger (as the fashion
> then was) but this Dr would be apt to draw out his dagger upon every
> slight occasion . . . His practise was not very great towards his later end.—
> He rode on horseback with a Footcloath [ornamental saddlecloth] to visitt
> his Patients, his man following on foote.

Aubrey's *Brief Lives*. Ed. by Oliver Lawson Dick.

Another example of a doctor in fashionable clothes occurs in "Comenius'
Visible World", 1664. At the bedside of his patient, the doctor is seen, in
petticoat breeches, the French fashion popularized by Charles II. These were
a very wide divided skirt. He also wears a cloak and a broad-brimmed hat.

Throughout the eighteenth century wigs were universally worn by men, over a shaved head. In the second half of this century members of the learned professions particularly favoured a style of wig which came to be known as the "physical wig" (physician's wig). (Fig. 231). It was white, very bushy and spread round the nape of the neck. Occasionally it had a very short queue.

231. Physician (Tobias Smollett, M.D.) wearing a "physical wig". *c.* 1761.

Goldsmith refers to the physical wig in *The Citizen of the World.*

> To appear wise, nothing more is requisite here, than for a man to borrow hair from the heads of all his neighbours, and clap it, like a bush on his own; the distributors of law and physic stick on such quantities that it is almost impossible, even in idea, to distinguish between the head and hair.
>
>   1762.

The doctor's wig with a queue is also mentioned by Goldsmith in *The Adventures of Ferdinand Count Fathom.*

> He [a would-be surgeon] appeared in the uniform of Aesculapius, namely, a plain suit full trimmed, with a voluminous tie-periwig; believing that in this place [Tunbridge] he might glide as it were imperceptibly into the functions of his new employment.
>
>   1753.

Until the late eighteenth century a doctor would call on his patient wearing a sword, since this was still the mark of a gentleman (See Plate 50a). When canes came into fashion he might even carry both.

Fielding describes "Gentlemen in tie-wigs, carrying amber-headed canes", 1743 (*Journey from this World to the Next*).

In the early years of the eighteenth century the massive full-bottomed wig was also worn:

> A suit of black (velvet if possible) a full-bottomed wig, a Muff and a gold or silver-headed cane formed the outward adornment of the physician.
>
> *c.* 1700. Ned Ward, *The London Spy.*

> A young physician . . . with a gilt-headed cane, a black suit of clothes, a full-bottomed flowing peruke, and all other externals of his profession.
>
> 1751. Francis Coventry, *Pompey the Little.*

In the nineteenth century smart clothes were the rule for doctors, and many continued to wear wigs through the first half of this century, though wigs in general were going out of fashion.

232. Dr Spraggs riding in tailcoat and breeches, away goes his hat and wig. *c.* 1834.

In 1834 Doctor Spraggs, when out riding, was wearing one (Fig. 232).

> But all in vain he tugged the rein
> The steed would not be stayed;
> The "Doctor's stuff" was shaken and
> A tune the vials played.

For in his pockets he had stowed
  Some physic for the sick;
Anon, "crack" went the bottles all,
  And formed a "mixture" quick.

His hat and wig flew off, but still
  The reins he hugged and haul'd;
And tho' no cry the huntsmen heard
  They saw the Doctor bald!

Seymour's *Humorous Sketches.*

An illustration in Ackermann's *Microcosm of London* (1808) shows a meeting of the College of Physicians. These all wear white tie-wigs, brown or black cut-away tailcoats, ruffled shirts (frilled down the front) and dark or plum-coloured breeches. This style of dress and wig continued to be worn by doctors throughout the first half of the nineteenth century.

> . . . mounted his dun pony . . . He the doctor . . . was dressed in orthodox black, with powder and a pig-tail [the tie-wig] drab shorts [breeches] and top boots.
>
> 1845. R. S. Surtees, *Handley Cross.*

Black appears to have been correct at this time for a doctor. Surtees describes another thus:

> his black suit fitted without a wrinkle and his thin dress boots shone with patent polish; turned back cambric wristbands displayed the snowy whiteness of his hand, and set off a massive antique ring or two. He had four small frills to his shirt and an auburn hair chain crossed his broad roll-collared waistcoat and passed a most diminutive Geneva watch into its pocket.
>
> 1845. R. S. Surtees, *Handley Cross.*

Country doctors, however, were not so smart in their appearance, as is shown in the following accounts of a country doctor's attire:

> A country-made snuff-coloured coat, black waistcoat, short greenish drab trousers with highlows.
>
> 1854. R. S. Surtees, *Handley Cross.*

Highlows were calf-length boots worn usually by country folk. Then again, in *Dr Bradley Remembers*, the doctor's outfit is thus described in 1887:

> The shapeless trousers were of striped cashmere, of a grey too light to be serviceable; the coat, a frock coat with ample skirtings and corded silk revers;

the waistcoat from the watch pocket of which a fob with signet dangled, was of striped brocade, cut high; the white linen collar glazed with starch— so tall at the back . . . and open at the front . . . a necktie of white piquet, its knot held in place by a cameo brooch . . . they were the uniform a professional man had been expected to wear in the year 1887 when Dr Bradley had qualified . . .

The sort of clothes in which Lister had operated were suitable for his disciple; though in the late nineties when he first took to tricycling on his round, Dr Bradley had exchanged the silk hat in which he started (and which was now shrouded in crepe and only worn at funerals) for a felt of the same height, with a rounded edge at the crown, and had gathered in the slack of the trouser-bottoms with steel-spring ankle-clips which in hours of abstraction he often forgot to remove.

Francis Brett Young, *Dr Bradley Remembers.*

In the early nineteenth century trousers began to replace breeches and in the second half the frockcoat gradually took the place of the tailcoat (Fig. 233).

233. Doctor's frock coat, trousers and top hat.

Frock coat and Vest 37/6 to measure.
In black Vicuna, Serges and Worsteds.
Special line Trousers 10/- to measure.
In latest patterns.   1897.

PLATE 49

PLATE 49

(*a*) Lamplighter with ladder and oil can. 1780's. See text, p. 286.

Carington Bowles, coloured print.

(*b*) Lamplighter with small boy assistant. 1805. See text, p. 286.

W. H. Pyne, Costume of Great Britain. *1808.*

PLATE 50

PLATE 50

(*a*) "The Benevolent Physician" in fashionable coat, waistcoat and breeches and carrying a sword. *c.* 1792.

Anonymous mezzotint. Impression in the Wellcome Historical Medical Museum.

(*b*) Group at St. Bartholomew's Hospital 1901. Back row, students. Front row, Sister Rahere and two physicians.

Photograph from Author's collection.

Women, who began to practise medicine in the second half of the same century, had no distinctive dress.

By the twentieth century a general practitioner on his rounds generally wore formal attire, a black "morning coat" and a top-hat. Students wore jackets. When cars took the place of carriages, convenience tended to replace convention, and jackets instead of "tails" were adopted, together with more casual wear, by the medical profession (see Plate 50b).

Lastly, in a few words, the resident staff of a hospital should be mentioned. In the early years of the twentieth century, both men and women house-surgeons and house-physicians, always wore, when on duty, a white washable coat generally knee-length. In the Royal Free Hospital the students wore similar coats, but they were buff colour, not white (see Plate 51a).

SURGEONS AND HYGIENE

It would seem obvious to us that the work of a surgeon or anatomy teacher would demand some form of protective clothing. This, however, does not always seem to have been the accepted view.

234. Surgeon operating on patient's eye. Both in embroidered tunics, but the surgeon wears a mantle. *c.* 1160.

In medieval days they appear to have relied on shortening or discarding garments rather than adding some form of protection. In a twelfth-century illustration the surgeon operating on the patient's eye wears a short tunic and mantle (Fig. 234). In another of the same date the surgeon who is operating on the patient's nose wears his tunic tucked up and relies on the bowl held

235. Brain operation. Surgeon in fashionable low-waisted gipon.
c. 1330–40.

by the patient to catch any nose-bleeding. In the brain operation of 1330–40 the surgeon wears his ceremonial fur-lined mantle over a low-waisted gipon (the forerunner of the doublet) and a hat with a close turned-up brim of fur (Fig. 235). The dentist of the same date is plainly clad in the style of his day, like his patient, in a gipon. Slung from his shoulder is a rope of enormous teeth advertising his profession (Fig. 236)!

Perhaps one of the earliest intimations that protective clothing existed is to be found in the rules laid down for those preparing for an anatomy lecture and demonstration in 1555. In that year the rules to be obeyed by such students are described as follows:

That they whiche be appointed for anathomye for yere next following and must sarve the Docter and be about the bodye he shall se and provyde that there be every yere, a matte about the harthe in the hall that Mr Docter may not take colde upon his feate, nor other gentlemen that do come and marke the anathomye to learne knowledge. And further that there be ii fyne rodds appointed for the Docter to touche the body where it shall please him and a waxe candell to loke into the bodye and that there be alwayes for the Docter two aprons to be from the sholder downewarde and two peyr of sleaves for his hole arme with tapes for chaunge for the sayed Docter and not to occupye one aporne and one payer of sleves every daye which is unseamly. And the Masters of the Anathomye that be about the bodye to have lyke aprons and sleves every daye both white and clean.

S. Young, *The Annals of the Barber-Surgeons*, pp. 308–9.

236. Dental extraction. *c.* 1330–40. See text.

Contrast this with the two seventeenth-century surgeons dissecting a victim of the plague in 1666 (Fig. 237). Surprisingly enough, they have no protective clothing at all, not even aprons. They are dressed in the fashion of the day, wearing doublets closely buttoned down the front and deep square falling bands, i.e. turn-down collars (Frontispiece to *The Manner of Dissecting the Pestilentiall Body*, by A. Thomson, 1666).

237. Surgeons doing a post mortem in ordinary clothes. 1666.

Smollett (himself a physician), however, in *Humphry Clinker* in 1771, refers to the York surgeon about to perform an operation thus:

> The operator, laying aside his coat and periwig, equipped himself with a nightcap [to cover his bald head], apron and sleeves.

This makes all the more remarkable the fact that Victorian surgeons operated in frockcoats.

The illustration shows such an operation in 1882, with the surgeons wearing no form of protective clothing, either for themselves or for the patient (see Plate 51b). The next picture shows a slight advance in that the surgeon wears an apron (see Plate 52a).

Rubber gloves were introduced for surgery in 1889–90. The gloves were worn, however, to protect the surgeon's hands from the carbolic acid in which the instruments were immersed, rather than to eliminate his hands as a source of infection.

238. (*a*) Doctor's short jacket in white washing drill with removable buttons. (*b*) Surgeon's operating coat in strong washing Holland with open back to allow of free ventilation. 1905.

White coats came in soon after. Those for men and women were practically identical, except that men's buttoned left over right, according to tradition, and women's right over left (see Plate 51a).

It was not until the turn of the century that the whole theatre outfit, white coats, caps, gloves, masks, etc., came to be regarded as essential and the influence of science won the day (Fig. 238 and 239).

239. Doctor's operating coat. Loose Prussian collar, fly front fastening, short sleeves with drawing strings. Inside "Raglan" patch pockets. 1909.

QUACKS

Quack doctors practised throughout the centuries, and were recognized in London as early as 1382 and called by Stow (1598) "Counterfeit-Physicians".

In a small book of 1651, entitled *Popular Errours or the Errours of the People in matters of Physic*, a curious quack female doctor is shown trying to oust the physician (in gown and ruff) standing by the patient's bedside.

The woman, wearing a tall hat, a ruff, a plain dress and apron, offers her remedies, but is thwarted by an angel.

> But loe an angell gently puts her backe
> Lest such erroneous course the sicke doe wracke.

In 1511 an act was passed for the regulation of medical and surgical practice with powers to suppress quack practitioners. Further powers to suppress were granted when the College of Physicians was founed in 1518, but quack doctors continued their work nevertheless!

The usual costume of a quack according to a writer in 1678 consisted of:

> a decent black suit . . . a plush jacket; not a pin the worse, though threadbare as a tayler's cloak, it shows the more reverend antiquity.

Sir William Read, who became oculist to her most gracious Majesty Queen Anne, is shown in a woodcut from one of his handbills operating on a patient in *c.* 1696. He was an unqualified surgeon, originally a tailor, who managed to rise and become the Queen's sworn oculist (Fig. 240).

240. Quack Surgeon in fashionable clothes. *c.* 1696. See text.

He is depicted wearing a full-bottomed wig and fashionable clothes. In the late eighteenth century the "Rapacious Quack" is also seen in fashionable clothes, wearing a tricorne hat and a "physical" wig (i.e. physician's wig). He carries a cane, now the mode (see Plate 53a).

Hogarth's quack doctor in 1745 wears a fashionable "suit of dittos", i.e. coat, waistcoat and breeches, all brown. His stockings are "roll-ups", being pulled up over his breeches at the knee, then the mode. He has a brown Campaigne wig and a "Steinkirk cravat". This was a long white neck-tie loosely knotted under the chin and then the ends passed through a button-hole of the coat.

Quack doctors abounded in the eighteenth century. Goldsmith describes one (Dr Richard Rock) in one of his "Chinese Letters";

This great man is short of stature, is fat and waddles as he walks. He always wears a white three-tailed wig, nicely combed and frizzled upon each cheek. Sometimes he carries a cane, but a hat never.

1760–61.

Quack doctors continued to flourish in the nineteenth century. See Fig. 241.

The modern Quack is a great cultivator of manners and appearance. Formerly, it was the custom of these gentry to dress like scarecrows, in order that they might be taken for men of learning; but now their apparel, with the exception of some slight touch of eccentricity—such, for instance, as a fur collar, which gives them what some folk are pleased to call a distingué appearance, only differs from that of the rest of the world in being rather more fine.

1841. *Heads of the People.*

241. The Quack Doctor wearing a coat with a fur collar. 1841.

The "Street" or "Travelling Doctor" was of a humbler type. He was known, in slang parlance, as a "Crocus". An intelligent member of the fraternity informed a questioner that as members of the medical profession they are bound to use what may be called "crocus" Latin. "Our profession is known, sir, as 'crocussing', and our dodges and decoctions as 'fakes'" (1877) (See Plate 53b).

Their attire was that of the ordinary man in the street.

PLATE 51

PLATE 51

(a) Group at Royal Free Hospital 1913.
House surgeons and physicians in white coats.
Students in buff coats. (Author, P.C., on the right.)
Sister in cap and apron.

Photograph from Author's collection.

(b) Operation performed with "complete antiseptic precau-
tions". The use of the Lister carbolic spray. 1882.

Engraving in W. Watson Cheyne's Antiseptic Surgery, *1882.*
By courtesy of the Wellcome Trustees.

PLATE 52

PLATE 52

Operation at the Royal Free Hospital *c.* 1892–6. This shows the nurses' uniforms as well as the ordinary wear of the surgeons.

APOTHECARIES

The earliest mention of apothecaries occurs in 1345, when Coursus de Grangeland received a pension of 6*d.* a day for life, for attending King Edward III "while lying sick in Scotland".

Apothecaries were at first grocers who supplied medicaments. In 1617 they separated from the Grocers' Company, becoming the Apothecaries Company only.

Because of the high fees charged by physicians, many people chose to be treated by apothecaries through the second half of the seventeenth century and all through the eighteenth century. Apothecaries were thus acting as general practitioners, but they did not take fees for treatment. From 1815, however, they were allowed to charge fees as well.

In the seventeenth century they either wore the clothes fashionable at the

242. Apothecary of 1822–3. See text.

time, sometimes protected with a blue apron, or sometimes a physician's gown, simulating a doctor of medicine. This also applies to the eighteenth century. In the accompanying illustration (see Plate 54a) of "The Apothecary" of *c.* 1750, he wears coat, waistcoat, breeches, stockings and shoes all typical of his date. On his head he wears a Campaigne wig, now going out of fashion. This wig had short side-locks with knotted ends and a very short queue behind. He also wears a protective apron.

In the next picture of *c.* 1822–3 (Fig. 242) the apothecary's clothes are in the fashion of the day, but he has added a long apron with a bib and elbow-length protective sleeves.

In a political satire of 1830 an apothecary is shown wearing a long green apron to his feet with the bib tied at the back of his neck. He also wears protective sleeves, green to match the apron. Aprons and protective sleeves appear to have been essential garments to apothecaries.

NURSES

Hospital Nurses and the History of Uniform

Nursing as a career for women began on a religious basis, when medieval piety in England founded hospitals for the sick, such as St Peters in York, built in 937, and St Bartholomew's in London, founded in 1123 by Rahere, who became an Augustinian Canon.

The more responsible nursing was done by nuns, hence the term "sister", and the habit worn was simply that of the religious order to which the nurse belonged. At St Bartholomew's Hospital in London, for example, the nurses wore the habit of the Augustinian Order, which consisted of a tunic and supertunic of grey cloth. It was expressly stated, however, that the tunic for the nursing sisters must not reach lower than the ankles. The head was always covered by the nun's veil and a mantle could also be worn (Fig. 243).

It is beyond the scope of this book to give descriptions of the uniforms worn in every hospital; therefore those developed by St Bartholomew's Hospital have been selected, since of the now famous English hospitals the most ancient is St Bartholomew's.

From the four sisters of the old foundation in direct descent comes the nursing staff of Barts in the present day. Strange to say, the number remained unchanged from 1123 for four hundred years, though subordinate helpers must have been employed.

The big break with tradition came with the dissolution of the monasteries. The hospital then became secularized and during the years 1544 to 1547 the reorganization took place. In 1546, by King Henry VIII's Deed of Covenant, the hospital and all its possessions were granted to the Mayor, Commonalty and Citizens of London.

243. Augustinian Nursing Sister. 1256. See text.

In 1544 five sisters were appointed and by 1551 there were twelve; one of whom was the matron. Since the sister was no longer a nun in conventual dress, her appointment carried with it a specified livery or habit, and at this time each received a yearly grant of 6 yards of cloth at 22s. 6d., of russet frieze for this purpose. In 1555, however, the colour was changed to watchet (i.e. light blue), and blue has remained the distinctive colour of the sister's uniform ever since. The matron was always distinguished from the rest by some slight difference in attire.

The headdress of the nursing staff indoors followed the fashion of the day and indeed continued to do so right into the nineteenth century. When ladies gave up wearing caps indoors in the 1880s nurses continued to do so.

It is interesting that the nurse's cap worn to this day is thus a relic of women's fashions of the past and is retained in spite of its apparent lack of function.

In 1686 the Board of Governors ordered, presumably for outdoor wear, that

> the sisters shall weare nightrales and hoods of white linen instead of livery gowns [long overgarments] anciently worn by them and the same to be this yeare provided by this House.

A woman's night rail—worn by day—was a white cape reaching to the waist or sometimes lower. This, then, may have been the origin of the cape which many nurses wear today instead of a coat. The night rails were finally abolished in 1843, according to the following statement in the Journal of the Board of Governors:

> Nightrail or white cloak worn at church or on View Day is discontinued 9 May 1843.

From earliest times the more responsible sisters were helped by subordinate nurses not entitled to a sister's uniform. These would wear ordinary clothes, with or without an apron, or else a different uniform. A print dated 1808 shows that at the Middlesex Hospital nurses wore ordinary working-class dress with mob-cap and apron. At Barts, on the other hand, in 1821 the nurses were ordered to wear a brown uniform, while the sisters continued in blue, as already stated.

In 1895 a contemporary writer made the following remarks about the nursing staff at Barts:

> The uniform is very serviceable and becoming though it is somewhat difficult in hot weather to keep the strings tied under the chin from looking limp and soiled.
>
> The sister . . . wears a flat cap consisting of two peaked frills, a dark blue gown, and an apron without straps; this too often necessitates the use of pins to the bib which never look quite tidy.
>
> The certificated staff-nurse wears an almost similar cap and apron with straps.

Dress of the Hierarchy

Differences in uniform have always tended to be used to distinguish the various grades in the nursing hierarchy. This is well exemplified at Barts in the twentieth century (Fig. 244).

PLATE 53

PLATE 53

(a) "The Rapacious Quack", c. 1792.
See p. 315.

*Anonymous mezzotint, c. 1792. By courtesy of
the Wellcome Trustees.*

(b) Street Doctor or "Crocus" in frock
coat and bowler hat. 1877.

*Photograph in Street Life in London, edited by
J. Thomson F.R.G.S. and Adolphe Smith,
2nd April, 1877.*

PLATE 54

PLATE 54

(a) "The Apothecary", c. 1750.

Engraving, after W. Shakespear, published by Ewart, c. 1750. By courtesy of the Wellcome Trustees.

(b) A Nightingale Nurse in cap and apron and long full skirt of the 1860's style.

Photograph of Mary Barker. c. 1860. By permission of the Governors of St. Thomas' Hospital.

All nurses enter this hospital as student nurses. They wear a light grey dress. Promotion is gained by passing examinations and a striped dress is then worn with a white belt. In the fourth year, as staff nurses, the white belt is changed for a blue belt and finally as sisters they wear the traditional blue uniforms. All wear cuffs, caps and aprons, and the dresses are of washable material. They have also a bonnet and cloak for an outdoor uniform.

The matron alone is dressed in black and wears a distinctive cap, but no apron.

244. Bart's Nurse. 1902. See text.

Uniforms in Other Hospitals

Generally speaking, what constituted a nurse's uniform was not style, which conformed more or less to the fashion of the day, but the colour of the dress (Fig. 245).

Here are a few examples from other hospitals.

At the Middlesex Hospital in the 1870s the "Lady Probationers" wore a violet-coloured dress with a small train, 3 inches long, which swept the floor behind them (as was then the fashion). To prevent these trains from becoming soiled, the nurses used to turn them up off the floor; but when the lady superintendent discovered this practice she soon put a stop to it. "I devised this little train," she said, "so that, when you lean over the bed to attend to your patient, your ankles will be covered and the students will not be able to see them."

245. Middlesex Hospital Nurse. 1888. See text.

At the same hospital in 1895 a contemporary wrote:

> The sisters wear a deep violet serge dress, a pretty frilled cap with strings loosely crossing the breast and a large white apron. The nurses wear blue cambric dresses, or grey gingham. The ordinary probationers wear black, grey or quiet cotton gowns.

At Guy's Hospital, founded in 1722, the only indication of a uniform in 1856 was the wearing of a round tin medal, hung round the neck, and inscribed with the name of the ward and the status of the nurse.

Outdoor as well as indoor clothes were provided.

The *Girl's Own Annual* of 1890, in an article about a competition on "The

Costumes of Hospital Nurses", has some startling descriptions of the dresses worn by nurses in provincial hospitals.

> We . . . quite agreed . . . that the two representatives of the nurses at the Putney Incurables Hospital, in their brown and black serges, pretty caps and aprons were perfect.
>
> The Norfolk and Norwich Hospital costumes are well worthy of the prize they gained—the monthly nurse in fawn-coloured cotton; the medical nurse in black serge; the fever nurse in blue zephyr with becoming and serviceable holland aprons and spotted cap.
>
> The University College Hospital sent a ward with its three nurses, the sister in a nun-like dress of black serge . . . the nurse in a blue serge and cap tied under the chin; the probationer in grey gingham.
>
> The Royal Albert Hospital, Devonport . . . the black cashmere and muslin cap with long strings and becoming apron were very attractive.
>
> The dress of the sisters of the Children's Hospital in Great Ormond Street is a departure from the general colours, being a dark red serge with characteristic cap and apron.
>
> The Kings College dress is very becoming and its colour Raphael green.

It will be noticed that in many of these uniforms unwashable dark serge was a favourite. It is only when we reach the twentieth century that hygiene was recognized as being more important than other considerations and washable dresses became the rule.

Uniforms "as supplied to the London Hospitals" are shown in Fig. 246.

(*a*) Special apron of stout linen–finish cloth. Large size and wide shoulder straps, 2*s*. 6*d*.

(*b*) For summer wear, in fine all-wool cravenetted cashmere cloth perfectly waterproof, 23*s*. 6*d*. In rainproof alpaca (will not cockle) 23*s*. 6*d*.

Florence Nightingale Nurses

Mention must now be made of Florence Nightingale, the true founder of modern nursing, who in 1854 offered her services to go to Scutari during the Crimean War. Under great difficulties she secured thirty-eight suitable nurses for the expedition. The uniform selected and supplied was not becoming, consisting of:

A grey tweed dress called a wrapper.
A grey worsted jacket.

246. Nurses' Uniforms, 1905. See text.

247. Private Nurse, 1732. See text.

A plain white cap.

A short woollen cloak, and

A holland scarf on which "Scutari Hospital" was embroidered.

In 1860 the Nightingale Training School for Nurses at St Thomas's Hospital was started, thus establishing an independent career for ladies. The first matron when on duty always wore kid gloves.

The *St James Magazine* of April 1861 described the uniform of the Nightingale School for Nurses thus:

> The nurses wore a brown dress and their snowy caps and aprons looked like bits of extra light as they moved cheerfully and noiselessly from bed to bed.

They had also to provide themselves with four holland aprons. A sharp criticism of their uniform was made in 1884 by Honnor Morten in *How to Become a Nurse and How to Succeed*. She wrote:

> The very earliest training school is cursed by too great a conservatism, and

248. Private Nurse in short waisted long green dress of the period, apron and mob cap. 1811.

thus its probationers have to work in a cold and unbecoming uniform consisting of striped cotton dresses, net caps, and brown holland aprons. On the score of cleanliness alone, white linen aprons and cotton gowns should be insisted on in all nursing uniforms.

Miss Nightingale had written in 1858, however:

> Better I think avoid washing stuffs; they require endless change to look decent (see Plate 54b).

Private Nurses (as opposed to hospital nurses)

Private nurses do not appear to have worn any special dress until the end of the nineteenth century.

In an early-fifteenth-century picture denoting the birth of the Virgin the nurse wears a blue surcote over a yellow kirtle (dress) and a white headkerchief, the usual costume of her time ("Speculum Humanae Salvationis", B.M. MS. Harl. 2838, f. 6V).

249. "Experienced Nurse" wearing shawl and jacket bodice. 1871.

In Lydgate's *Life of St Edmund* (1433), midwife and maid alike wear dresses which conform with the fashion of the day, consisting of long white kirtles, with or without girdles, and tall horned headdresses. No aprons are shown, although this protective accessory was a common adjunct with humble folk.

In the eighteenth century the nurse is generally shown wearing a waisted thigh-length jacket and skirt, then called a petticoat, and a mob-cap (Fig. 247). This was the usual costume of working women. In the nineteenth century, apart from caps ordinary plain clothes were worn (Fig. 248 and 249).

A last word must be said about the midwives, who were so satirized in the first half of the nineteenth century and made immortal by Dickens's Sairey Gamp in *Martin Chuzzlewit*. She wore no uniform, but merely ordinary clothes of her day; but from among her varied belongings her stumpy umbrella has added a new word to our language (Fig. 250).

250. Sairey Gamp. *c.* 1850. See text.

CHAPTER XIV

EVOLUTION OF PROTECTIVE CLOTHING

In this and the next chapter it is proposed to deal with some general topics connected with working dress, and to exemplify them particularly by reference to occupations that did not lend themselves to the historical treatment of the earlier chapters.

Sartorial devices for extra protection will be considered first. The hat or glove protects the body directly, but most protective wear consists in specially durable and/or specially washable garments shielding the rest of the clothing, rather than the body itself, at tactical points—and these points vary with the job in hand. A wide variety of protective garments of both kinds has gradually evolved.

APRONS

The apron is the most widespread of all such garments, since the commonest hazards are due to what the hands are doing in front of the body. The apron's origin would appear to go back to Adam and Eve. For centuries it was worn by working men as well as women, so much so that the plebeian Parliamentary party during the Civil War were contemptuously known as "aproneers".

Leather Aprons

In earlier times, for men, it is not the washable but the leather apron that is most in evidence. This relic of pre-textile days has persisted down to today.[1] It was consistently worn, as we have seen, by metalsmiths and coopers to protect them from sparks and friction. Made often of a whole skin and therefore four- or five-pointed, one corner of it would generally be used to form the bib. Of the many ways of supporting bibs the one shown in Plate 58a is rare. Perhaps because he represents Tubal Cain himself, this smith pins it up

---

[1] Only in recent years has anything more durable been found. Coopers now wear a fabric containing man-made fibres which they say wears better; and van-men find that used pieces of "printer's cloth" are an economical material.

with a handsome brooch. Attachment by button-hole to a coat or waistcoat button is the usual method. If the bib was square it had a loop at the back of the neck—a typical example in the Manx Museum is the "brat" worn by one of the last of the local lead-spoon makers, who died in 1897.

The leather apron is also highly characteristic of shoemakers and cobblers (Fig. 251), who were always protected from the rubbing and the black cobbler's wax by a bibbed "black flag".

251. Cobbler in leather apron, the "black flag". 1655.

Woodworkers used them, too (see pp. 82–85 and also Plate 62). R. Holme[1] (1688) gives an apron not only to the smith, tinker and joiner, but also to the tanner. Tanners and slaughtermen both used leather aprons as shields against splashing and knife injuries. Indeed, Pyne in 1805 depicts them with a second apron made of sheepskin (wool outwards) worn underneath an ordinary one of rawhide (Fig. 252). Tanning fluids stain indelibly. Francis Thynn describes a tanner, even when on a journey, as having hands that "were stained both the skyn and naile; Full many peece of barke they hadden rent". (About 1568, *Debate between Pride and Lowliness*.)

Leather aprons $\frac{1}{4}$ in. thick are still sold to butchers, and indeed measures

[1] *Academy of Armory*.

252. Feltmonger at tannery. Hide apron over sheepskin apron; leg
shields. 1805.

are being sought to make them obligatory for the safety of employees in
certain dismembering operations.

Even a "primitive" feature, as the biologist might call the leather apron,
can be subject to what he terms "specialization". Mayhew[1] describes the
women who spent their lives sieving rubbish for salvage, as wearing in 1851

> a strong leather apron from their necks to the extremity of their petticoats,
> while over this was another leather apron, shorter, padded thickly, . . . they
> pushed the sieve from them and drew it back again . . . against the outer
> apron with such force that it produced a hollow sound. . . .

[1] H. Mayhew, *The London Poor*.

Cloth Aprons

Cloth aprons were worn by men and women alike for a steadily increasing variety of occupations right up to the end of the nineteenth century. These were made at first of linen, for example dowlas (sixteenth century down to the present day) or Holland (mostly after 1600) and were neither bleached nor dyed.

More durable types were originally of coarse woollens such as the cloth, often dyed red, called stamin in the sixteenth century and later stammel. "My best stamyn apron" is mentioned in one of the Rattlesden Wills in 1539. Other woollens used were the serges, from medieval to recent times: "This material works clean as the dirt rubs off", writes a gardener in 1960.[1] For similar reasons it was used by fish-sellers, of whom Mayhew writes:

> These [costers] who deal wholly in fish wear a blue serge apron, whereas "cloth coats" are regarded by them as an extravagance of the highest order, for the slime, scales and fish stick to the sleeves and shoulders.[2]

Dickens writes:

> The fishmonger pulls off his hat and his men cleanse their fingers on their woollen aprons.[3]

Baize, introduced by Walloons in 1561, was softer although strong. Dyed green it became in the nineteenth century the universal choice for the aprons of furniture-removers.

Canvas, a very stout linen cloth, generally imported, came to be an alternative to wool for men's work, and a mixture known as linsey-woolsey was a favourite for women.

A sort of inverted camouflage was adopted by masons and millers, who would choose a white cloth because of dust and flour. The most popular dye in the food trades has long been indigo, giving a permanent "butcher blue" after washing.

Further "adaptive radiations" evolved in the nineteenth century, for example hessian (hemp or jute), which is still in use by woodcutters in the twentieth century, and oilskin for fishermen. Butchers had the choice of oilskin or the damp-resisting cotton or wool "flesher" aprons, or even

[1] E. Catt in *Country Life*, Vol. 128, 8th July 1960.
[2] Ibid.
[3] 1864. *Our Mutual Friend.*

"macintosh" aprons like those of surgeons. Finally heavy rubber came to be used in fish and meat markets, chemical works, etc.

Cotton was at last getting cheaper than linen as a washing material and it provided everything from unbleached drill to the finest white starched apron for the nurse or parlourmaid. Aniline dyes added their quota to the ever-increasing variety of material.

The earliest cloth aprons were bibless. When worn by women, even for work on the farm, they were often, in the fourteenth century, embroidered across the top (Fig. 24, p. 41). One is reminded of these by Flora Thompson's[1] village schoolmistress. Though she lived 500 years later she not only clung to "Holland" aprons, but wore them "one embroidered with red one week and one embroidered with blue the next".

As skill in dressmaking advanced, bibs became commoner, but they must still have been rather rare when Cobbett (1821)[2] wrote that the Norwich market women wore "white aprons and *bibs* (I think they call them) going from the apron up to the bosom". The cloth bib was supported by straps or pins—an adjustable strap being invented only in about 1900. There was, and still is, a "fall-over" type used by butchers where the bib has no support but turns down to provide an extra layer across the front. The milk woman in Plate 55b seems to have had the same idea.

Finally there was a waterproof bibbed apron favoured by women herring-gutters which wrapped right round the body like a skirt (see Plate 56a). This recalls the tarred petticoat of sailors, shown on p. 60.

Prevalence of Aprons

At first the chief female wearers of aprons were the farmworkers; chief male wearers were the leather-aproned men mentioned above and the masons and cooks. In the seventeenth century the number of users increased, though slowly, and included men working in the fields. In an edition of Comenius's illustrated Latin Primer *Visible World*, dated 1664, twenty-two trades and crafts are depicted, yet only six have aprons or any other protective clothing. Even the baker is apronless (no cooks are shown). The twelfth edition of the same book, dated 1777, has a different set of engravings, apparently furnished for the eleventh edition of 1731. Here aprons are given also to the carpenter

[1] *Lark Rise*, 1941.
[2] *Rural Rides*.

and mason (quite usual from the fifteenth century onwards), but, in addition, to the groom, miller, baker, butcher, "landress" and barber. This would seem to show an increase in the sense of hygiene between mid-sixteenth century and mid-seventeenth century. Many industrial workers at this time also wore small aprons (Figs. 253).

253. Artisans and miller, all in short aprons. 1647.

In the eighteenth and nineteenth centuries the garment became increasingly popular with domestic servants (see Chapters VI and VII) and among shopkeepers, street vendors and industrial workers.

There were many retailers, even after the development of the factory from *c.* 1700 onwards, who were their own manufacturers and habitually wore an apron at the counter as they did at the bench. One such trade which survived into recent times was the hatter's. F. Willis, who was brought up to the

Mayfair hat-making trade in the heyday of the silk topper, as late as the 1890s, writes as follows:[1]

> Hatters worked in very high temperatures arising from constant heating of irons, so they wore only a singlet, an old pair of trousers and a white apron. . . .

At the counter customers

> expected tradesmen to look like tradesmen, in white shirt sleeves and white apron.

Thus the shopkeeper was typically an apron wearer and this remained true even for those who, by the end of the seventeenth century, constituted a distinct class—namely the shopkeepers who did not themselves either make (or bake) their wares. Thomas Allspice is a modest salesman of grocery and hats in 1808 and wears an apron as a matter of course. Only after his election as sheriff does his daughter aspire to lift him out of the class to which aprons belong. After that, even his assistant says:

> I daren't go before my mistress with my apron on—she says it is vulgar.
>
> 1808. T. Morton, *The Way to Get Married*, II. ii.

In Victorian times an apron was usual not merely for grocers and chemists but for any retailer; for example, in a smart shoe shop in the 1880s ladies were served by elderly men who knelt before them in aprons. But in the twentieth century, under the stigma of vulgarity, the apron of the shopkeeper soon vanished unless he handled food.

Street vendors were for 300 years great users of the apron, both for protection and as an aid in carrying their wares (see Chapter V and also p. 355). Nearly all factory workers used them. Illustrations in the various educational Books of Trades of the nineteenth century show potter, weaver, printer, nail-maker, glass-blower, watchmaker, indeed nearly everyone wearing long aprons. These garments look unsuited to the machine age, but they persisted alike for men, women and boys, at least as late as the 1860s (Fig. 254).

As machinery advanced skilled mechanics and engineers attained among factory workers a special prestige. Their work clothes, described by one of their number, looking back in the 1860s[2] to his youth, included a washable

[1] *A Book of London Yesterdays*, 1960.

[2] 1867. *A Journeyman Engineer* [Thomas Wright], *Some Habits and Customs of the Working Classes*.

"shop jacket" or "slop" and "moleskin or cord trousers, or *overalls*", and no apron. This is an early mention of what later prevailed everywhere—some form of overall, giving better protection than an apron. There had long been, and is to this day, an overall for slaughtermen and others, cut like an immense shirt and still called by the old word "smock" or "slop" (Fig. 93b). The newer, trousered, overalls—the safest style with machinery—appear in the catalogues of a Liverpool manufacturer of "Trade Attire" for the first

254. Boy factory-hand making lace-tags. Typical apron; unusual type of cap. 1844.

time as recently as 1907, under the names of "boiler suit" and "mechanic's overalls". At first these had detachable hoods; they were made of "brown denim" or "blue dongaree" (a calico first imported in the seventeenth century)—hence "dungarees".

An alternative, starting in 1905, was advertised as "American style overalls with patent brace fasteners"—none other than the bib-and-brace overalls used by almost every workman at the present day.

White coats were beginning to be worn by butchers, bakers, dairymen, etc., in early Victorian times. In the twentieth century, not only in all the food trades, but in hairdressing, in domestic, factory, laboratory and retailing jobs, the vogue for hygiene and smartness swept the country. Soon all went into washable coats as dazzling white as the doctor's and the day of the mere apron was done.

OVERSLEEVES

To prevent damaging and dirtying the sleeves when working, women have often simply worn short ones, but men have seldom done so, preferring to roll up the shirt sleeve or hitch it up with a sleeve band as would the butcher in Fig. 255 (compare "Yarks", p. 35).

However, a coat, the sleeves of which will not roll up, may have to be

255. Butcher. Band for hitching up shirt sleeve; apron. (Detail from Hogarth's Hudibras.) 1726.

PLATE 55

My rest you'd disturb early in the morn,
Leave me in bed comfortless and forlorn
Milk and water will not with me agree,
Therefore I'll nothing have to do with thee.

PLATE 55

Milk woman. Apron with turn–down bib (? acting as pocket);
open overskirt, darker underskirt; neckerchief, mob cap,
bonnet. c. 1810.

Contemporary print. Photograph by Reading University Museum of Rural Life.

PLATE 56

PLATE 56

(*a*) Manx herring-gutters "washing down". Oilskin "brats" with bibs and skirts that wrap right round. *c.* 1890.

Photograph (detail) by courtesy of the Manx Museum.

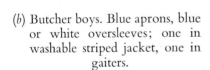

(*b*) Butcher boys. Blue aprons, blue or white oversleeves; one in washable striped jacket, one in gaiters.

W. H. Pyne, Costume of Great Britain. *1808.*

worn. It may be needed for warmth, as with street vendors (who suffer exposure, without having very active work), and with road-menders and butchers in winter conditions. It may be wanted for appearance' sake, as with surgeons, or to protect against contact with hot oven doors, etc., as with cooks. In all these cases the answer has been found in the use of protective oversleeves.

They have also proved popular with nurses and women domestics to preserve their dress-sleeves from dirt.

All these uses have been exemplified already and here we need only make a few comparisons. Oversleeves are a fairly old device, though before the invention of elastic (in the 1820s) they must have been troublesome to keep up. No doubt they were cut on the bias or knitted, and often tied at the top. A Spitalfield weaver in great poverty was described in 1841[1] as wearing a pair of green "stocking sleeves"; they may have been "relics" of this primitive form of oversleeve or merely cut-down stockings. Compare agricultural women labourers' wearing cut-down trousers in lieu of leggings or gaiters.[2]

Some of the earliest examples of oversleeves, as already described, were those of an anatomist in 1555 and those of butchers in 1664. They were popular in the eighteenth century, when coat-sleeves had particularly bulky and ornate cuffs, hence the gardener's use of oversleeves in Fig. 256—blue to match his apron, like those of many butchers in his day (see Plate 56b).

Outdoor workers, except in medieval times, often used blue, grey or brown canvas oversleeves. Nineteenth-century vendors of cockles, eels and fried fish would quite likely have them in black calico; but white for washable sleeves increasingly prevailed and by 1900 became the rule.

Waterproof oversleeves have been used for a variety of jobs and made of oilskin they could be seen in wear by Manx fishermen in 1900. Leather sleeves strapped on and called arm-guards are worn at the present day by welders to protect them, as do their leather aprons and leg shields, from splashes of molten metal.

By contrast a recent development of the protective sleeve is the little muslin object the size of a cuff, which by means of its elastic holds the dress sleeve rolled up at elbow-level. This is favoured by hospital sisters, as it allows of their wearing a dignified long sleeve to the dress without jeopardizing even an oversleeve while actually nursing.

[1] A. Armitage in *Heads of the People*.
[2] F. Thompson (recalling the 1880s), *Lark Rise*, 1941.

Oversleeves may protect in still another way—from sunburn (Fig. 30, p. 50 and Plate 10a). In 1873 in Wiltshire:

> in the hay harvest . . . women had loose sleeves which they pinned on to their "shift sleeves" and which covered their arms to the wrist, from the sun.
>
> *Kilvert's Diary.* Edited by W. Plomer, 1944.

256. Gardener. Apron of characteristic blue colour, oversleeves to match. 1794.

HEAD PROTECTORS, FAN-TAILS, SHOULDER CAPES

Except for the helmets of police, firemen and miners (see Chapters III, X, and XI), there have been few skull protectors for working people in the past. But in Strangers' Hall, Norwich, there is an ancient dome-shaped hat, made of plaited reeds, that belonged to a gamekeeper. This is extremely hard and so enormous that it would fit over an ordinary hat with room for padding in between. It must surely have been a helmet for defence against poachers.[1] The hazard to builders from falling masonry has only been met by suitable headgear in very recent years and heat hazards to furnacemen, firemen and

[1] "What is the matter?" said Sir James. "Not another gamekeeper shot I hope." 1872. George Eliot, *Middlemarch*.

others could not be dealt with properly until the industrialization of asbestos-ized cloth (containing mineral fibres) in the present century.

To protect the ears from excessive noise little was done until quite recently, and it was an understood thing that riveters would lose much of their hearing by middle age. There was, however, a sort of helmet with ear-flaps for the use of boiler-makers as far back as the 1840s, and this presumably gave some protection.

The dustman and coal-heaver, as we have seen, used to protect the head and the back of the neck from dirt by a so-called fan-tail hat—a cap or hat, often of oilskin, with a strong flap hanging behind. Its (surviving) prototype is a piece of sacking thrown over the back of the neck, as seen in a drawing by G. Scharf of a rural-looking London scene, where men are "unloading grass [in baskets] at Rhoad's Dairy, Hampstead Road" in 1836. Scharf shows a fan-tail, labelling it "brown leather-covered hat", on London Street cleaners and on men carrying baskets of builders' refuse in about 1848.

A true fan-tail hat is shown by Hogarth as worn by a porter in the middle of the eighteenth century. It has a "knot" attached to it (see p. 369).

H. Mayhew in 1851 illustrates the fan-tail on dock labourers, coal-porters, Thames lightermen and fish-porters.

As a protection from water dripping from the roof it was worn by men working in the sewers, such as flushermen and ratcatchers (Fig. 259).[1]

An allied garment is the shoulder cape evolved for market meat-porters. The more elaborate of these is a small cape made of oilskin lined with serge and buttoning in front. The shoulder waistcoat is similar, but narrower and longer. These are still in use, but fan-tail hats seem largely to have died out.

GLOVES, HANDLEATHER, BRAIN-BAND

Gloves for workers were used to protect the hand not so much from cold as from friction. Hence their wide use, gauntleted wrists and all, by country workers in the fourteenth century. Their decline as far as labourers were concerned was presumably for economic reasons alone, and was never complete.

Made without divisions, then with a thumb and one or two fingers (Fig. 257), they were at first known as mittens, and for the poor were made of coarse cloth rather than leather. In the *Creed of Piers Plowman* (late fourteenth century) a very needy ploughman had:

[1] Cf. The "tarpaulin hat" of sailors (p. 60).

Tweye meyteynes . . . maad al of cloutes [rags], the fyngres weren for-wered [worn out].

The ploughman in Fig. 5 (who looks more prosperous) wears the then popular parti-coloured gloves which are seen, for example, on shepherds in other manuscripts.

257. "Mitten or Glove to Hedg with". 1688.

At this time even women wore gloves for work, e.g. when beating mattresses (p. 199) or waiting on their clients at an inn (Fig. 155, p. 200).

By the seventeenth century only labourers doing specially rough work wore protection for the hands. R. Holmes in 1688 describes a workman's glove as follows:

> *Mitten.* This is of some termed a *Hedged* Mitten and Glove to Hedg with; a *Tethering Glove.*

"Hedginge mittens" are also mentioned in an account-book in 1673.[1] As late as the 1890s a Herefordshire hedger was wearing an exactly similar "mitt" to that illustrated by Holme (compare Fig. 257 and Plate 6b). Thus mitts have probably been in continuous use by hedgers since medieval times—a primitive yet perfect adaptation to this extremely tough work.

Other work specially hard on the hands is that of woodlanders and reapers, and these, too, have always liked mitts and gloves. Thomas Tusser, the Elizabethan writer, advises farmers: "Give gloves to thy reapers a larges(se) to crie."[2] Describing late-nineteenth-century rural life, G. E. Evans says: "The reapers used gloves to prevent their hands being pricked by thistles as they curved them round the corn when using the serrated sickle." The cornstalks themselves, of course, are harsh, and in some areas a hooked stick is used instead of the gloved hand.

[1] *The Account Book of Sarah Fell . . . 1673–1678.* Edited by N. Penney, 1920.
[2] D. Hartley, *Thomas Tusser* 1931. "Largesse" was still being "cried" in Suffolk at the end of the nineteenth century, though the harvesters' reward was then in the form of money.

PLATE 57

PLATE 57

(a) Thigh pads suspended from a belt, used in turfing to protect thighs. ? 20th century.

Photograph of specimen in Museum of English Rural Life, Reading.

(b) Thatcher trimming spars. Leather knee pad to protect thigh or knee. 20th century.

Photograph: Rural Industries Bureau.

PLATE 58

PLATE 58

(*b*) Post-boy's boot with spur-leather. (Top damaged.) Specimen in North-ampton Museum. 17th century.

Photograph of specimen in Northampton Museum.

(*a*) Tubal Cain the Smith. Leather apron, its bib fastened by brooch; apron-fronted boot, like the moulder's boot of today. *c.* 1360.

British Museum. MS. Egerton 1894.

(*c*) "Mersea pattens" (backsters) for pro-tection from sinking into mud on shore. 20th century.

Author's collection.

Quite another use for gloves is cited by G. E. Evans. He recalls their being worn in the 1880s by lads who had to catch new bricks as they were thrown down from the mouth of the brick kiln.[1]

Against the rubbing of the reins, coachmen, cabmen, grooms, and postilions have, of course, worn gloves of leather, wool or string from very early times. Dogskin gloves are mentioned on page 249.

Against the claws, beaks and teeth of animals, thick leather gloves or mitts are an ancient protection. In the evolution of costume the glove, perhaps

258. Falconer. Decorated leather gauntlet glove; falconer's pouch on belt; fashionable dress befitting a high-ranking servant. 1575.

owing to its importance in armour and its tendency to acquire symbolic meanings, soon reached its highest level of complexity and beauty, the peak coming in the fifteenth century.[2] Thus the gauntlet-shaped gloves of the chief falconer to Queen Elizabeth I could be tasselled and ornamented in a manner fitting to his rank and hers—even more elaborately than in Fig. 258. But

[1] *Ask the Fellows who Cut the Hay*, 1956.
[2] There was a Company of Glovers in London already in *c.* 1349, and they were granted armorial bearings in 1463.

Jack Black, "Rat Catcher to Queen Victoria", was doubtless content with the simple mitt, like his confrère in Fig. 259.

In the 1820s the discovery of how rubber could be moulded to fit parts of the body led eventually, as it did in footwear, to a spate of adaptive radiations among gloves. In 1889–90 rubber gloves were introduced for surgeons and dressers against the irritant effects of antiseptics (see p. 313). Later, of course, the medical world adopted them against transmission of micro-

259. Rat-catcher in London sewer. Fan-tail hat and leather mitt. 1851.

organisms, because, unlike the hands they could easily be sterilized. But in factories they have continued to protect from irritants, such as detergents, acids, etc., because of their chemical inertness and imperviousness to water.

A remarkable example of the revival of a long-lost type has been the development of the modern "chain mail" and "metal-studded" leathers used for making foundrymen's gloves. The latter unconsciously imitate the gauntlets of the medieval knight, for once again they are composed of leather beset with metal rings or studs.[1]

[1] Armoured gauntlets can be seen at Canterbury Cathedral which are believed to have belonged to the Black Prince. Strictly speaking, their modern counterparts come just outside our period, the studding machine having evolved out of the Vickers automatic gun of the 1914 war.

Two varieties of incomplete glove have been used for special jobs probably for centuries, and can still be found in parts of the country today. These
are the thatcher's palm and the shoemaker's hand-leather. Like the thimble,
each is simply a device that offers protection to the hand exactly where, and
only where, the rub comes. The former is a leather pad strapped to the hand
so as to protect the palm when the thatcher is "pushing home spars" or
"palming the butts of reeds", i.e. pressing against the cut ends to make them
flush.[1] The shoemaker who sews manually uses a band of leather encircling
the hand, with a hole for the thumb (Fig. 260). This protects the back and

260. Shoemaker sewing. Hand-leather protecting back of left hand, brain band restrain-
ing the hair, leather apron with beard tucked
in. *c.* 1900.

margin of the hand from the rub of the thread looped round it, and the
leather is often reinforced at the crucial point on the hand's edge; it may also
be fringed for decoration.

Brain-band

While on the subject of shoemakers it may not be wholly out of place to
mention their "brain-bands", although these can hardly be termed protective. Thomas Hardy describes in the corner of a cobbler's shop:

> An apprentice with a string tied round his hair (probably to keep it out of
> his eyes).
>
> 1872. *Under the Greenwood Tree.*

Hardy's guess was correct. The brain-band was called for by the very stooping posture, since a shoe to be sewn was gripped between the knees. Thomas

[1] Rural Industries Bureau, *Thatcher's Craft*, 1961.

Wright in *The Romance of the Shoe* (1922) gives the following account. The old stitchman, "Beard-in-Bib" (Fig. 260), in *c.* 1900

> wore his hair long, rolled up behind and kept back by a band of leather called at Leicester a "brain-band" and at Northampton the "brow-band". (The last [to wear one] in Olney was old Samuel Wright.) His beard he tucked into the bib of his apron.

The alternative to a brain-band was a flat velveteen "cobbler's cap", of which there is a mid-nineteenth-century specimen in the Central Museum, Northampton.

LEGWEAR

Legwear, like footwear, may protect from pressure, sparks, splashing by chemicals, from dirt, mud and water.

A primitive form of plough, and a turf-cutter used even in recent times, both involved the worker in pushing a blade through the resistance of the soil by the thrust of his upper thighs against a long T-shaped handle. In Fig. 261 (1871) the man turfing is wearing a short "leather apron with two boards in front of the groin, the apron being buckled round the waist and round the

261. Turf cutting. Short leather apron faced with two boards to protect groin and upper thigh; short gaiters. *c.* 1840.

upper part of the thighs".[1] In the Museum of Rural Life, Reading, and the Curtis Museum, Alton, are similar pairs of boards, not fastened to an apron, but suspended from a waist belt and secured by straps, either round the legs or to each other. These are called thigh-pads, clappers or ploughman's beaters, and serve the same purpose (see Plate 57a).

For the knee, pads to relieve pressure and chafing have been used at least as long as thatching has been practised. The thatcher's knee-pad is a piece of leather strapped to the leg, with two different uses. He spends most of his time kneeling on the thatch or on a ladder and it then saves his knees. But when seated, trimming spars of hazel, which rest across his lap, he hitches up the pad to protect his thighs from the rub of the wood (see Plate 57b). A flint-knapper's or stone-breaker's knee-pad can be seen at Strangers' Hall, Norwich. Strapped on and made of layers of canvas glued together, it takes the rub of the stone in the same way. In refined form it was made of leather with extra thickness in the middle, as in the specimen at Alton.

Finally, miners who have to work kneeling still use leather pads strapped on in the same way as a thatcher's knee-pad.

A different sort of hazard, that from sparks or splashes, is met (if an apron is inadequate) by several kinds of shields. These vary from types covering

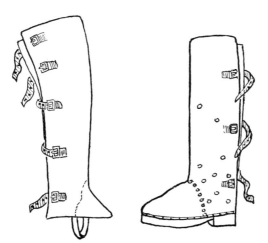

262. (*a*) Slaughtermen's leg-shields, buckled behind. (*b*) Ditto, attached to wooden soles ("killing clogs"). 1912.

[1] H. Stephens, *Book of the Farm*, I (4th Ed.).

the whole leg and even groin, down to ankle spats[1]. Some are of canvas and other cloths, but many, even of the spats, are leather. What we will call "leg-shields" overlap the instep like ordinary gaiters, but differ from these and true leggings in being strapped at the back like cricket pads and in modern times fitted with "quick-release" buckles. Those of butchers (Fig. 262) were sometimes combined with wooden soles. In a primitive form, leg-shields must have been in existence in medieval times, for a mid-fourteenth-century poem describing smiths at work says: "Their shanks are sheathed against sparks of fire."[2]

To protect against splashing, typical leg-shields are shown in W. H. Pyne's drawings of a tanner (Fig. 252), a slaughterman and a man watering horses at a cab-rank (Plate 33). Men printing cloth in the 1840s, who were at risk from dyes splashing, at the same time had to be very mobile, as they worked a hydraulic press. The result was a remarkable specialization, for they wear full-length leg-shields conjoined at the top to make an apron reaching the waist (Fig. 263).

The more ordinary leg protection used by outdoor workers against cold, wear and tear and dirt were either wrapped round, primitively, or else buttoned or buckled at the side. Of his "leather-legged chaps", the Sussex woodlanders, in 1822 Cobbett writes:

> As God has made the back to the burden, so the clay and coppice people make the dress to the stubs and bushes. Under the sole of the shoe is iron; from the sole 6″ upwards is the highlow [short boot], then comes a *leather bam* to the knee, then comes a pair of leather breeches . . . and the wearer sets brush and stubs and thorns and mire at defiance . . .

"Bam" is dialect for what was not called "legging" until the nineteenth century, but existed as a cloth "gamash" in the seventeenth. Even recently in some areas a bam in the form of cloth wound round the legs like puttees was enamoured especially of shepherds. Leather leggings in the nineteenth and twentieth centuries were used by farmworkers in wet weather; also by grooms in lieu of riding-boots—and thus they passed down to chauffeurs in the early days of motoring (see Plate 26b).

Spatterdashes (1670s onwards) often reached above the knee and, from the eighteenth century onwards, could have an instep strap. These were worn by

---

[1] A primitive spat made of hay is mentioned on p. 225.
[2] British Museum MS. Arundel 292, f. 72b.

country gentlemen and farmworkers alike, in the late eighteenth century and early nineteenth century (see Plate 8a), but then gave place to modern gaiters. Typically with instep strap, gaiters reached barely to the calf.[1] They are frequently seen on nineteenth-century carters and farmworkers, as in Fig. 261, but the favourite with navvies, dustmen, etc., was the even shorter spat. Made of buff-coloured cloth or canvas, it bore little resemblance to the elegancies of that name as worn today.

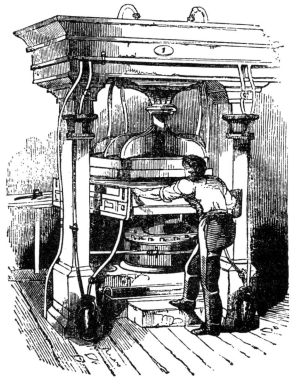

263. Dyeing bandanas. Leg-shields and apron combined. 1844.

FOOTWEAR

Space will not allow of the mention of more than a few examples of special footwear.

[1] A short gaiter, covering half the foot, but lacking instep strap, is described by R. Holme, 1688, under several names that were later applied to boots. It is seen in wear by a ploughman in an illustration to W. Ellis's *Farmer's Instruction*, 1747.

An early form designed to protect from molten metal and falling metal objects has lasted six hundred years. The fourteenth-century smith in Plate 58a is wearing a boot with a flap front and, except that here the flap is fastened by a pin or a leather thong, the design is almost identical with the moulder's boot or clog manufactured today (Fig. 264).

264. Blucher-shaped clog; flap buckled over laces to protect from splashing; wooden sole. 20th century.

Tall riding-boots fitted with spurs became common in the seventeenth century on, for those whose work kept them constantly in the saddle (see Plate 58b). High boots seem to have been less popular with labourers than shoes combined with gaiter-like leg coverings, because the former hampered ankle movements, and were costly to make.

> He is a gentleman, I can assure yee, Sir, for he walks alwaies in boots.
>   1616. S. Rowlands, *Cupid's Whirligig.*

Boots, if worn by workmen at all, were generally quite short—the startups of the sixteenth and seventeenth centuries and the highlows of mid-seventeenth century onwards. The makers of labourers' coarse serviceable boots and shoes were known as "strong shoe men". In 1839[1] those in London were said to have mostly hailed from the provinces. They formed a society of their own, so different were their products from those of other shoemakers. The soles were thick and hobnailed and the parts were stitched with extremely coarse hemp (later riveted). Of advantage in wet undergrowth was the side fastening occasionally seen even today. This exactly resembles the fastening of a boot in a fifteenth-century brass at Faversham.

A former labourer, who did wear tall, heavy boots (called in Essex

[1] J. D. Devlin, "The Shoemaker", in *Guide to Trade.*

PLATE 59

PLATE 59

Leech–gathering. "These little blood-suckers attach themselves
to the feet and legs and are from thence transferred by the fair
fingers of the lady to a small keg . . . suspended at her waist."
Short petticoats and necessarily bare legs; aprons. 1814.

Engraving after G. Walker, in Costume of Yorkshire. *1814.*

PLATE 60

PLATE 60

Grave-digger in Shakespeare's time; also church caretaker, hence dog-whip carried in his belt, and keys. Old fashioned long-skirted jerkin over doublet; small ruff; skull cap (unusual and possibly an "occupational" speciality). 1594.

Portrait at Peterborough Cathedral. Photo: copyright Walter Scott, Bradford.

"fences"), in the early twentieth century, describes some of their features thus:

> The "gore" was a piece inserted in the back of the boot to give more freedom around . . . the ankle . . . most essential, as some of the boots were ten inches high. . . .
> The tongue was stitched on either side to the . . . uppers, thus forming a water-tight boot. Some of the wearers preferred "straights", which were boots made to be worn on either foot, thus ensuring even wear.
>
> F. L. Wallace in *The Essex Countryside*, XIV, 211, 1966.

Clogs in the sense of wooden or wooden-soled shoes, not merely pattens and overshoes, have been used by working people only, but in a variety of conditions. It is difficult to say when they were first used in England. They seem never to have been universally adopted, as by some of the peasantries abroad, and examples have not so far been recognized in illuminated manuscripts. But according to Dr Pococke's *Travels Through England* (1750) they were at that time habitual for working women in the north-west, and often worn without stockings. J. Devlin (1839) states with regard to the makers of clogs:

> In Northern England there are still workmen of this [the clogger's] profession . . . [most of whom] . . . travel from place to place . . . the trade has long been on the wane.[1]

Wooden-soled clogs and the rarer wholly wooden "sabots" were always more prevalent in the north, and even in the twentieth century Yorkshire mill-girls clattered to work in clogs as a matter of course. A stableman's pair, hand-made in the twentieth century, can be seen in the Central Museum, Northampton. These have iron rims on the sole, and a leather upper like that in Fig. 264.

Being resistant to water, non-conducting of heat and yet not "airless", wooden soles are still ideal in damp yards and have been fitted (e.g. for slaughtermen) with uppers of leather or rubber, even in Wellington style (Fig. 265).

Allied to the clog is the "backster", "splasher", "mud-board" or "Mersea patten" worn by longshoremen, for instance on the Essex coast today. This is a wooden or cork board, fastened to the boot with ropes or straps which,

[1] Ibid.

by its flatness and large area, prevents him from sinking into loose sand or mud—in fact, it functions like the splayed foot of a camel or the webbed foot of a duck (see Plate 58c).

265. Butcher's Wellington boot, leather with wooden sole. 1912.

Actual immersion with no protection at all was obligatory for those who gathered leeches by the method of personal attraction (see Plate 59).

For others inevitably immersed, the battle against wet and mud has never really been won, since what is impervious to water is generally impervious to air. In the Middle Ages no fight was put up by the working man. Well-diggers, like those in Plate 64, simply stripped from the waist downwards. However, nineteenth-century "well-diggers' boots" can be seen at Strangers' Hall, Norwich. Very high boots for excluding water were uncommon till the seventeenth century, when they were only gradually adopted for angling and other occupations which involved standing in water. J. Dowie (1861) says that the leather would be

> filled with grease or any of the many repellants now used for keeping out water.[1]

(A primitive repellant still used by country folk is neat's-foot oil.) H. Mayhew reports a conversation with a man whose job it was to stand in the London sewers and flush them with water:

> We stand up to our fork in water, right to the top of our jackboots and sometimes over.
>
> 1851. *London Labour and the London Poor.*

[1] *The Foot and its Covering.*

Such very high boots were, of course, extremely wide at the top and had no fastenings. A similar style was used by men watering the streets in the 1820s, but at the same time Bewick draws many anglers standing in water with no protection at all.

The application of rubber for proofing footwear constituted a major "break-through". Devlin writes that he had

> about the year 1830 purchased a quantity of the native caoutchouc goloshes then introduced for the first time from South America.
>
> *The Shoemaker.*

The word galoshes had been used for leather overshoes since the fourteenth century,[1] but this was the first appearance of rubber footwear. Gradually rubber boots and shoes came in, at first only for the well-off,[2] later for fishermen; but it was three-quarters of a century before they became normal for agricultural labourers working in the wet and mud. Even for fishing, thigh-length wader boots were still made of leather in the twentieth century. A pair can be seen at the Central Museum, Northampton, the shanks of which show the interesting technique of pegging, i.e.

> fastening together of sole and insole with wooden pegs, a method . . . specially useful for seamen's footwear and others used in water, as the wood swells and does not rot too quickly, birch or maple being used.
>
> 1966. J. M. Swann, Assistant Curator, Central Museum, Northampton. Personal communication.

The art of "pegging" is an old one. Of the husbandman mentioned on p. 24 we read:

> A payre of startuppes had he on his feete . . .
>   And in their soles full many a wooden pegge.
>
> 1568. *Debate between Pride and Lowliness.*

A pair of hand-made dyking boots, 27 in. high, now in the Reading Museum, show that the art of making water-resisting leather thigh boots was still lively in about 1910. But human conservatism and the price of rubber

---

[1] Galosh-makers were incorporated with the patten-makers under Charles II.

[2] Against "rheumatism or chills" they are recommended in *Every Lady her own Flower Gardener,* by Louisa Johnson, 1840. Mine-inspectors wore them in 1881.

were both breaking down, and by the end of our period rubber Wellingtons became the normal wear for fishermen, ditchers, navvies, cowmen and many others needing protection from damp.

In this survey of the evolution of protective garments perhaps the only surprising fact to emerge is that in the past they have been so few, so feeble and so fixed in their design. A glance at some of the factors that may account for this anomaly is taken at the end of the chapter which follows.

CHAPTER XV

SOME SPECIAL RELATIONS OF CLOTHING TO WORK

CLOTHING IN RELATION TO CARRYING

The unique ability of Man to foresee his own needs, together with his ingenuity in devising means to meet them result in a propensity for carrying objects about with him which is likewise unique. Not only is his anatomy adapted for this but his clothing has been pressed into the service in a great variety of ways. Examples will obviously come from four classes: those whose work is not in a fixed place (labourers, herdsmen, doctors); those who need an implement always immediately to hand, as does a barber or a man on a ladder; street vendors of all kinds, and finally, of course, porters.

Pockets

To us, the most obvious adaptation for carrying is the pocket, so widely distributed that it is hard to believe that it was unknown in medieval garments. It seems first to have been introduced into the trunk hose in the sixteenth century, and then into breeches. Coat pockets did not appear until the seventeenth century. Even then they were more often an ornament to a gentleman's suit than a "functional" device for artisans. However, they served to carry the doctor's medicaments. By now the workman had pockets in his apron, seen for the first time in the late seventeenth century. These came in usefully for the jobbing carpenter's saw, the decorator's brush, the barber's scissors and a multiplicity of other objects. Lauron's Song-seller (1689) uses her apron pocket to hold the song sheets.

Special double pockets for money, made to tie round the waist and sold in 1906 as "market women's pockets", were identical with those used by an eel-wife in 1750 and her contemporary, selling "Hot Dumplens". Presumably these were preferable to the usual purse when fingers were sticky (compare Fig. 266 with Fig. 267).

In the nineteenth century, with improvements in machinery, and cheapening of materials, pockets became a normal part of a workman's coat and waistcoat As internal hanging "poacher's pockets" they were also fitted into

266. "Buy my live Eeles!" Check apron with double pocket tied on in front; cloak; hat over mob cap. *c.* 1750.

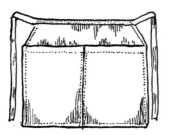

267. Market woman's double pocket. 1906. Cf. Fig. 266.

smocks, and finally they appeared in overalls and dungarees with all the uses familiar to us. Several special types were devised, for example the patented pocket in a painter's jacket "so designed as to prevent the knife from falling out when the wearer stoops" (catalogue of Messrs John Peck, Liverpool).

Skirts

Undoubtedly the most primitive way of using the clothing for carrying is that illustrated in Fig. 23. Here Ruth is gleaning corn behind the reapers and simply gathers it into the voluminous skirt of her supertunic. In the same way men often carried in their tunics seed for sowing or stones to sling at birds, squirrels and foxes (Fig. 268). The skirt of an apron has endlessly been used

268. Carrying stones in the tunic for slinging at birds. *c.* 1340.

in the same way. In a twelfth-century Bestiary[1] men are shown with aprons full of stones, tied round their necks.

In 1689 Lauron draws a newsvendor with an apron full of *London Gazettes*, and his seller of "Hot Baked Wardens" (pears), with a pottery tub on her head, carries other fruit for sale in the same way. Itinerant coopers and cobblers carried much if not the whole of their kit in the bibs or folds of their stout leather aprons.

For a man working on a ladder the problem of carrying without pockets is acute—the eighteenth-century lamplighter solved it simply by turning his apron into a sling for the support of his wick-trimming scissors, etc. (Pl. 49).

[1] Cambridge University Library.

Apron-strings and Belts

Apron-strings, like waist belts, provide a handy way of suspending implements such as the cooper's pincers and the butcher's steel.

Belts have been used for carrying an enormous variety of objects. Labourers and craftsmen naturally stuffed into their waist bands when going to work their mitts (Fig. 269) or their hoods, or any tools of accommodating

269. Shepherd carrying mitt on his belt; colleague playing a double pipe (often carried in same way). *c.* 1340.

shape, like a billhook. The medieval reaper did this with his sickle while he stopped to bind a sheaf (Fig. 23) and porters did the same with their rope:

> They have a *Leather Girdle* about them with a strong Rope of two or three Fouldings hanging thereat, which they have in readiness to bind the Burthen to their backs.
>
> 1688. R. Holme, *Academy of Armory.*

The sexton-verger shown in Plate 60 had to keep the church free from the stray dogs so ubiquitous in his day. Hence a whip in his belt[1] (opp. p. 349).

---

[1] The North Porch-room at Exeter Cathedral is called the Dog-whipper's Room to this day.

Street vendors, naturally, used the waist belt for whatever it would carry, even their wares themselves sometimes. A woman crying "Cunny skins" had rabbit pelts festooned all round her. Another of Lauron's London Criers had the awkward job of selling ink in the streets from a barrel borne on his back (Fig. 270). He had a funnel and measuring ladle with their handles hooked on

270. Ink seller, carrying funnel and measurer on his belt (quills in his hand). 1689.

to his belt. That of yet another vendor supported a walking-stick, two baskets and a wooden box while he clutched glassware in his right hand and blew a horn with the help of his left (Fig. 271).

Waist and shoulder belts have suspended a variety of pouches and receptacles made for special purposes. Some of the earliest, apart from weapon sheaths, were the little leather pouches of the thirteenth century, drawn up by a string at the top, and the leather escerelle of the fourteenth century which hung by two short straps from the waist band. These were used even by ploughmen and servants at work.

271. Seller of Singing Glasses, etc. Carrying with help of belt; he wears a small apron. *c.* 1689.

Fastened to medieval messengers' girdles were the small leather wallets in which they carried their masters' letters (see page 233). Though he may arrive helmeted and on a motor-cycle the telegraph boy of today uses an exactly similar device.

Medieval medical men and those who gave veterinary treatment, in the absence of pockets and doctors' "bags", carried all their remedies in three or four small containers, sometimes with lids, strung on their belts (Fig. 272).

272. Veterinarian dosing a hound. He carries medicaments on his belt. 1575.

A similar arrangement was used by shepherds, whose work might take them far from home for as much as a day and a night at a stretch. As well as the invariable crook, they had to carry all their own requirements and also medicines and instruments that might be needed in tending the sheep. In the Middle Ages a shepherd is often portrayed with three neatly made little receptacles of different shapes suspended from his girdle (Fig. 273). One doubtless contained a small knife and at least one held veterinary medicaments. A "tar box" for these last, as described by Thomas Tusser[1] in the sixteenth century, was still carried thus by shepherds in the twentieth century in Suffolk. A reed pipe to help pass the time might be suspended from the girdle and a horn slung over the shoulder.

[1] *Thomas Tusser.* Edited by D. Hartley, 1931.

273. Shepherds carrying knife, medicaments, etc. suspended on belt. *c.* 1345.

In the sixteenth and seventeenth centuries shepherds seem to have put most of their belongings into a shoulder bag like a satchel (Fig. 10) or into a single large pouch at the waist. Such pouches, often tasselled, were very widespread. An extra large one was carried by falconers and contained again medicaments and surgical implements (Fig. 258).

A writer's description in 1568 of a miscellaneous group of people in the country gives some good examples of carrying with the help of belts. He says of the bricklayer:

A trowell at his gyrdle weared he . . .

Of the husbandman:

A mightie pouche of canvas at his belt.

Of the informer:

A blacke bagge from his girdle hung downe
It was a great bagge like a fawconere [falconer's]
And hong upon his girdle by a ring:
And hundred writtes at least within it were.[1]

A ratcatcher carried a "painefull Bagge of Poisons" on his belt (Fig. 274) and a costermonger might put such a pendant purse to multiple uses:

With a basket on his head . . .
and in his purse a paire of Dice
for to play at Mumchance.

1612. *Ballad* in Pepys' collection (I.206, B.L.).

[1] *Debate between Pride and Lowliness.*

Indeed, such was the prevalence of pouches that we are told of a street seller who regularly accepted not only shoes and old buskins but "ould Pooch rings" as legal tender from those who bought his brooms.

274. Rat-catcher, carrying "painful bagge of poisons" on his belt. 17th century.

By the nineteenth century waist bands were much less used for suspension. Shepherds and harvesters, however, had a belt to carry their supply of home-brewed ale, either in an earthenware bottle (a costrel),[1] tied by its handle, or in a little keg. A mower's belt carried a small pouch at the back to hold a sandstone for whetting the scythe (Fig. 275). An exactly similar "rub-bag" was still carried by reapers in Suffolk near the end of the nineteenth century. Right up to modern times women vendors, like ladies on journeys, carried money in pouches slung from the waist beneath their skirts. See also Fig. 39.

A curiosity is the ingenious belt shown in Fig. 276. Worn by Mr James Smith, founder of the famous umbrella firm, it had a special metal fitting to act as a base for a bow drill.

[1] G. E. Evans in *Ask the Fellows that Cut the Hay* states that a costrel made in Suffolk in 1834 still exists; kegs for the purpose can be seen, Museum of Rural Life, Reading.

275. Mower carrying whetstone for scythe in a sling on his belt. 1802.

276. Founder of James Smith (Umbrellas) Ltd. with fitment on his
belt acting as base for the reel of a bow drill. 1830.

Associated with shoulder belts is the shoulder band or tab on the coat originally designed to prevent the sword belt from slipping. This became typical of the uniform of the armed forces and thence of servants' livery. For a long time "a vestigial structure", it acquired recently the new function of carrying a doorman's and a page boy's white gloves (see p. 191). The servant's gloves are no new idea, but in the past other ways of carrying them had been improvised.

Headgear

> *King Lear:* What hast thou been?
> *Edgar:* A serving man, proud in heart and mind,
>   That curl'd my hair and wore gloves in my cap.
>
> 1608. Shakespeare, *King Lear* III. iv. 85.

277. Vendor carrying hats for sale on top of his own and basket-ware on his belt. *c.* 1640.

A man's hat, (its occasionally a resting-place for his railway ticket today) has often acted as a vehicle in connection with his work. Sellers of straw hats and baskets would perch the hats for sale on top of their own, and itinerant old-clothes dealers, their arms and backs burdened with clothes and even old swords, would do the same with hats (Fig. 277 and 278). A popular song of the 1860s features a dealer who

> drove a trade, and prospered well,
> In skins of cats and ancient hats . . .
> A gentleman in three old tiles.[1]

More important was the miner's hat in its role as a mobile candlestick (Fig. 43).

278. Old clothes man carrying hats on top of his own; second hand swords in hand. 1689.

[1] Tile=slang for hat.

Back in the Middle Ages headgear, but this time in the form of the hood, again proved handy for transport. Its use for carrying a baby is outside the scope of this book, but, as Fig. 279 shows, the hood was sometimes turned back to front and employed as a temporary fruit-bag by a man up a tree.

279. Boy using his hood for collecting fruit. *c.* 1340.

Miscellaneous Items

A small item that has often served an extra purpose by supporting things is a coat- or a waistcoat-button. By this has depended the key, and even the clapper, of a watchman, the whistle of a gamekeeper, and the licence discs of cabbies and conductors (Fig. 178, p. 228). A London street vendor in the 1830s used to have a bunch of kettle trivets hanging from one button and two or three flat-iron-stands from another (Fig. 280).

Even a yark (see p. 35) can have a secondary function. A spade-cleaner (called "the old man" in Dorset) would be tucked into it when a man was hoeing.

280. Street Vendor carrying hardware suspended from coat buttons. 1839.

Pressure Pads

There are many devices for introducing in the clothing a pad to absorb pressure and reduce friction. All the main parts of the body have been provided with buffers at one time or another, and some of them have been discussed under "protective clothing". Those concerning us now are related to the carrying of heavy loads.

Starting at the top we have the cloth wound on itself to make a *head-pad*, for the carrying of weights on the head with comfort and easy balance. Figure 281, grotesque though it be, illustrates the way this has been used in water-carrying all over the world. Many market people and street vendors used these pads through the whole of our period (Fig. 282). Women wore them over their caps or headkerchiefs, and frequently over a hat as well. Muffin-men, surviving into the early twentieth century, still used a pad over a soft peaked cap to carry their wooden trays. An alternative was sometimes resorted to by men with loads of builders' material. They would make a buffer by stuffing newspaper into the crown of a bowler hat.

Allied to the head-pad is the *porter's knot*, a pad resting on the back of the neck, supported by a strap over the forehead. When P. Kalm visited England

281. Carrying a jug with help of a head-pad. Combined operations. (An early 14th century grotesque.)

in 1748 he was understandably struck by the way women at the Kentish chalk kilns carried loads of chalk and coal. Nearly doubled up, they carried on head and shoulders three baskets at once. An old man's hat served as a head-pad, and a primitive type of porter's knot was used at the same time. The latter was a board with

> a band laid by a noose over the upper part of the head . . . they have, . . . under the piece of wood and the band, a bunch of hay, that the wood and the cord may not injure the back.

Hogarth's engraving (Fig. 283), shows clearly the porter's knot in its

282. Carrying with the help of a head-pad. Covent Garden "Basket woman". 1859.

fullest form. Here it is an integral part of a specialized fan-tail hat (see also Fig. 284). J. O'Keefe writing of the years around 1800 says:

> When I lived in Acton I sometimes walked to Oxford Street . . . John walking before me, through the most crowded streets . . . if anything on a person's head, whether hamper, trunk, furniture, etc. he would put up his hand and turn it away

incurring the abuse of

> applewomen, fishwomen, *porters with knots on their heads*. . . .
>
>   1826. *Recollections of the Life of John O'Keefe*, written by himself.

283. "Porter's knot", a cushion strapped to the hat. The porter has deposited his load while delivering a letter. (Detail of print by Hogarth.) 1755–58.

284. Porter carrying load with help of porter's knot on his back. 1818.

Objects of unwieldy length are most conveniently carried over the shoulder, hence the *shoulder-pad*. George Scharf, in London in the 1840s, sketches a man driving a cartful of iron sheets and rods. He carefully labels the "shoulder piece" which the man is wearing to help him in unloading.

This padded portion of the coat has its parallel in the twentieth century in the buckled leather shoulder-pad lined with felt, used by dustmen and others, and in the shoulder waistcoat of butchers. The latter is not only damp proof but is padded with serge to ease the pressure of the carcass on the man's collar-bone.

The hip itself can take the weight of a load and has accordingly been known to acquire an appropriate *hip-pad*. In a Midlands brickworks within living memory women carried enormous bricks (made for special purposes) by resting them on the hip. Most of the girls carried four bricks at a time. These "weighed 26¾ lbs. each and were generally held in a . . . pile by the left arm, the bottom brick supported on a belt of sacking. . . ."[1] The sacking would be bunched on the left hip to make a sort of bolster under the load, which amounted to almost a hundredweight. With improved methods of transport and greater concern for industrial welfare this, and indeed many of the more highly evolved devices for carrying, were destined for extinction in the present century.

SARTORIAL SYMBOLS

That costume can convey messages need hardly be stated. It may be worth while to analyse shortly the sort of information it can give as to the wearer's work, group allegiance and status within his working group.

The most obvious examples of costumes that make such assertions are definite uniforms or liveries and the distinctive attire of the clergy, which is so deep-rooted in the past that the expression "the cloth" has come to mean the very clergy themselves.

Uniforms and servants' liveries have been dealt with in earlier chapters, and clerical dress is outside our province, but the subject of the liveries of London Companies (grown out of the Guilds) will be touched on here. Although not worn strictly speaking for work, these bulked largely in the wardrobe of already forty-eight types of master craftsmen or traders by the end of Edward III's reign—and later of very many others. Distinctive of his own craft, he would wear the livery at regular fraternal meetings, where it symbolized his competence in their special skill.[2] As the Mercers put it in 1347, a livery was adopted as one of the means:

[1] Report No. 44 of Industrial Fatigue Research Board (M.R.C.), 1927.
[2] There was, of course, honorary membership, too, but this is irrelevant here.

PLATE 61

PLATE 61

(a) Straw boater as a butcher's sign outside his shop at Glastonbury. 20th
century.

Photograph by courtesy of J. P. Lucas, M.A., M.C.

(b) Shoeblack in red uniform jacket, red
banded peaked cap, apron. 19th
century.

*Song written and composed by S. Bevan, printed by
W. Cornish.*

PLATE 62

PLATE 62

A Jack-of-all-Trades on the stage. R. Suett in the role of "Dicky Gossip". Woodworker's leather apron, over barber's white apron, both with button-holed bib. 1797.

Portrait by S. de Wilde. Photograph by courtesy of the Ashmolean Museum, Oxford.

For cherishing the unity and good love among them and for the common profit of the mistery.[1]

Ordnance quote by G. Unwin in *The Guilds and Companies of London*, 1908.

So important was the livery that to attain membership was called "to be clothed"; but by the fifteenth century in many companies the wealthier members (merchants) constituted an *élite* called the "livery", and only they were entitled to the full garb. Thus it expressed simultaneously both membership and rank.

The clothing varied with time, with the wealth of the company, and with the rank of the member. It ranged from simply a badge, "the cognizance" (e.g. gold knots and silver trefoils for the goldsmiths), with or without a distinctively coloured hood, up to an entire suit—hood, coat or surcote, with a cloak or gown for ceremonials. The Grocers' Company began with a meet-

285. Members of Grocers' Company of London in livery gowns each holding his symbolic hood by its long apex (liripipe). It resembles the original Medieval hood except for lacking the shoulder piece. 1588.

ing in 1345 of twenty-two "pepperers" all attired simply in the same-coloured surcote. Its full livery is shown in Fig. 285. By this date (1588) a company's livery was all the more striking, since gowns and hoods were no longer people's ordinary wear. The livery hood was now purely symbolic, degenerate and peculiar in form and not even, strictly speaking, *worn* at all.

[1] Mistery = craft or group of craftsmen.

But its origin from the medieval hood can easily be recognized when the latter is seen carried in the same way by its tippet or liripipe (Fig. 286)[1]. J. Stow in his *Survey of London* (1598) says that in medieval days the gown and hood of a livery had been parti-coloured:

> These Hoods being made . . . according to their gownes; which were of two Colours . . . but now of late time they have used their gownes to be all of one Colour and that of the saddest.

286. Medieval hood held by liripipe, for comparison with Fig. 285.
The circular aperture is for the face. (Man scaring birds.) *c.* 1340.

Thus the Carpenters in 1673 had:

> A Livery gowne of black cloth, lined and faced with Budge [lambskin] and a whod [hood] of black and red cloth.
>
> > Quoted in E. B. Jupp's *Historical Account of the Worshipful Company of Carpenters*, 1848.

Particulars regarding the butchers' livery are given in Chapter V, p. 115.

Interesting examples exist of workers wearing an alien livery out of deference to its proper owner. (Cf. the royal crest on a tradesman's notepaper today, with the words "By appointment to H.M. the Queen".) At celebra-

---

[1] cf. p. 303. The academic hood is already differentiated.

tions of the second marriage of Edward I (1300) the loyalty of the citizens of London to their respective companies was expressed by their

> wearing the Cognizances of their Mysteries embroidered upon their Sleeves.[1]

But their loyalty to the throne was also displayed, for they all turned out in the royal colours of red and white. Somewhat more mundane were the symbols of a loyalty to the monarch which erupted on the recovery of George III from a breakdown in 1789. Fanny Burney records from Weymouth:

> All the labourers wear "God Save the King" in their hats

and the ladies in the royal service

> wear it in their bandeaus on their bonnets to go into the sea; and have it again, in large letters round their waists to meet the waves.[2]

A curious instance is on record of servants' costume being used to confer not a compliment but an insult. After Charles II and his Court in 1666 had adopted a new style of dress ("vest" and "tunic"), to assert its independence of French fashions, Pepys reports:

> The King of France hath, in defiance, . . . caused all his footmen to be put into vests . . . this makes me mighty merry, it being an ingenious kind of affront.
>
> *Diary of Samuel Pepys.* Entry for 22nd November 1666.

There are countless examples, among trades, of small arbitrary conventions of dress which, without amounting to uniform, proclaim the wearer's work in the same way. As we have seen, the colour of an apron (blue for gardeners, checks for barbers, etc.) and even the direction of stripes on an apron or a waistcoat can be adhered to by a professional group for generation after generation.

Even where the custom began on a utilitarian basis its persistence can often be explained only by the wearers' love of having a recognized trade-mark in common with his group. White was used for masons' aprons for practical reasons, as we have seen, but Wardens of the Freemasons, most of whom never handled stone, also wore white aprons at their meetings as a symbol

[1] J. Stow, *Survey of London.* Edited by Strype, 1720.
[2] *Fanny Burney—Selections from the Diary.* Edited by John Wain, 1961.

of their loyalty (Fig. 287). For butchers the straw "boater" became so much a trade-mark that there is a butcher's shop in Glastonbury to this day whose street sign depicts simply an enormous boater hat (see Plate 61a).

An example of a costume asserting membership of a working group, but, unlike the livery of a guild, actually worn at work, was the brightly coloured jacket that shoeblacks adopted when in the mid-nineteenth century they

287. Warden of Freemasons. Symbolic white apron. Cognizance (square and dividers) emblazoned on apron and worn round neck. 1804.

formed themselves into local clubs. The first "Shoeblacks' Brigade", "The City Reds" (see p. 382), was followed by nine other London societies, each in its own area and each with its own colour scheme for the jacket. The South London society wore yellow, West London purple, Notting Hill blue with red facings and so on (see Plate 61b).

It is interesting to notice what clothing is seized upon by cartoonists, illustrators, writers and actors to convey, as it were in shorthand, the occupation of the person they portray.

Up to the late nineteenth century the apron was in such general use for all jobs that its name in literature and its appearance in pictures (provided it was neutral in colour) became a sort of generic term or symbolic attribute denoting the "working man" (compare p. 328).

Thus in Coriolanus we find this ironical gibe against the fallen leaders who had relied on the rabble of Rome:

> You have made good work
> You and your *apron-men*: you that stood so much
> Upon the voice of occupation . . .
>
> 1607. Shakespeare, *Coriolanus*, IV. vi.

Cobblers' aprons have received special attention. When Pope wants to contrast men's fundamental inequality with their superficial differences he uses "a cobler apron'd" to stand for the menial worker and a "parson gown'd" for one of the others. Gowns were made of prunella cloth; hence:

> Worth makes the man and want of it the fellow:
> The rest is all but leather and prunella.
>
> 1758. *Essay on Man.*

At least three public orators in England made humble starts in life as cobblers, two of them being members of Cromwell's Parliament and another being a preacher in the nineteenth century. All three were shown in contemporary cartoons, declaiming from platform or pulpit in long more or less blackened leather aprons.[1]

The caricature in Fig. 288 of the Duke of Wellington in the role of a cobbler asserts his calling by the leather apron and strap as certainly as it conveys his individuality by the facial features. The blackness of cobblers' and tinkers' aprons was so characteristic that a man in a black apron would be recognized for one of them at once (Fig. 251).

As we have seen, the long smock was almost a uniform for carters in the eighteenth and nineteenth centuries. In a lampoon of 1848 on D'Oyly Carte, called "Le Diable à Carter—an Operatic Notion", he is displayed for all to recognize with a whip and a smock-frock.

Obviously costume that corresponds with occupation has special significance on the stage. Richard Suett in the part of Dicky Gossip[2] conveyed

---

[1] Barbon or "Barebones", a Leatherseller, and John Hewson, a cobbler, were the Cromwellians. The subject of the nineteenth-century cartoon has not been identified.

[2] This character in Prince Hoare's *My Grandmother* (1797) was actually barber, apothecary, tailor and coffin-maker.

vividly to his audience that he was a woodworker on the one hand, and a barber and apothecary on the other by wearing two kinds of aprons at the same time (see Plate 62).

288. Cartoon of Duke of Wellington in role of cobbler. Characteristic leather apron buttoned to waistcoat. 1830.

Similar information in a sort of sartorial code used to be given at hiring fairs. In the days of illiteracy working people had to present themselves to potential employers without previous advertisement or correspondence.

Started probably in the fourteenth century and continued even into the twentieth, statute fairs ("statty fairs" or "mops") were held periodically in the country to act as employment exchanges. Workers of all sorts had to appear *en masse*, and it was an important function of their dress to convey what occupation it was that they followed. The way the women could be sorted out is explained by Samuel Curwen, describing a fair at Waltham Abbey in 1782.

> The females of the domestic kind are distinguished by their aprons, viz. cooks in coloured, nurserymaids in white linen and chambermaids in lawn or cambric.

The men wore appropriate emblems, which probably varied with locality. At a fair at Studley, Warwickshire, in 1830:

> The men wore clean white frocks [smocks] and carried in their hats . . . insignia of the situation they . . . were desirous to fill: for instance a waggoner or [a] ploughboy had a piece of whip-cord in his hat some of it ingeniously plaited in a variety of ways and entwined round the hat band; a cowman, after the same manner had some cow-hair; to these there was sometimes added a piece of sponge; a shepherd had wool; a gardener had flowers.
>
> Letter in W. Hone's Table Book I.

Permanent badges for identification connected with employment are, of course, legion. Such labels on hats, shoulder tabs, arm bands, neck ribbons or even the backs of coats, have given official status to porters, easy recognition to couriers, authority to watchmen (Plate 40), and the very right of plying their trades to cabbies and Thames watermen of the old days (Fig. 198).

Identification badges, like the number plates of cars, have often been prescribed by law, so as to facilitate the prosecution of their owners if need arose. At Smithfield Market as early as about 1820:

> . . . by order of the Lord Mayor each drover was compelled to wear a number painted on a piece of leather to be strapped on the arm, by which anyone of their body detected wantonly ill-using the cattle, might be identified and prosecuted.
>
> 1827. W. H. Pyne, World in Miniature.

Compare the use of badges for chimney-sweep boys described on p. 281.

It is a solemn thought that a negro servant in the eighteenth century sometimes had to wear an irremovable silver collar engraved with his master's name and address to prevent his escape from a servitude bordering on slavery. Even paid workers have sometimes been made to wear identification marks simply to prevent their escape from their employers. In the fourteenth century:

> The building industry was essentially capitalist . . . the principal employers being the monarchy and the Church . . . Workers were subject to impressment by the Crown . . . and the tendency of conscripts to withdraw in pursuit of higher wages led the Sheriff of York to supply the men he impressed with red caps and liveries "lest they should escape from the conductor".
>
> M. McKisack, *Oxford History of England—14th Century*, 1959.

Quite another kind of identification mark is the status symbol which is used to differentiate the wearer from lower forms of life. Some of these are discussed elsewhere. We shall merely illustrate here, first, a general tendency of high-ranking individuals to wear a costume that makes them look tall, and secondly the apparently fortuitous yet rigid character of some of the other status symbols.

Tallness and dignity are so closely associated in the average mind that "high hat" and long gown are the commonest symbols used by the heads (the very word is significant) of working groups. The medieval master craftsman generally wore a conspicuous hat, and a survival of this is seen in the black hat of the "Master Mason" presiding at Freemasons' meetings.

A similar tradition held for the head of a sheep-shearing team in Stuart times. G. E. and K. R. Fussell write:

> Shearing in Sussex . . . was done in companies, often of more than thirty men under a captain in a gold laced hat and a lieutenant wearing one adorned in silver.
>
> *The English Countrymen—A.D. 1500–1900*, 1955.

A pale reflection of this sort of differentiation was described by an elderly Essex farmer not long ago:

> When I was a little old boy in Dengie Hundred only the farmers and head horsemen wore lum hats.[1]

Among men cooks the master cook or "chef" became, in the twentieth century, the wearer of one of the tallest hats ever to dignify man (see Plate 21b).

[1] Personal communication ("lum hat" = top-hat).

F. Willis sums it all up in the words:

> This matter of hats is a very important one. . . . Consider how the awful authority of old Mr Osborne in *Vanity Fair* would have suffered if he had walked round Russell Square at night without a hat. Remove the policeman's helmet and you destroy his authority . . . abolish the bank messenger's silk hat and you aim a blow at the heart of British finance.
>
> *A Book of London Yesterdays*, 1960.

Since a hat increases height, its absence indicates deference, as many a custom shows. The Frenchman, H. Misson, in his *Memoirs* (1698) writes:

> An apprentice is a sort of slave; he wears neither hat nor cap in his master's presence.

but the translator[1] adds (in a footnote):

> Unless he is in the last year of his time. Thus I remember a 'Prentice . . . being call'd to the Coach side by one of his Customers, after he was got half way into the street, ran immediately back again to clap on his Hat to shew his prerogative.

Incidentally a nice example of grade within grade!

At the opposite end from the hat, long flowing garments also, of course, convey an impression of height and therefore dignity. Long gowns were justified for the eminent in an ancient university in the following words:

> In . . . 1358 . . . in a congregation of the regents . . . it was ordained that any tailor who cut or made a gown to be used in the university should make . . . it properly so that the masters and beadles should have gowns not narrow or short but wide and reaching to the ankles . . .
>
> . . . For it is decent and consonant with reason that those to whom God had granted the privileges of mental adornment beyond the laiety should also be outwardly different in dress . . .
>
> *Munimenta Academica I.* Edited by G. Anstey.

Even today the Oxford undergraduate's gown, though vestigial for commoners, is full length for scholars. In the late fifteenth century the clergy were accused of overdoing the dignity. "A Balad against Excess in Apparel, especially in the Clergy" contains the words

[1] 1719. *M. Misson's Memoirs and Observations in his Travels over England.* Translated by John Ozell.

Ye holy prestis full of presumcion
Make shorter your taylis [trains] . . .

For dignity, then, a gown must be long—not only absolutely but relatively
to the gowns of lesser folk. This (besides economy) was the idea behind the
Elizabethan decree that the gowns of working people should be restricted in
length to the level of the calves unless they were over sixty.

The enforcement of such sartorial distinctions, made for distinction's sake,
rests often on very subtle, almost unspoken tradition; but in the past they
have sometimes been imposed, as we have seen, with all the force of law.

> In 1582 the Common Council [of London] ordered that no apprentice to
> presume to wear any apparel but what he received from his Master. . . . A
> ruff only of 1½ yards long. Stockings only white blue or russet.[1]

In 1611 the Council further decreed that an apprentice should not wear a
hat costing over 5s; he must not wear Spanish shoes nor have his hair

> with any tufte or lock, but cut short in decent comely manner.

Finally a word on vicarious dignity expressed in dress. The status of a
servant varies not only according to his rank in the household but according
to the rank of his master in society. The black cockade, indicating that a
gentleman was in the royal service, might be worn only by the servants of
commissioned officers. Even servants of "Gentlemen who are N.C.O.'s and
privates in Volunteer Rifle Corps do not wear cockades"[2]. (Originally the
badge of the Hanoverians, the black cockade is seen in Plate 9b).

The wearing of insignia of any sort savours of advertisement. In the section
which follows some bizarre uses of costume for purely commercial advertising will be discussed.

COSTUME FOR ADVERTISEMENT

Since a moving advertisement tends to be more eye-catching than a still one,
a perambulating human being in a startling costume has often been used to
further mercenary ends.

An example of the use of curious attire to draw attention is afforded by the
eccentric quack-doctor-turned-dentist, Martin Van Butchell, a one-time
pupil of John Hunter (Fig. 289).

[1] Quoted in W. Harrison, *History of London*, 1776.
[2] 1859. *Notes and Queries*, 2nd Ser., IX, 129.

He was . . . noted for the eccentricity of his manners. His long beard and extraordinary costume [note his hair and peculiar hat] astonished all beholders and it was his custom to ride [in Hyde Park] on a white pony which he sometimes painted all purple or sometimes with . . . spots.

1803. R. S. Kirby, *Wonderful and Scientific Museum.*

His mode of advertisement seems to have done him nothing but good—his practice was enormously lucrative.

289. "The celebrated Martin van Butchell", quack doctor and dentist. Self-advertisement by eccentric costume, beard, and pony painted with spots. 1803.

Renown has been gained by sheer singularity of attire on humbler levels of employment than van Butchell's. At least two street vendors in the eighteenth century, who could be seen wherever a concourse of Londoners collected, both made themselves conspicuous in this way. "Tiddy Doll", who would be selling gingerbread, arrested attention by combining with his white apron an imitation of court dress, topped off by a gold-laced hat with a feather. One can catch sight of him in the crowd in Hogarth's "Execution of the Idle Apprentice". See Fig. 290. His contemporary, James England, the "Flying Pieman", went to the opposite extreme and presented the then extraordinary sight of a man out of doors neatly dressed and aproned, but wearing his own hair, powdered and *en queue*, instead of the universal wig; and—still more remarkable—lacking any hat whatever. Anything to be different.

290. "Tiddy Doll" the gingerbread seller dressed, for advertisement, like a person of rank—lace ruffled shirt, laced and feathered hat, white stockings (all combined with an apron).
1747.

Shoeblacks were generally small and at work were always seated—all the more important therefore that their clothes should show up in the street. Shoeblack boys were first organized into a sort of livery company, with a true lodge of its own, by the philanthropist John McGregor in 1851. Visitors to the Great Exhibition had their shoes cleaned—and some twenty-five waifs and strays gained a livelihood. They were put into bright scarlet jackets, so conspicuous that when they later settled down in licensed pitches in central London they came to be known as City Reds. When shoeblack little boys became extinct this scarlet jacket was taken over by a well-known firm of boot-polish manufacturers and, with the firm's name embroidered on the velvet collar, has turned into a highly effective advertisement of their wares (see Plate 63).

A broad sash across the shoulder has not only been used to denote the Order of the Garter or the Bath. Appropriately designed, it could equally

PLATE 63

PLATE 63

Wally Jones, Shoeblack. Advertisement by means of scarlet
jacket and trimmings, 20th century.

Photograph by kind permission of Messrs Chiswick Products Ltd.

PLATE 64

PLATE 64
Well-diggers. Absence of protective clothing. *c.* 1360.
British Museum, MS. Egerton 1894.

well, for several centuries, signify a gelder or a ratcatcher. These men were specialists, doing a skilled job, and until quite recent times each would serve the public throughout a wide area, over which he had to walk. A famous ratcatcher of about 1615 advertised his presence by carrying a banner with rats portrayed on it and when possible by suspending his actual victims from

291. Itinerant Gelder. Special shoulder sash for advertisement. 1689.

its staff (Fig. 274 shows that he was rather fashionably dressed). But by the end of the seventeenth century gelders and ratcatchers would call attention to themselves by blowing a horn[1] and wearing a broad shoulder-sash ornamented by a row of horseshoes (for the gelder) or of rats (for the rodent operator (see Figs 291 and 292). Their striking garb has made these men a

[1] Hogarth introduces a gelder with his horn into his satirical picture "Musician's Lament".

292. Ratcatcher. Special shoulder sash for advertisement. 1803–5.

293. Jack Black, ratcatcher to Queen Victoria. Advertisement by means of arresting colours and special sash with royal arms between rats. 1851.

subject for artists from the seventeenth century onwards. Jack Black, "Rat and Mole destroyer to her Majesty" (Queen Victoria), has been immortalized by H. Mayhew, who reports him as saying:

> I used to wear a costume of white leather breeches and a great coat and scarlet waistcoat, and a gold band round my [top] hat, and a belt across my shoulder. I used to make a first rate appearance, such as was becoming the uniform of the Queen's rat-ketcher.

1851. London Labour and the London Poor.

Between the rats embroidered on his shoulder band were a crown and the letters V.R. (Fig. 293). Here was a relic of the ancient custom whereby any tradesman or craftsman might wear the heraldic crest of a family he served (see p. 162).

294. Newsvendor. Newspaper displayed in his hat. 1820–30.

295. "Mad Hatter". Hat worn for advertisement. (From *Alice in Wonderland*.) 1865.

The hat, being the garment most likely to be seen in a crowd, has been used for advertisement in various ways. Its band may blazon forth a name, as with couriers or hotel doormen: at one time it used to display a sample of the newsvendor's papers (Fig. 294): again it may constitute an advertisement in itself, as with the Mad Hatter (Fig. 295).

Representatives of a business may make their public appearances all the more effective by fancy dress. Certain manufacturers of "trade clothing" in Edwardian days advertised as follows:

> We make a speciality of Advertising Uniforms for Bill Distributors, Messenger Boys, Sandwich men, etc.,

and added discreetly:

> Arrangements can be made to confine any particular style to any particular district.

The illustration to show what could be done when "original ideas were worked up to suit requirements" shows a group of lads in duck suits, puttees and Indian turbans with a poster reading: "There is no tea like Phillip's."[1]

A well-known example of a complete costume used as an industrial advertisement is that of the draymen who parade the streets of London in the twentieth century wearing the livery adopted by their firm in 1750. Here the antique design of coat, hat, breeches and buckled shoes arrests attention by its historic associations and its violent contrast to the lorry-drivers' clothes of today. The £150 it costs for each man is seen by the company as a highly profitable outlay in advertisement, cf. p. 139.

THE RATIONALE OF IRRATIONAL CLOTHES

If a single generalization had to be made on the facts presented in this book it might be that the costume worn by a worker is, more often than not, ill adapted for its "practical" purpose. Why is this? Some of the reasons are simple enough—lack of means, lack of available materials, lack of invention. These are sufficient alone to explain, for example, the comparative uniformity which in the remoter past characterized the dress of all workers no matter how diverse their occupations. Then there are the psychological reasons which are more difficult to assess—those to do with sex, aesthetics, fashion, pride, fear of ridicule and finally conservatism.

It is hardly necessary to cite examples of inconvenience due to poverty and lack of materials. Sheer scarcity of needles and scissors largely accounts for the

[1] 1908–9. Catalogue of Messrs John Peck & Co., Liverpool.

unpractical flapping garments so characteristic of early medieval times. The non-existence of "elastic", which did not appear until the nineteenth century, meant that the labourer had either to use unstretchable garters, or else fasten up his hose to his braies-girdle or his doublet by buttons and strings (Fig. 296) which were always breaking at the back when he stooped to

296. Joseph divested of his coat. Footless hose fastened to braies girdle by buttons and inelastic strings. (The back suspenders not showing.) *c.* 1360.

work.[1] In the absence of rubber for gum-boots men ditched and delved either in ill-proofed boots of enormous weight, or else stripped from the waist down (see Plate 64).

As to ingenuity—this was probably no more lacking at one time than another, and the mother of invention was always present. But after the necessary materials have become available the gestation period for any invention is notoriously slow. Ignorance of the simple art of knitting accounts for the wrinkled and descending cloth hose of Piers Plowman, which overhung his shins and got "beslomered" in the mud (Chapter I).

It is obvious that women, even doing the same work as men, have been relatively hampered by their clothes for the whole of our nine centuries. Women chased away foxes, milked goats (Fig. 297 and 298) and worked machines, in dresses down to their feet. They covered their hair in wind-catching caps or veils. The maintenance of decency or propriety on the one hand, sex appeal on the other, must have determined a multitude of discomforts for women workers—and not a few for men.

Aesthetic considerations were again often militant against a worker's convenience—hence, surely, the hat, so universally worn, however unsuitable for the job in hand, right down to the end of our period. Hence, too, the

[1] Indeed in describing a smart man's appearance, Chaucer thinks it worth mentioning that all his suspenders were intact: "Ful faire and thikke been the poyntes set" ("Miller's Tale").

coster girls' white caps and gay kerchiefs that needed constant washing and the coster boys' brass buttons that were always being polished.

The sheer love of "fashion" has often been strong enough to overcome all other considerations. Why else did working men wear white ruffs when

297. Inconvenience of a ground-length kirtle when lambasting a fox with a distaff. Early 14th century.

298. Billowing skirts no hindrance when milking a goat? 1757.

gardening, or wigs when ploughing, and why in the 1860s did women insist on wearing crinolines in match factories to the danger of their lives? Even so down-to-earth a worker as a miner is subject to the influence of what happens to be the fashion among his immediate fellows. A Royal Commission on Mines, in 1842, opined that only this could explain the fact that in one mine the men all wore singlets, trousers and shoes, while in another, where physical conditions were identical, they went stark naked.

Adherence to fashion is closely bound up with one of the overruling motives in dress, that of asserting importance and prestige.

As we have seen, what confers dignity of appearance, on the one hand, and what is convenient for moving about in, on the other, are rarely the same. "Length" helps the one and hinders the other. Chaucer's Parson deplores:

> The superfluity in length of the aforesaid gowns, trailing in the dung and in the mire, on horse and eke on foot, as well of man as of woman.[1]

The conflict between dignity and fitness has bedevilled the dress of artisans and servants (especially the domestic) for all time. Wide or trailing sleeves are peculiarly ill adapted for almost any work, yet servants in later medieval times, rather than be out of fashion, wore them through thick and thin— indeed, literally, for it is recorded that those of waiters often dipped into the soup.

Such sleeves also prevented a man from defending his master in an assault:

> . . . what help will he,
> Whose sleeves so wide and cumbrous trail,
> Give to his lord? He is of no avail
>   He helpeth no more than a woman can.
>
>> 1411/12. T. Hoccleve, *The Regemente of Princes*. Edited by
>> F. Furnivall, 1897.

Again, in 1525, J. Fitzherbert gives a lively (if ungrammatical) account of the unsuitability of servants' dress when they aped their masters in his day.

> See mens' servants so abused in their array their coats be so syde [long] that they be fain to tuck them up when they ride as women do their kirtles . . . And furthermore they have ruffs upon their sleeves above their elbows, that they could not shoot one shot to hurt their enemies till he have cast off his coat or cut off his sleeves . . . it endeth in pride, presumption and poverty.
>
>> *Book of Husbandry* (Spelling modernized).

---

[1] *Canterbury Tales, c.* 1387, edited by W. Skeat, 1894.

The love of "status symbols" discussed above has often involved the worker in wearing a costume positively antagonistic to its practical purpose. It was surely of a living dairyman's wife that Thomas Hardy wrote, in reference to her "respectability":

> . . . Mrs Crick . . . wore a hot stuff gown in warm weather because the dairymaids wore prints.
>
> 1891. *Tess of the D'Urbervilles.*

The words of the craftsman hatter, whose reminiscences of the 1890s have been mentioned earlier,[1] suggest another example.

> The white apron was the hallmark of the skilled man, it inspired confidence in the Olympian [customer] and pride in the tradesman. Lesser fry wore baize aprons or any old apron, but we, the aristocrats of labour, wore white aprons, dressed by the laundry.

Any of the other aprons would have been more serviceable, and the white one actually involved the man in extra expense—but it was the status symbol of his respected trade.

It is also very noticeable that as an individual rises in rank in his trade group he tends to reduce or shed various items of useful protective clothing, since they are now regarded as symbols of menial work. Thus the aprons of chefs and nursing sisters are whittled down in size compared with those of apprentice cooks and student nurses. The horticulturist in Fig. 299, wearing tall hat and tails has abandoned his apron altogether. And when a man becomes a head waiter he, too, generally gives up his apron and wears a black tail coat instead of a washable jacket. When a hairdresser at the turn of the present century was eminent enough to call on his lady clients in person, he left his apron behind and wore a black frockcoat with no protective clothing at all.

These are, as it were, negative symbols of rank. Many of the positive are unpractical, too, and some of the worst have been the dignities vicariously conferred on the servants of the mighty. One could hardly conceive of more unsuitable clothes than the "gaudy and fantastical" liveries of the eighteenth and nineteenth centuries, especially for young page boys and in the days before dry cleaning. A page's gay livery in 1847 in the words of his mistress (who had designed it) "in not more than a week . . . was not fit to be seen".[2]

---

[1] F. Willis, *A Book of London Yesterdays.*
[2] H. and A. Mayhew, *The Greatest Plague of Life . . .*

A curious and quite different sort of pride has been a serious deterrent in the adoption of health and safety devices in industry, especially when these had to be worn on the person. An age-old problem, this has been emphasized

299. Flower gardener. Old-fashioned breeches but up-to-date tail-coat and tall hat; no apron. 1821.

lately by the Chief Inspector of Factories, who is quoted in a leaflet by the "Golden Shoe Club" as saying:

> One of the difficulties in the way of their greater use [safety boots, goggles and helmets] is resistance by *workpeople*, particularly where the need is not obvious. There are many obstacles. Not the least of these is *ridicule by work-mates* . . .

The leaflet continues:

> "Ridicule by workmates"—this epitomizes the problem of safety experts in industry. For while older men in general adapt themselves to safety footwear, the young . . . dread being thought "soft".
>
>   1962. Golden Shoe Club, *Protection with Style in Safety Footwear*.

Finally against every practical improvement in working dress there operate the subtle forces of tradition. Indeed, in the handbill quoted above even the younger industrial worker's resistance is said to be partly because he is "innately conservative".

Whether we can go all the way with him or not, it is interesting that after an exhaustive survey of the state of the poor, Sir Frederick Eden, in 1797, gives it as his serious opinion that:

> If he [the penurious labourer] does not reap the full reward of his labours . . . it is because, either through ignorance, custom or prejudice, he adheres to ancient improvident systems in dress, in diet, etc.
>
>   1797. *Annals of Agriculture*, 28, 449.

Such conservatism may have disastrous results from the purely practical point of view, but in origin it is not necessarily evil, and in some of its effects it need not be deplored. Workers having the same calling obviously cling to common custom for a number of subtle reasons. When new conditions have made their traditional costume quite inappropriate in a utilitarian sense it may be preserved by a laudable solidarity within the group and a vague loyalty to generations past. Moreover, whatever this may entail in discomfort for the wearers, it proves, as this book has sometimes shown, no ill wind for the chroniclers of costume. For the working Englishman, as he walked through history, has left us a trail of surviving customs, and these, as much as records in ink and in paint, help to give body to our vision of his past, enabling us to answer a confident "yes" to his question:

> Thou villain base,
> Know'st me not by my clothes?
>
>   *Cymbeline*, IV. ii. 81.

BIBLIOGRAPHY

Manuscripts

For the Medieval period, the principal sources used have been illuminated MSS. especially those at the British Museum, and others mentioned in the Sources of Plates and Figures. Among valuable facsimiles available are those in the following books.

Illustrations of the Book of Genesis ["Egerton Genesis" (*c.* 1360)] Oxford, Roxburghe Club, 1921.

Ellesmere Chaucer [Fifteenth-century Ed.]. Manchester University Press, 1911.

English Illuminated MSS. Vol. I. 10th to 13th Centuries. Vol. II. 14th and 15th Centuries. Eric G. Millar. (Paris Lib. Nat. d'Art et d'Histoire.) 1926, 1928.

Holkham Bible Picture Book. [*c.* 1330.] W. O. Hassall. Dropmore Press, 1954.

Illustrations of a Hundred MSS. in Library of H. Yates-Thompson. (7 Vols.) H. Yates-Thompson. Chiswick Press, 1907-18.

Luttrell Psalter. [*c.* 1340.] Eric G. Millar. British Museum, 1932.

Queen Mary's Psalter. [*c.* 1320.] Sir George Warner. British Museum, 1912.

Vetusta Monumenta. [6 vols. of reproductions from MSS.] Society of Antiquaries, 1747. Index by N. Carlisle, 1810.

Printed Books

Publication is in London unless otherwise stated.

Abbreviations: ed. = edited by
Ed. = edition.

Abel-Smith, Brian. *The Hospitals, 1800–1948,* Heinemann, 1964.

Adams, Samuel and Sarah. *The Complete Servant.* Knight & Lacey, 1825.

Aitken, James (ed.). *English Diaries XVI, XVII, XVIII Centuries.* Pelican Books, 1941.

Archenholz, Johann W. von. *A Picture of England.* . . . Dublin, 1791.

Ashton, John. (ed.). *Chap-books of the Eighteenth Century.* Chatto & Windus, 1882.

Ashton, John (ed.). *Real Sailor – Songs.* Leadenhall Press, 1891.

Ashton, John. *Old Times.* . . . Nimmo, 1885.

Ashton, John. *Social Life in the Reign of Queen Anne.* Chatto & Windus, 1882.

Babee's Book etc., The, ed. F. J. Furnivall, E.E.T.S., Ed. 1868 and Ed. 1931 under title: *Early English Meals & Manners.* See also Rickert, E.

Bagley, J. J. *Life in Medieval England.* Batsford, 1960.

Bailey, Nathan. *An Universal Etymological English Dictionary.* C. Hitch; C. Davis, 6th Ed., 1733.

Baldry, George. *The Rabbit Skin Cap*, ed. L. Rider Haggard. 2nd Ed. Collins, 1950.

Barker, T. C. and Robbins, M. *A History of London Transport*. Vol. I. Allen & Unwin, 1963.

Best, H. *See* Robinson, C. B.

Blackstone, G. V. *A History of the British Fire Service*. Routledge & Kegan Paul, 1957.

Bond, Francis. *Wood-Carving in English Churches*. Vol. I, Misericords. 1st Ed. 1907.

Bovill, E. W. *English Country Life, 1780–1830*. Oxford University Press, 1962.

Boyd, R. Nelson. *Coal Pits and Pitmen*. Whittaker, 1832.

Browne, Douglas. *The Rise of Scotland Yard*. Harrap, 1956.

Burke, T. *Travel in England*. Batsford, 1949.

Busby, T. L. *Costume of the Lower Orders of London*. Baldwin, 1820.

Busby, T. L. *Costume of the Lower Orders of the Metropolis*. T. L. Busby, 1835.

Byrne, M. St. Clare. *Elizabethan Life in Town & Country*. Universal Paperbacks Ed. 1961.

Chaucer, Geoffrey. *The Complete Works of Geoffrey Chaucer*, ed. W. W. Skeat. Oxford, Clarendon Press, 1894.

Churchyard, Thomas. *Churchyardes Chippes*. Printed by Thomas Marshe, 1578.

Coate, Mary. *Social Life in Stuart England*. Methuen, 1924.

Cobbett, Wm. *Rural Rides . . .*, ed. P. Cobbett. Reeves & Turner, 1893.

Coghlan, F. *The Iron Road Book*. . . . Baily, 1838.

Commenius, J. A. (Komensky). *Visible World*. . . . Trans. C. Hoole. Kirton, Ed. 1664 and 12th Ed. 1777.

Conder, Edward (ed.). *Records of the hole crafte and fellowship of Masons*. . . . Swan, Sonnenschein, 1894.

Corbett, M. and Norton, M. *Engraving in England—XVI & XVII Centuries*. Cambridge University Press. 1964.

Costume of Yorkshire. Leeds, Robinson, 1814.

Courtesy Book, A Fifteenth Century, ed. R. W. Chambers. E.E.T.S. 1914.

Couts, J. *Practical Guide for the Tailor's Cutting Room*. Glasgow, Blackie [1848].

Cryes of the City of London, see Tempest.

Cunnington, C. W. and P.E., and C. Beard. *Dictionary of English Costume, 900–1900*. A & C. Black, 1960.

Cunnington, C. W. and P. *Handbook of English Medieval Costume*. Faber, 1960.

Cunnington, C. W. and P. *Handbook of English Costume in the 16th century*. Faber, 1962.

Cunnington, C. W. and P. *Handbook of English Costume in the 17th century*. Faber, 2nd Ed., 1967.

Cunnington, C. W. and P. *Handbook of English Costume in the 18th century*. Faber 2nd Ed., 1964.

Cunnington, C. W. and P. *Handbook of English Costume in the 19th century.* Faber 1959.

Defoe, Daniel (pseudonym "Andrew Moreton"). *Everybody's Business is Nobody's Business.* Warner, 1725.

Defoe, Daniel. *A Tour Through the Whole Island of Great Britain.* 1st Ed. 1724. Ed. Dent, 1962.

Devlin, James. *The Shoemaker.* Knight, 1839.

Dickens, Admiral Sir Gerald. *The Dress of the British Sailor.* H.M.S.O., 1957.

Dickens, Charles. *Sketches by Boz.* Macrone, 1833–5.

Dickens, Charles. *Novels.*

Dodd, George. *Textile Manufactures of Great Britain.* Knight, 1844.

Dodd, George. *British Manufactures. Series II – VI.* Knight, 1844–6.

Dodsley, Robert. *The Footman's Friendly Advice. . . .* Worrall, 1731.

Dodsley, Robert. *A Muse in Livery.* Dodsley, 1732.

Dodsley, Robert. *A Select Collection of Old English Plays* originally published by Robert Dodsley. Ed. G. Carew Hazlitt. Reeves & Turner, 1874.

Domestic Life in England. . . . By Editor of *Family Manual. . . .* Tegg, 1835.

Dowie, James. *The Foot and Its Covering.* Hardwicke, 1861.

Drew, Bernard. *The Fire Office. . . .* Essex and Suffolk Equitable Insurance Society, 1952.

Edwards, A. C. *English History from Essex Sources, 1550–1750.* Essex Record Office, 1952.

Egan, Pierce. *Tom and Jerry—Life in London.* Hotton, 1869. (1st Ed. 1821.)

Egan, Pierce. *Finish to the Adventures of Tom, Jerry and Logic. . . .* Reeves, 1887. (1st Ed. 1828.)

Ellis, C. Hamilton. *Popular Carriage.* Brit. Transport Commission, 1962.

Emmison, F. G. *Tudor Secretary. . . .* Longmans, 1961.

Eulogium Historiarum . . . ad Anno Domini 1366, ed. F. S. Haydon. Longmans, Green, 1863.

Evans, George Ewart. *Ask The Fellows Who Cut The Hay.* Faber, 2nd Ed. 1965.

Fairholt, F. W. (ed.) *Satirical Songs and Poems on Costume. . . .* Percy Society, 1849.

Fairholt, F. W. *Costume in England.* 4th Ed. Dillon, 1885. (1st Ed. 1846.)

Fitzherbert, John. (?) [Also attr. to Sir A.] *Booke of Husbandry.* Ed. 1525? and Awdely, 1568.

Forrester, Alfred. (pseudonym "Crowquill") *Seymour's Humorous Sketches.* Routledge, 1838.

Fuller, John. *Chef's Manual of Kitchen Management.* Batsford, 2nd Ed. 1966.

Fussell, G. E. and K. R. *The English Countryman.* Melrose, 1955.

Fussell, G. E. and K. R. *The English Countrywoman.* Melrose, 1953.

Fussell, G. E. *The English Rural Labourer. . . .* Batchworth Press, 1949.

Garment Making—Part III. Williamson (nineteenth century, undated.)

Glossographia anglicana. . . . Isaac Newton, Blunt, *et al.* Dan. Brown etc., 1707.

Goddard, Henry. *Memoirs of a Bow Street Runner.* Museum Press, 1956.

Goldsmith-Carter, G. *Sailors, Sailors.* Hamlyn, 1966.

Gray, Mrs Edwin. *Papers & Diaries of a York Family, 1764–1839.* Sheldon Press, 1927.

Great Western Railway. *Standard List of Uniform Clothing.* 1907.

Grinling, C. H. *The Ways of our Railways.* Ward, Lock, 1911.

H., N. (Merchant in the City of London). *The Complete Tradesman.* Dunton, 1684.

Hadfield, Miles. *Gardening in Britain.* Hutchinson, 1960.

Halstead, W. S. *Surgical Papers.* Baltimore, 1924.

Hammond, J. L. and L. Barbara. *The Village Labourer, 1760–1832.* . . . Longmans, Green, 4th Ed. 1927.

Hammond, J. L. and L. Barbara. *The Town Labourer, 1760–1832.* . . . Longmans, Green, new Ed. 1925.

Hammond, J. L. and L. Barbara. *The Skilled Labourer, 1760–1832.* Longmans, Green, 2nd Ed. 1920.

Hanway, Jonas. *Journal of Eight Days' Journey.* Woodfall & Henderson, 1847.

Hardy, Thomas. *Under the Greenwood Tree.* (Chatto & Windus, 1872) and other novels.

Hare, Augustus J. C. *The Gurneys of Earlham.* Allen, 1895.

Harrison, Molly and Royston O. *How They Lived (Vol. II), 1485–1700.* Oxford, Blackwell, 1963.

Harrison, W. *Harrison's Description of England in Shakespeare's Youth,* ed. F. J. Furnivall, etc. New Shakspere Society, 1877–1908.

Hartshorne, Charles H. *Ancient Metrical Tales.* Pickering, 1829.

Hassall, W. O. *How They Lived. (Vol. I.) 55 B.C.—1485 A.D.* Oxford, Blackwell,, 1962.

Haydon, A. L. *The Book of the Fire-Brigade.* Pilgrim Press, 1912.

Heads of the People. See Meadows.

Heath, Richard. *The English Peasant.* Fisher Unwin, 1893.

Hecht, J. Jean. *The Domestic Class in 18th Century England.* Routledge & Kegan Paul, 1956.

Herbert, Williams. *History of the Twelve Great Livery Companies.* Published by the author, 1837.

Heywood, John. *The Spider and the Flie.* 1st Ed. Tho. Powell, 1556.

Hind, Arthur. *Engraving in England, Parts I & II.* Cambridge U. P., 1952. (For *Part III* see Corbett, M. and Norton, M.)

Hindley, C. L. *A History of the Cries of London.* Hindley, 2nd Ed. 1884.

Hole, Christina. *English Home Life, 1500–1800.* Batsford, 1947.

Holme, Randle. *Academy of Armory or a Store-house of Armory and Blazon.* Holme, 1688.

Hone, William. *Table Book.* Thomas Tegg, 1830.

Howard, George (i.e. F. George Kay). *Guardians of the Queen's Peace.* Odhams Press, 1953.

Howard Household Books (1) *Manners and Household Expenses . . .* [years 1462-69] ed. B. Botfield. (Roxburghe Club, 1841). (2) *Household Books of John Duke of Norfolk . . .* [years 1481–90] ed. J. P. Collier (Roxburghe Club, 1844–5).

Howitt, William. *Book of the Seasons.* Colburn & Bentley, 1831. 9th Ed. 1851.

Hull, William. *History of the Glove Trade.* E. Wilson, 1834.

Jackson, Mason. *The Pictorial Press . . . 1588–1885.* Hurst & Blackett, 1885.

Jarrett, Dudley. *British Naval Dress.* Dent, 1961.

Jenkin, A. K. Hamilton. *The Cornish Miner.* Allen & Unwin, 3rd Ed. 1962.

Judges, A. V. (ed.) *The Elizabethan Underworld.* Routledge & Kegan Paul, 2nd Ed. 1965.

Jupp, E. B. *An Historical Account of the Worshipful Company of Carpenters of the City of London.* 2nd Ed. Pickering & Chatto, 1887.

Kalm, Pehr. *Account of his Visit to England. . . .* Trans. J. Lucas. Macmillan, 1892. (1st Ed. 1753.)

Kay, F. George. *Royal Mail.* Rockliff Publishing Corporation, 1951.

Kilvert, F. *Kilvert's Diary, 1870–1879,* ed. Wm. Plomer, Jonathan Cape, 1944.

Lanceley, Wm. *From Hall-boy to House Steward.* Arnold, 1925.

Lant, Thomas. *Funeral Procession of Sir Phillip Sidney,* engraved after T. Lant, 1588.

Lee, Charles E. *The Horse Bus as a Vehicle.* Brit. Transport Commission, 1962.

London and North Eastern Railway. *Clothing Regulations,* 1905

M[arkham], G[ervase]. *A Way to Get Wealth. Book VI. A New Orchard and Garden,* by Wm. Lawson. 2nd Ed. J. Harison, 1638.

MacCausland, H. *The English Carriage.* Batchworth, 1948

Mayhew Brothers, [H. and A.]. *The Greatest Plague of Life. . . .* Bogue, 1847.

Mayhew, Henry. *London Labour and the London Poor.* Bohn, 1861–2.

Mayhew, Henry and others. *London Characters.* Chatto & Windus, 1874.

McKisack, May. *Oxford History of England, 14th Century. 1307–1399.* Oxford, Clarendon Press, 1939.

Meadows, Joseph K. *Heads of the People. . . .* Drawn by Kenny Meadows. Tyas, 1841.

Merryweather, J. C. *The Fire Brigade Handbook.* Merritt & Hatcher, 1888.

M. Misson's Memoirs and Observations in his Travels over England. . . . Trans. John Ozell. Browne etc., 1719.

Monro, I. S. and Cook, D. E. *Costume Index*—a subject index. . . . New York. Wilson, 1937.

Morris, O. J. *Grandfather's London*. Putnam. 2nd Ed. 1961.

Morten, Honnor. *How to become a Nurse*. Scientific Press. 3rd Ed. 1895.

Moule, Thomas. *Bibliotheca Heraldica*. . . . Lackington, 1822.

Nutting, M. A. and Dock L. L. *A History of Nursing*. Putnam, 1907.

O'Keef(f)e, John. *Recollections of the Life* of John O'Keefe written by himself. Colburn, 1826.

O'Keefe, John. *Tony Lumpkin in Town*. Cadell, 1780.

Parliamentary Papers, 1842, Nos. 380, 382 (in Vols. XV and XVII). *Report of Royal Commission on Employment of Children* (*Mines*).

Paston, George. *Social Caricature in the Eighteenth Century*. Methuen, 1905.

Paston Letters, ed. John Fenn, re-ed. A. Ramsay. Knight, 1840.

Pearson, Lu E. *Elizabethans at Home*. Stamford University Press, California, 1957.

Pepys, Samuel. *Diary, 1660–1669*. Dent (Everyman's Ed.), 1954.

Phillips, Margaret and Tompkinson, Wm. *English Women in Life and Letters*. Oxford University Press, 1926.

Phillips, Sir Richard. *Modern London*. R. Phillips, 1805.

Post Office Uniforms. See Raynham.

Purefoy Letters, 1735–1753 ed. George Eland. Sidgwick, 1931.

Pyne, W. H. *Costume of Great Britain*, written drawn and engraved by W. H. Pyne. Miller, 1808.

Pyne, W. H. *Microcosm*. Pyne & Nattes, 1803–6.

Pyne, W. H. *Rustic Figures*. Ackermann, 1813.

Pyne, W. H. *The World in Miniature*. Ackermann, 1827.

Raistrick, Arthur. *Mines & Miners of Swaledale*. Clapham, Yorks. Dalesman, 1955.

Raynham, F. J. and Calvert, W. S. *Post Office Uniforms*. P.O. Green Paper 27A, 1936.

Rickert, Edith. *The Babee's Book—Medieval Manners for the Young, Done into Modern English*. New York, 1908.

Rickert, Edith (compiled by). *Chaucer's World*. Oxford University Press, 1948.

Rickert, Margaret. *Painting in Britain : the Middle Ages*. Penguin Books, 1954.

Riley, Henry. *Memorials of London Life . . . 1270–1419*. Longmans, 1868.

Robinson, C. B. (ed.). *Rural Economy in Yorkshire in 1641 . . . Account Books of Henry Best*. Durham, Andrews, 1857.

Robinson, Howard. *Britain's Post Office* . . . .Oxford University Press, 1953.

Rollins, H. E. (ed.). *A Pepysian Garland . . . Ballads of 1595–1639*. . . . Cambridge University Press, 1922.

Rowlandson, Thomas. *Rowlandson's Characteristic Sketches of the Lower Orders*. Leigh, 1823.

Roxburghe Ballads, ed. Chappell, W. (9 Volumes). Ballad Society, 1869, etc.

Rural Industries Bureau. *The Thatcher's Craft*. 1961.

Saxl, F. and Meier, H. *Catalogue of Astrological & Mythological Illuminated MSS. of the Latin Middle Ages*, Part III. Warburg Institute, 1953.

Sekon, G. A. *Locomotion in Victorian London*. Oxford University Press, 1938.

Souvenir of the Cookery Annual . . . ed. C. Herman Senn. Food & Cookery Publishing Agency, 1907.

Seymour, R. See Forrester, A.

Seymer, Lucy R. *General History of Nursing*. 3rd Ed. Faber, 1954.

Shoppee, C. J. *Description of Pictures . . . in the Hall . . . of the Worshipful Company of Barbers*. G. Barber, 1883.

Smith, John Thomas. *The Cries of London*. Nichols, 1839.

Smith, Albert and Reach, Angus B. (ed.). *The Man in the Moon*. Clarke, 1847-8.

Smith, Albert (ed.). *Sketches of London Life and Character*. Dean, 1859.

Smollett, Tobias. *The Exhibition of Humphry Clinker*. Hutchinson, 1905. (1st Ed. 1771.) and other novels.

Smyth, C. P. *Sailor's Wordbook*. Blackie, 1867.

Spenser, Edmund. *The Shepheardes Calendar*. Singleton, 1579.

Steer, F. W. (ed.). *Farm and Cottage Inventories of Mid-Essex, 1635-1749*. Chelmsford. Essex Record Office, 1950.

Stephens, Henry. *Book of the Farm*. 3rd Ed. Edinburgh, Blackwood, 1871.

Stow, John. *A Survey of London*, ed. C. L. Kingsford. Oxford, Clarendon Press, 1952; ed. J. Strype, 1720. (1st ed. 1598.)

Strutt, Joseph. *Manners and Customs of the English*, etc. Published by himself, 1775

Strutt, Joseph. *Dress and Habits of the People of England*. . . . ed. Planché, 1842 (1st Ed. 1796).

Stuart, Dorothy Margaret. *The English Abigail*. Macmillan, 1946.

Stubbs, S. G. B. and Bligh, E. W. *Sixty Centuries of Health and Physick*. Sampson Low, 1931.

Surtees, R. S. *Jorrocks' Jaunts and Jollities*, (with coloured Plates by H. Alken). Folio Society, 1949. (1st Ed. 1831-4). Also other novels.

Tempest, P. (publisher). *Cryes of the City of London*: engravings after M. Lauron. 1st full Ed. 1689; similar Ed. 1711. (Modified Ed. by Sayer, *c.* 1750.)

Textile Terms, Glossary of. Manchester, Marsden, 1921.

Thompson, Flora. *Lark Rise to Candleford*. (A trilogy.) Oxford University Press, 1945.

Thompson, Charles J. S. *The Quacks of Old London*. Brentano's, 1928.

Thompson, Gladys Scott. *The Russells in Bloomsbury, 1669-1771*. Jonathan Cape, 1940.

Thynn(e), Francis (doubtfully attributed). *Debate between Pride and Lowliness*, ed. J. P. Collier. Shakespeare Society, 1841. (1st Ed. *c.*1568.)

Tomlinson, Charles. *See* Trades.

Trades, Books of:
  Book of Trades . . . or . . . Library of the Useful Arts. Tabart, 1804–5; Phillips, 1811
    etc.; enlarged, under title:
  Book of English Trades. Phillips, 1824; Rivington, 1827.
  Book of Trades or Circle of the Useful Arts. Glasgow, Griffin, 1835.
  Complete Book of Trades. . . . by Whittock, Bennett, etc. Tegg, 1842.
  Illustrations of Trades by Charles Tomlinson. S. P. C. K. 1856.
  Little Jack of All Trades. . . . by W. Darton. Darton & Harvey, 1806.
  Panoramic Alphabet of Trades. Darton, 1856.
Trevelyan, G. M. *Illustrated English Social History.* Longmans, Green, 1949.
Turbervile, George. *Booke of Faulconrie. . . .* Barker, 1575.
Turbervile, George (trans.) *Noble Arte of Venerie or Hunting.* Barker (?1575).
Thomas Tusser, ed. Hartley, Dorothy. Country Life, 1931.
Unwin, George. *Gilds and Companies of London.* Allen & Unwin, 1908.
Vale, Henry Edmund T. *The Mail-Coach Men of the late 18th Century.* Cassell 1960.
Vecellio, Cesare. *Habiti Antichi et Modernie.* Venice, 1598.
Whitbread, J. R. *The Railway Policeman.* Harrap, 1961.
Whitbread's, The Story of. Whitbread & Co. (published by). 3rd Ed. 1964.
Whitteridge, G. and Stokes, V. *A brief History of the Hospital of St. Bartholomew.*
    Governors of the Hospital, 1961.
White, R. J. *Life in Regency England.* Batsford, 1963.
Williams, Ernest N. *Life in Georgian England.* Batsford, 1962.
Willis, Frederick. *Book of London Yesterdays.* Phoenix House, 1960.
Wolley, Hannah (?). *The Compleat Serving Maid.* Passinger, 1685. (1st Ed. 1677.)
Wolley, Hannah. *The Gentlewoman's Companion.* Thomas, 1675.
Wood, J. and R. (Publishers). *Catalogue of Printing Types. c.* 1855–1879.
Wright, Thomas. *A History of Caricature and Grotesque.* Virtue, 1865.
Wright, Thomas. *Romance of the Shoe.* Farncombe, 1922.
Young, Arthur, *Six Weeks Tour. . . .* 2nd Ed. 1769. (1st Ed. 1768.)
Young, Francis Brett. *Dr. Bradley Remembers.* Heinemann, 1938.
Young, Sidney (ed.). *Annals of the Barber-Surgeons of London.* Blades, East & Blades,
    1890.

Periodicals

Farmer's Magazine, 1832–1874.
Fireman, 1880–1.
Gentleman's Magazine, 1731–1833.
Graphic, 1869–.
Illustrated London News, 1843–.
London Chronicle, 1757–1823.

Notes and Queries, 1850–.
Punch, 1841–.
Tailor and Cutter, 1867–.
Universal Magazine, 1747–1814.
Folk Life."The Countryman's Smock", by Anne Buck, in Vol. I (1963).

Museums

The following museums have specimens or pictures illustrative of occupational costume:
Alton—Curtis Museum
Cambridge and County Folk Museum
Cardiff Welsh Folk Museum
Colchester—Holly Trees
Exeter—Royal Albert Memorial Museum
Hereford—City Library, Museum and Art Gallery
Ipswich—Christchurch Mansion
Leicester—City Museum & Art Gallery
Leeds—City Museum
London—British Museum
          British Railway Transport
          Hogarth House, Chiswick
          Industrial Health and Safety Centre
          London Museum
          National Maritime, Greenwich
          Tottenham Corporation Postal Museum
          Victoria and Albert
Luton—Museum and Art Gallery
Manchester—Gallery of English Costume, Platt Hall
Manx Museum, Douglas, I.O.M.
Northampton—Central Museum
Norwich—Bridewell, Museum of Local Industries and Rural Crafts
          Strangers' Hall Museum of Domestic Life
Reading—Museum of English Rural Life
Saffron Walden Museum
Salisbury—S. Wilts. and Blackmore
Shaftesbury—Local History Museum
York—Castle Museum
          Railway Museum

SOURCES OF FIGURES

Figures which directly reproduce original prints or drawings are marked with an asterisk. All others are from tracings made from the sources stated.

Where the names of publishers are not given, these may be found in the Bibliography.

Abbreviation: B.M. = British Museum.

CHAPTER I

1 B.M. MS. Cot. Tiberius B.V. (Saxon Calendar). 11th Century.
2 Ibid.
3 B.M. MS. Add. 42130. *c.* 1340.
4 B.M. MS. Cot. Nero D.1 by Matthew Paris. *c.* 1320–59.
5 B.M. MS. Add. 42130. *c.* 1340.
6 B.M. MS. Add. 47682 (Holkham Bible Picture Book). *c.* 1330.
7 Fitzwilliam Museum, Cambridge. MS. 370. *c.* 1280.
8 B.M. MS. Harl. 2332. 1400–10.
9 Detail of engraving in *Boke of Husbandrye* by J. Fitzherbert. *c.* 1525.
10 Woodcut in *Shepheardes Calendar* by Edmund Spenser. 1579. (Detail.)
11 *Woodcut in *The Orchard and the Garden*, London, Islip, 1954.
12 Engraving in Tract No. 188, Thomason Collection, Vol. II. B.M. 1642.
13 Woodcut in *Roxburghe Ballads* (Original broadsheets) Vol. II, 308. B.M. 17th Century.
14 Engraving in *A New Instuction* [sic] *of Plowing* by E. Maxey. 1601.
15 17th Century woodcut "The Great Boobee", reproduced in *A Century of Ballads* by J. Ashton. 1887.
16 *Engraving in *Academy of Armory* . . . by R. Holme. 1688.
17 *Ibid.
18 W. H. Pyne, *Microcosm.* 1803–7.
19 Aquatint by J. Bailey after J. L. Agasse—"Stage Waggon" (detail). 1820.
20 W. H. Pyne, *Microcosm.* 1803–7.
21 G. Cruikshank—Illustration to Dickens's *Pickwick Papers* (detail). 1836–7.
22 Drawing in *The Graphic.* 1870.
23 *Lambeth Bible* MS., Lambeth Palace. (Detail of miniature.) *c.* 1150.
24 B.M. MS. Add. 42130 (*Luttrell Psalter*). *c.* 1340.
25 B.M. MS. Roy. 2 B.VII. *c.* 1320.
26 *Engraving by W. Hollar in *Ornatus Muliebris Anglicanus.* 1640.

27 Woodcut *c.* 1640 reproduced in *Roxburghe Ballads,* edited by C. Hindley. 1874. Vol. II.

28 Woodcut *c.* 1670–80, *Roxburghe Ballads* (Original broadsheets) Vol. II, 347. B.M.

29 17th Century woodcut reproduced in *Chapbooks of the 18th Century* by J. Ashton. 1882.

30 Engraving after G. Walker. *Costume of Yorkshire.* 1814.

CHAPTER II

31 13th Century *Bestiary,* University Library, Cambridge, MS. I. i.4.26.
32 Andrew Boorde, *First Book of Knowledge.* 1547.
33 Cesare Vecellio, *Habiti Antichi e Moderni* (Venice), 1598.
34 *Fishmongers' Pageant on Lord Mayor's Day, 1616.* (Guildhall Library.)
35 Etching in B.M. 1737.
36 W. H. Pyne, *Costume of Great Britain.* 1808.
37 *The Book of English Trades,* edition 1827. Published by R. Phillips.
38 C. Keene, *Punch*—(a) 1862, (b) 1876. (Details.)
39 *The World in Miniature,* edited by W. H. Pyne. 1827.
40 *Punch,* September 29th, 1866. (Detail.)

CHAPTER III

41 17th Century drawing reproduced in *A History of Technology* by C. Singer *et al.* Oxford; Clarendon Press, 1958.
42 See Bibliography: Parliamentary Papers, 1842.
43 Detail from illustration in *Mines and Miners or Underground Life* by L. Simonin, translated, adapted and edited by H. W. Bristow. London, 1869.
44 *Engraving after M. Lauron in *Cryes of the City of London,* Tempest, 1689.
45 Engraving in *World in Miniature* edited by W. H. Pyne. 1827.
46 T. L. Busby, *Costume of the Lower Orders of the Metropolis.* 1835.
47 *Sketches of London Life and Character* edited by Albert Smith. 1859.
48 *Roxburghe Ballads* (Original broadsheets) II, No. 383. Early 17th Century. B.M.
49 *Punch*—(a) J. Leech, 1846, (b) C. Keene, 1861. (Details.)

CHAPTER IV

50 B.M. MS. Claudius B.IV. 11th Century.
51 B.M. MS. Royal 10 E.IV (detail). Early 14th Century.
52 Engraving (1698) reproduced in *English Costume* by C. W. Fairholt. Ed. 1896.

53 Engraving in *Academy of Armory* by R. Holme. 1688.
54 Ibid.
55 W. H. Pyne, *Microcosm*. 1803–7.
56 Ibid.
57 *The Complete Book of Trades* by Whittock, Bennett and Badcock. 1842.
58 C. Keene, *Punch*. 1867. (Detail.)
59 C. Keene, *Punch*. 1878.
60 (a) Drawing by J. Tenniel in *Alice Through the Looking Glass* by Lewis Carroll. 1872.
   (b) "Happy Families" (Playing-cards). *c.* 1860.
61 ★Wood's Catalogue of Printing Types, *c.* 1860, kindly lent by Mr. A. A. Wolpe.
62 *Illustrated London News*. 1842.
63 Illustration in G. Dodd's *British Manufactures*. Ser. VI. (1846.)
64 Political Cartoons by J. Tenniel, 1863. *Punch*, XLIV, 263 and XLV, 99. (Details.)
65 Drawing by J. Barnard in *David Copperfield* by C. Dickens. 1849–50.
66 B.M. MS. Cotton Nero D.I. (1220–59.)
67 Trinity College Dublin, MS. E.I.40 *Life of St. Alban*. 13th Century.
68 B.M. MS. Egerton, 1894 (*Genesis*). *c.* 1360.
69 ★Woodcut from *The Game and Playe of the Chesse*, translated by William Caxton. 1483. B.M.
70 Detail from panel of the Legend of St. Etheldreda. By courtesy of the Society of Antiquaries. *c.* 1425.
71 R. Holme, *Academy of Armory*. 1688.
72 W. H. Pyne, *Microcosm*. 1803–7.
73 ★*Book of English Trades and Library of Useful Arts,* 12th edition. Published by R. Phillips. 1824.
74 B.M. MS. Add. 47682, *Holkham Bible Picture Book*. *c.* 1330.
75 *Roxburghe Ballad* "In Praise of the Blacksmith" (Original broadsheet.) *c.* 1661. B.M.
76 Painting on a Worcester vase reproduced in *Coloured Worcester Porcelain of the First Period* by H. Rissik Marshall. 1959.
77 W. H. Pyne, *Microcosm*. 1803–7. (Detail.)
78 Ibid.
79 *Punch* XIII, 160. (Detail.) 1847.
80 B.M. MS. Roy. 2 B.VII (*Queen Mary's Psalter*). *c.* 1320.
81 B.M. MS. Roy. 10 E.IV. Early 14th Century.
82 Tubal-Cain's sister. B.M. MS. Egerton, 1894. *c.* 1360.
83 ★Tract printed at London for Thomas Lambert. 1636.

84　Engraving after G. Walker in *Costume of Yorkshire*. 1814.
85　Engraving after W. Hogarth, "The Rake's Progress, I". (Detail.) 1735.

CHAPTER V

86　B.M. MS. Cot. Nero C.IV. *c.* 1150–60.
87　*Roxburghe Ballads* (Original broadsheets.) Vol. III. "The Lamentable Complaints of Hop the Brewer and Kilcalf the Butcher", 1641. B.M.
88　W. H. Pyne, *Microcosm*. "Cottage Group". (Detail.) 1803–7.
89　R. Dighton, "A Pleasant way to lose an Eye". 1824.
90　Illustration by G. Cruikshank in *The Finish to Adventures of Tom and Jerry* by P. Egan. 1828.
91　*J. Leech, *Punch*. 1851.
92　J. B. Partridge, *Punch*. 1893. (Detail.)
93　Catalogue, 1909–12, kindly lent by Messrs. G. Rushbrooke (Smithfield) Ltd.
94　B.M. MS. Roy. 10 E.IV. Early 14th Century.
95　*Engraving in *Noble Arte of Venerie* . . . Translated by G. Turbervile. 1575(?). (Detail.)
96　*Engravings in *Academy of Armory* . . . by R. Holme, 1688.
97　Engraving after M. Lauron in *Cryes of the City of London*. 1689.
98　*Book of Trades and Library of the Useful Arts,* published by R. Phillips, edition 1811.
99　Coloured engraving by W. Craig in *Modern London* by R. Phillips, 1805. (Detail.)
100　Sketch by G. Scharf I. (Detail.) 1850. B.M.
101　Caricature by Hine in *Man in the Moon*, edited by Albert Smith & A. Reach. Vol. I. (1847.)
102　*The Chef*, Vol. II, No. 33. (1896.)
103　Advertisement, John Peck & Co., Liverpool. 1905.
104　*Catalogue, 1906 (reprinted 1912), kindly lent by Messrs. John Peck, Liverpool.
105　B.M. MS. Claudius B.IV. 11th Century.
106　B.M. MS. Roy. 2 B.VII. (*Queen Mary's Psalter*.) *c.* 1320.
107　B.M. MS. Roy. 10 E.IV. Early 14th Century.
108　Misericord. All Hallows Church, Wellingborough, Northants. (after Thomas Wright).
109　*Roxburghe Ballads*, edited by C. Hindley. Vol. I. (1873.)
110　J. Ashton, (Ed.) *Chapbooks of the Eighteenth Century*. 1882.
111　*Book of English Trades and Library of Useful Arts*. Published by R. Phillips. 12th Edition. 1824.
112　W. H. Pyne, *Costume of Great Britain*. 1808.
113　T. L. Busby, *Costume of the Lower Orders of London*. 1820.

114 Lithograph by Day. Published by Ackermann, 1855.
115 Print by E. Buckman: "The Brewer's Drayman". 1871–73.
116 *Woodcut, one of 32 *Cries of London. c.* 1640. B.M. (See M. Corbett & M. Norton, *Engraving in England*, III, item 83.)
117 (a) B.M. MS. Add. 42130. *c.* 1340.
     *(b) R. Holme, *Academy of Armoury.* 1688.
118 Engraving after M. Lauron in *Cryes of the City of London.* 1689.
119 Engraving (from photo) in *London Labour and the London Poor* by H. Mayhew. Edition 1865.
120 *Engraving after M. Lauron in *Cryes of the City of London.* 1689.
121 Paul Sandby, *Cries of London.* 1759.
122 K. Meadows in *Heads of the People.* 1841.
123 Engraving (from photo) in *London Labour and the London Poor* by H. Mayhew. Edition 1865.
124 Engraving after G. Walker in *Costume of Yorkshire.* 1814.

CHAPTER VI

125 B.M. MS. Egerton, 1894. *c.* 1360.
126 MS. 775. Pierpont Morgan Library. *c.* 1470.
127 B.M. MS. Roy. 6 E.VI. *c.* 1330.
128 K. Meadows in *Heads of the People.* 1841.
129 B.M. MS. Add. 42130 (*Luttrell Psalter*). *c.* 1340.
130 B.M. MS. Cot. Nero C.IV. *c.* 1150–60.
131 B.M. MS. Add. 42130 (*Luttrell Psalter*). *c.* 1340.
132 Trinity College, Dublin, MS. E.1.40. 13th Century.
133 Engraving in *Booke of Faulconerie* . . . by G. Turbervile. (Detail.) 1575.
134 Engraving by T. de Bry after T. Lant in *Funeral Procession of Sir Phillip Sidney.* 1588.
135 *Engraving in *Noble Arte of Venerie* . . . Translated by G. Turbervile. 1575(?).
136 *Woodcut in *Academy of Armory* by R. Holme. 1688.
137 17th Century woodcut reproduced in *Roxburghe Ballads*, edited by C. Hindley. Vol. I. (1873.)
138 *Engraving by W. Hogarth. *Industry & Idleness VI.* (Detail.) 1747.
139 Caricature by W. Heath. 1812.
140 *C. Keene, *Punch.* 1879. (Detail.)
141 *Coloured print after drawing by W. M. Thackeray for his *Mrs. Perkins's Ball.* 1847.
142 (a) Drawing after B. Wilson's *Portrait of Francis Fountayn*. Temple Newsam House, Leeds. 1770–80.

(b) After drawing by R. Doyle, senior, 1831. Both by courtesy of Messrs. Faber & Faber.

143 *J. Leech, *Punch.* 1857.

144 *G. du Maurier. "The Height of Magnificence" (detail). *Punch.* 1880.

145 *C. Keene, *Punch.* 1869.

146 G. du Maurier, *Punch.* 1883.

147 *G. Cruikshank. Illustration in *The Greatest Plague* . . . by bros. Mayhew 1847.

148 J. F. Herring, "Harnessed Carriage Horse" (detail). Walker Art Gallery, Liverpool. *c.* 1840s.

149 Illustration in *Hone's Everyday Book II.* (1828.)

150 J. Leech, *Punch.* 1848.

CHAPTER VII

151 B.M. MS. Add. 42130 (*Luttrell Psalter*). *c.* 1340.

152 J. Highmore, illustration to *Pamela* by S. Richardson. 1745.

153 J. Gillray, "The Stays". 1810.

154 B.M. MS. Roy. 10 E.IV. Early 14th Century.

155 B.M. MS. Add. 47682 (*Holkham Bible Picture Book*). *c.* 1330.

156 Engraving in *The Spider and the Flie* by J. Heywood. 1556.

157 Portrait by unknown British artist. (Lady Hart Dyke Collection.) *c.* 1625–30.

158 Caricature by C. Williams, "The Titsworth Frolic" (detail). 1804.

159 Hand-coloured print after G. Woodward, "A Sudden Emotion" (detail). 1804.

160 Cartoon: "Robertina Peelena Maid-of-all-Work" by W. Heath. (Detail.) *c.* 1829.

161 W. Heath. *c.* 1829.

162 G. Cruikshank in Dickens's *Pickwick Papers.* 1836–7.

163 Drawing by W. M. Thackeray in his *Christmas Book, Our Street.* 1848.

164 *Punch* XLV. "Servantgalism" (detail). 1863.

165 *Wood's Catalogue of Printing Types. *c.* 1860.

166 *Advertisement in *Cassell's Shilling Cookery.* 1890.

167 *Gordon Browne, *Punch.* 1899.

168 Illustration in Catalogue, Messrs. John Peck, Liverpool. 1910–12.

169 Photo: supplied by Radio Times Hulton Picture Library. 1892. (Detail.)

CHAPTER VIII

170 *Punch.* 11th Sept:, 1852. (Detail.)

171 *Our Own Magazine.* 1886.

172 *Chatterbox,* No. XLIII. (1910.)
173 *Illustrated London News.* December 7th, 1844.
174 Engraving (*c.* 1680) reproduced in *Cries of London* by J. T. Smith. 1839.
175 Drawing by C. Khan reproduced in *Social Caricatures in the 18th Century* by G. Paston. (Detail.) 1905.
176 *Mayhew's London,* edited by P. Quennell, Kimber. 1951.
177 *J. Leech, *Punch.* 1861.
178 *Punch.* August 25th, 1866.
179 F. Pigrum, *Punch.* 1904.

CHAPTER IX

180 B.M. MS. Roy. 10 E.IV. Early 14th Century.
181 Original illustration. 1613. By courtesy of H.M. Postmaster General.
182 Woodcut from *The London Post,* January 1647.
183 Engraving by W. Hogarth, "Industry and Idleness IV". 1747. (Detail.)
184 Contemporary illustration reproduced in *Royal Mail* by F. G. Kay. 1951.
185 *Post Office Uniforms* (P.O. Green Paper No. 27A.), 1936.
186 Illustration (1838), reproduced in *Royal Mail* by F. G. Kay. 1951.
187 T. Rowlandson, *Characteristic Sketches of the Lower Orders.* 1823.
188 *Post Office Uniforms* (P.O. Green Paper No. 27A.), 1936.
189 Ibid.
190 Photo: in *Grandfather's London* by O. J. Morris. (2nd edition, 1961.)
191 Photo: by courtesy of H.M. Postmaster General.
192 *Engraving (1821) in Bruce Castle Museum. By courtesy of H.M. Postmaster General.

CHAPTER X

193 *Luttrell Collection. B.M.
194 T. L. Busby, *Costume of the Lower Orders of the Metropolis.* 1835.
195 Political satire on Sir Robert Peel by John Doyle ("H.B."). 1829.
196 J. Tenniel, *Punch.* March 20th, 1869. (Detail.)
197 J. Tenniel, *Punch.* 1869. (Detail.)

CHAPTER XI

198 *Book of English Trades* ... 12th edition, 1824. Published by R. Phillips.
199 *Engraving (1727) by courtesy of Sun Alliance Insurance Group.
200 *Engraving (1735) by courtesy of The Chartered Insurance Institute.
201 T. L. Busby, *Costume of the Lower Orders of London.* 1820.
202 Print (1834) in the collection of the Fire Protection Association. (Detail.)

203 Lithograph by Day. Published by Ackermann. 1855.
204 *The Fireman,* Vol: IV. (1881.)
205 G. V. Blackstone, *A History of the British Fire Service.* 1957.
206 Ibid.
207 *Engineers' and Mechanics' Encyclopaedia.* 1841.

CHAPTER XII

208 "Parish Characters" by Paul Pry (i.e. W. Heath). 1829. Print kindly lent by The Parker Gallery, London, W.1.
209 *Engraving after M. Lauron in *The Cryes of the City of London.* 1689.
210 T. L. Busby, *Costume of the Lower Orders of London.* 1820.
211 Photo: in *Grandfather's London* by O. J. Morris. (2nd edition 1961).
212 Woodcut (*c.* 1670–80) reproduced in *Chapbooks of the 18th Century* edited by John Ashton. 1882.
213 Print after J. McArdell: "Teague's Ramble at Charing Cross". 1747. (Detail.)
214 Print (*c.* 1770) reproduced in *The English Townsman* by T. Burke. 1949.
215 Photo: (1899) by R. Thiele kindly lent by Messrs. Ashton & Mitchell, London.
216 Woodcut in *Academy of Armory* by R. Holme. 1688.
217 Frontispiece to *An Essay in Defence of the Female Sex* by (?) Mary Astell. 1696.
218 Print published by Darley, 1776. (Detail.)
219 Colour-print by Carington Bowles. 1776.
220 *Punch,* June 5th, 1869.

CHAPTER XIII

221 B.M. MS. Add. 42130 (*The Luttrell Psalter*). *c.* 1340.
222 Detail from painting (1541) by Holbein at the Royal College of Surgeons of England.
223 Caricature by I. Cruikshank (detail). 1797.
224 Print (1804).
225 B.M. MS. Harl. 1585. *c.* 1160.
226 (a) and (b) details from Bodleian MS. Ashmole 399. 13th Century.
227 Portrait of Dr. Wm. Gilberd, 1570. Castle Museum, Colchester.
228 Portrait of William Bullein, 1562. Woodcut from *Bulwarke . . . againste . . . sicknes* by W. Bullein.
229 Detail from engraving by T. de Bry after T. Lant in *Funeral Procession of Sir Phillip Sidney.* 1588.
230 Contemporary woodcut of William Cunningham from his *The Cosmographical Glasse.* 1559.

231 Detail from portrait by N. Dance. *c.* 1761.

232 Illustration by Alfred Crowquill in *Seymour's Humorous Sketches. c.* 1834.

233 Advertisement in *British Medical Journal.* 1897.

234 B.M. MS. *Medical Treatise,* Harl. 1585. *c.* 1160.

235 B.M. MS. Roy. 6 E.VI. *c.* 1330–40.

236 Ibid.

237 *Frontispiece to *The Manner of Bissecting the Pestilentiall Body* by A. Thomson. 1666.

238 Catalogue (1905) kindly lent by E. & R. Garrould Ltd., London.

239 Catalogue (1909), kindly lent by John Peck & Co. Ltd., Liverpool.

240 Woodcut in a hand-bill published for Sir William Read. *c.* 1696.

241 Drawing by K. Meadows in *The Heads of the People.* 1841.

242 Detail from a coloured lithograph by C. Philipon. *c.* 1822–3.

243 Drawing in *Histoire des Ordres Monastiques.* (Anon.). Published by J.-B. Coignard, Paris. 1715.

244 Drawing in *A Short History of Nursing* by W. R. Bett. 1960.

245 *The Nursing Record,* December 20th, 1888.

246 Catalogue (1905), kindly lent by E. & R. Garrould Ltd., London.

247 Detail from "Harlot's Progress V". 1732.

248 Caricature by C. Williams: "Sic Transit Gloria" (detail from print).

249 C. Keene, *Punch.* 1871.

250 Drawing (1850) in *A Professional Nurse's Diary,* 1907–8. By courtesy of The Wellcome Trustees.

CHAPTER XIV

251 Detail from woodcut in *The Witch of the Woodlands* by Lawrence Pierce. Edition *c.* 1670.

252 Drawing and engraving (dated 1805) by W. H. Pyne in *Costume of Great Britain.* 1808. (Detail.)

253 *Woodcut in *These Tradesmen are Preachers* . . . a tract in Thomason Collection, B.M. (Detail.)

254 *Engraving in *Textile Manufactures of Great Britain* by G. Dodd. 1844.

255 W. Hogarth's illustration III to *Hudibras.* (Detail.) 1726.

256 "The Effects of Hope". (Detail.) Coloured engraving by I. Cruikshank after G. Woodward.

257 R. Holme, *Academy of Armory.* 1688.

258 G. Turbervile, *Book of Faulconerie.* 1575. (Detail of woodcut, slightly simplified.)

259 Drawing (after a daguerrotype) in *London Labour and the London Poor* by H. Mayhew, Vol. II. (1851.)

260 Portrait reproduced in *Romance of the Shoe* by Thomas Wright. 1922.
261 ★Engraving in *Book of the Farm* by G. H. Stephens. 4th edition. *c.* 1840.
262 Catalogue (1912), Messrs. G. Rushbrooke (Smithfield) Ltd.
263 ★Engraving in *Textile Manufactures of Great Britain* by G. Dodd. 1844.
264 ★Catalogue (20th Century), Messrs. Wallach Brothers Ltd. London.
265 Catalogue (1912), Messrs G. Rushbrooke (Smithfield) Ltd.

CHAPTER XV

266 Engraving after Broitard in *Cryes of the City of London*, published by Sayer. *c.* 1750.
267 Catalogue of Messrs. John Peck & Co. Ltd., Liverpool. 1906.
268 B.M. MS. Add. 42130 (*Luttrell Psalter*). *c.* 1340.
269 Ibid.
270 ★Engraving in *Cryes of the City of London* after M. Lauron. 1689.
271 ★Ibid.
272 ★Engraving in *Noble Arte of Venerie . . .* by G. Turbervile. 1575(?).
273 From a misericord, Gloucester Cathedral, *c.* 1400.
274 ★Woodcut to a 17th Century Ballad, reproduced in a *Pepysian Garland* by H. E. Rollins. 1922.
275 W. H. Pyne, *Microcosm.* 1803–7.
276 Portrait in possession of Messrs. James Smith (Umbrellas) Ltd., London. 1830.
277 ★One of 32 *Cries of London. c.* 1640. (See source of fig. 116.)
278 ★Engraving in *Cryes of the City of London*, after M. Lauron. 1689.
279 B.M. MS. Add. 42130 (*Luttrell Psalter*). *c.* 1340.
280 Engraving by J. T. Smith in *Vagabondiana.* 1839.
281 B.M. MS. Roy. 10 E.IV (early 14th Century).
282 Engraving in *Sketches of London Life and Character* by Albert Smith. 1859.
283 ★"An Election" drawn and engraved by W. Hogarth. (Detail.) 1755–8.
284 Caricature by G. Cruikshank, "The Art of Walking the Streets of London". (Detail.) 1818.
285 Engraving by T. de Bry after T. Lant in *Funeral Procession of Sir Phillip Sidney.* (Detail.) 1588.
286 B.M. MS. Add. 42130 (*Luttrell Psalter*). *c.* 1340.
287 Print after G. Woodward, first published 1804, reprinted in *Woodwards' Humorous Caricatures*, published by Wilson 1821. (Detail.)
288 Cartoon by W. Heath, "The Cobblers Last". 1830.
289 Engraving, after "drawing from the life" by A. Mills, in *Wonderful Science Museum* by R. S. Kirby. 1803.
290 W. Hogarth, "Idle Apprentice Executed at Tyburn". (Detail.) 1747.

291 *Engraving after M. Lauron in *Cryes of the City of London*. 1689.

292 W. H. Pyne, *Microcosm*. 1803–7.

293 Illustration (from a photograph) in *London Labour and the London Poor* by H. Mayhew. 1851.

294 G. Scharf I. Sketches, Vol. II. (B.M.)

295 Illustrations by J. Tenniel in *Alice in Wonderland* by Lewis Carroll. 1860. (Detail.)

296 B.M. MS. Egerton 1894 (*Genesis*). *c.* 1360.

297 B.M. MS. Roy. 10 E.IV (early 14th Century).

298 S. Wale, frontispiece (detail), *Journal of Eight Days Journey* by Mr. H.[anway]. 1757.

299 *Book of English Trades.* . . . Edition 1821. Published by R. Phillips.

INDEX OF AUTHORS QUOTED VERBATIM

Adams, S. and S., 188
Addison, Joseph, 144
Archenholz, J. W. von, 173
Ashton, John, 44, 137
Aubrey, John, 304

Barham, R. H., 52, 189
Boord, Andrew, 55
Braidwood, James, 267
Bulwer, John, 83
Bunyan, John, 234
Burney, Fanny, 373
Byng, Hon. John, 240

Catt, E., 36
Chaucer, Geoffrey, 41, 52, 122, 302, 389
Cibber, Colley, 113
Cobbett, W., 332, 346
Coleman, Terry, 78
Colman, G., 248
Coventry, Francis, 306
Cowper, W., 49
Creevey, T., 181
Curwen, Samuel, 377

Dee, John, 198
Defoe, Daniel, 68, 157, 195, 203, 204
Dekker, T., 72, 201
Deloney, T., 106
Devlin, J., 349, 351
Dickens, Charles, 38, 98, 193, 224–5, 248, 249, 331
Dodsley, R., 174
Dowie, J., 350

Eden, Sir Frederick, 48, 392
Eliot, George, 47, 240
Evelyn, John, 286

Fairholt, F. W., 60–61
Farquhar, G., 174
Fielding, H., 305
Fitzherbert, J., 169, 389
Fitz Stephen, W., 123

Gay, John, 284, 291
Goldsmith, Oliver, 305, 315
Gower, John, 20

Gray, Mrs Edwin, 109

Hall, Mrs S. C., 151
Hamilton, Lord Frederic, 188, 379
Hanway, Jonas, 281
Hardy, Thomas, 32, 33, 34, 35, 50, 99, 343, 390
Hartshorne, Charles, 22
Haydon, B. R., 118
Hoccleve, T., 164, 389
Holme, Randle, 83, 91, 138, 176, 289, 340, 356
Howitt, W., 32

Jenyns, Soame, 157

Kalm, P., 30, 31, 46
Kay, G., 232
Kilvert, F., 47, 338
King, B. Franklin, 11
Kirby, R. S., 381

Lamb, Charles, 282
Langland, William, 19, 41, 339
Lee, William, 281
Lennox, Lord William, 248

Massinger, P., 170
Maxey, E., 27
Mayhew, H. and A., 37, 74, 76, 148, 152, 158, 186, 191, 194, 330, 331, 350
Merryweather, J. C., 272
Middleton, T., 167
Misson, H., 379
Mitford, Mary, 34
Morten, Honnor, 325
Morton, T., 334

Nimrod (Charles James Apperley), 249
Nightingale, F., 326

O'Keefe, J., 177, 368

Pepys, S., 73, 108, 143, 251, 280, 282, 360, 373
Pope, A., 375
Pyne, W. H., 237, 277, 377

Richardson, S., 197
Robertson, J. & M., 206

Roland, Mme J. M., 48
Rowlands, S., 27, 348
Russell, John, 161

Scott, Sir Walter, 237
Shakespeare, William, 82, 115, 167, 168, 169,
    233, 279, 363, 375, 392
Silliman, B., 174
Smith, Albert, 74–76, 142
Smith, Horace, 267
Smollett, T., 58, 173, 249
Stow, J., 372

Stubbs, P., 67, 167
Surtees, R. S., 89, 100, 179, 180, 184, 210, 307

Thompson, Flora, 35, 51, 100, 104, 105,
    246

Ward, Ned, 306
Webb, M. W., 188
Willis, F., 119, 333, 390
Wolcot, Dr John (Peter Pindar), 140

Yates, Edmund, 227

INDEX

Page numbers in *italics* indicate an illustration in the text, but in the case of articles of clothing, where written reference is made on the same page as an illustration ordinary type is normally used.

Categories of workers are indexed under the main employment—e.g. Butler under "Servants"; Engine driver under "Railwaymen".

Advertisement, 380–6 (*See also* Publicity)
Agriculturist, *see* Landworker
Aigulet, 183
Ale-wife, *136*
Apothecary, *317*, Pl. 54
Apprentice, 379
Apron, prevalence of, 332–6
Aproneer, 328
Apron-men, 375
Aprons, Men's, 328–36
   Agricultural labourer's, 27, *28, 29*
   Barber's, 289–93, *298*, Pl. 62
   Bibbed, *105*, 117, 131, 139, 290, 293, 328, Pl. 15, Pl. 62
   Blue, 36, 108, 117, 155, 277, 278, 318
   Brewer's, 137
   Butcher's, 114–17, 120, 121, Pl. 19
   Butler's, 168, 180
   Carpenter's, 82
   Checkered, 289
   Cobbler's, 329, 375
   Cook's, 124–6, 134, 163, *164*, Pl. 20
   Cooper's, 138, 139
   Coster's, 149
   Doctor's, 311, 312
   Dustman's, 277, 278
   Fisherman's, 61
   "Flesher", 121, 331
   Gardener's, 36, *37*
   Green, 108, 180, 318
   Leather, 74, 82, 94, 95, 101–4, *105*, 116, 117, 137, 138, 142, 328–30, 344, Pl. 22, Pl. 58, Pl. 62
   Mackintosh, rubber, 121, 332
   Mason's, 95, *96*, 99
   Miller's, 123
   Oilskins, 121
   Pinner, 34
   Porter's (fire), 265
   Serge, 331
   Sheepskin, 329, *330*
   Smith's, 101, Pl. 17
   Striped, 121, 155, 285, Pl. 19
   Tasselled, 102
   Tarred, 60
   Weaver's, 108
Aprons, Women's, 328–36
   Agricultural, 41, *45, 46*, 48, 49
   Barm cloth, 41
   Bibbed, *101*, 204, *212*, 213, 320, 332, Pl. 31, Pl. 55
   Blacksmith's, 101
   Checked, *205, 206*, 207
   Coster's, 149
   Domestic, 197–9, 201, 377, Pl. 30, Pl. 31
   Fisherwomen's, 64, *65*, 332, Pl. 56
   Milkseller's, 154
   Nurse's, 320, 321, *322*, 323, *324*, Pl. 50, Pl. 52
   Sack as, 51, 214, 224
   Silk, 201
   Spinner's, *107*, 109
   Starched, *211*, 213
   "Trouser", 71
Apron-strings, -ties, 116, 133, 356, Pl. 21
Arm band, sleeve band, *336*
Armlet, police duty, 256–7, Pl. 40
Arm patch, collier's, 70

Backster, 349, Pl. 58
Badge, 377
   District messenger's, 287, 288
   Fireman's, 261, 263, 266, 273, Pl. 43, Pl. 46
   Letter carrier's, 237
   Police, 257, Pl. 40
   Post boy's, 235, 237
   Railwayman's, 217, 218, 221
   Tramway, 229
   See also Licence
Baize, 331
Baker, 123, *124, 126, 128*

Baker's boy, 127, Pl. 21
Bal-maiden, 71
Bam, 346
Band, 172, 312
Banyan, 112
Barber, 288, *289–93*, 294
Barber-surgeon, *295–9*, Pl. 48
Barbette and fillet, 39, 101, Pl. 9
Barm cloth, 41
Basecoat, 166
Bedgown, 47, 48
Bellman, *see* Postal services *and* Watchman
Bell punch, 227, 229
Belt, shoulder, 217, 287, 357, 363, Pl. 32
Belt, waist, 65, 222, 232, *233*, 234, 259, 265, 270, 273, 287, 321, 356–61, *362*
Benjamin, surtout, 188
Billycock, *see* Hat, men's
"Black flag", 329
Blacksmith, *see* Smith
Blouse, 51, 215, 281
Blue, colour worn by servants, 167
Bluet, bluett, bluette, 121
Boatman, *see* Sailor
Bodice, 43, *45*, 64; basqued, *44*, 196; décolleté, 46, Pl. 23; fur-lined, 195; jacket, 47, 150, Pl. 9, Pl. 10
Boiler suit, 335
Bollinger, *see* Hat, men's
Bonnet, 48, 64, 65, *304*; Phrygian, *300*, 301; round, *297*; sun, 51; Turkey, 54
Boots—
    Ankle, 31, 32, Pl. 3
    Buskin, 95
    "Fences", 349
    High, 55, 348
    Highlows, 31, *37*, 74, 118, 285, 346, 348, Pl. 7
    Jack, 188, 223, 260, 350
    Moulder's, 348
    Napoleon, 272
    Post-boy's, 234, Pl. 58
    Riding, 348
    Rubber, 276, 351, 352
    Startups, 25, *27*, 56, 77, 348, 351
    Thigh, 51, 61, 350
    Top, 118, 188, 267, Pl. 26, Pl. 27
    Wader, 351
    Wellington, 269, 272, 273, 349, *350*, 352
    Wooden-soled, 142
Bow Street Patroles, 252, 254, 257
Bow Street Runners, 252
Bo-yank, *see* Yark

Braces, 62, 111
Braies, 15, *16*, 52, 54, 135, Pl. 1
"Brat", 329
Breeches, 25, 27, 74, 164, 180, 230, 265, 266, 277, 280
    Canvas, 56
    Corduroy, 248, 250
    Footman's livery, 166, *181*, 182
    Leather, 28, 35
    Oval, 137
    Petticoat, 177, 304, Pl. 24
    Plush, 173, 182, 186, 187, 267
    Riding, 189
    Round, 30
    Sailor's, 56
    Venetians, 26, 67, 77, *78*
    Women miners', *70*
Brewers, 136–42. *See also* Drayman
Brickmakers, Pl. 16
Brow-band, Brain-band, 344
Buff Jerkin, *see* Jerkin
Builders, 91–100; bricklayers, 97, *99*; masons, 91–100, Pl. 16; painters, *90*, 100; paper-hangers, 100
Bullbeggar, 296, 297
Bus, *see* Omnibus
Buskins, *see* Boots
Bustle, 44, 46, 49, 208, 210, *211*
Butchers, 114–22, *336*, 374, Pl. 19, Pl. 61
Butcher's boy, 117, *118*, Pl. 56
Buttons, 20, 26, 79, 313, 365, Pl. 3, Pl. 5
    Coster's, 153
    District messenger's, 287
    Domestic servant's, male, 168, 170, 175, 183, 185, 188, 189, 191, Pl. 26, Pl. 27
    Fireman's, 266–8, 270, 272, Pl. 44
    Police, 256
    Postman's, 243
    Transport worker's, 217, 221, 225, 227–9
"Buttons" (Page-boy), 191
By-bag, *see* Letter bag

Cab driver and cabman, 224–*226*, 228
Cab, taxi, 229
Cad, 224, Pl. 33. *See also* Omnibus crew
Canvas, canvice, 56, 331
    Coat, 30
    Labourer's doublet, 22
    Miner's clothes, 67
    Sailor's suit, 56
    Shirt, 78
    Smock, 281
    Trousers, Pl. 32

Cap, Men's—
  Brewer's (or fisherman's), 61, 78, 117, 138, 141, Pl. 22
  Cauliflower, 130, *133*, Pl. 21
  Cheese-cutter, *216*, 217, 272, Pl. 42
  Cloth, 63, 100
  Cobbler's, 344
  Cook's, 129–*133*, Pl. 21
  Flat, 170
  Forage, 215–18, 272, Pl. 32
  Glengarry, 272
  Leather, 265
  Mail guard's, 239
  Miner's, 68, Pl. 14
  Monmouth, 56
  Paper, 86–90, 138
  Peaked, 225, 227–9, 247, 257, 281. *See also* cheese-cutter *and* forage
  Pillbox, 191, 287
  Policeman's, 222
  Pork pie, 130, *133*
  Round, 102, 115, 116, Pl. 17
  Skin, 98
  Skull, 152, Pl. 60
  Smith's, *102*
  Stocking—*see* Cap, brewer's
  Tam-o'-Shanter, 127, 129, 131–3, 138
  Toque, 129, *133*
  Velvet, 100, 130, *131*, 177
  See also Nightcap
Cap, Women's—
  Maid's, *207–11*, 214, Pl. 30
  Mob, 48, 150, 197, 203–*205*, 291, *325*, Pl. 10
  Nurse's, 319, 320, 322, 323, *324*
  Nursemaid's, *212*
  "Pinner", Pl. 30
Cape, 72, 226, 256; hooded, *20*, Pl. 1, Pl. 3; nurse's, 320; policeman's, 256; shoulder, 339
Carpenter, *80–88*
Carter, 32, *33*, 34, 375, Pl. 6
Carême, Antoine, 129
Carrying with aid of clothing, 353–70; aprons, 353; belts, 356–62; headwear, 363–9; pockets, 353, 354; pressure-pads, 366–70; skirts, 355
Cary, *19*
Cassock, 166, 296
Chaperon, 95, *164*
"Charley", 251–4
"Checkered-apron men", *see* Barber
Chef, *see* Cook, male
Chemise, 39

Chimney sweeps, 279–*283*
Clapper, *see* Rattle
Clappers, 345
Cloak, men's, 167, 237; sheepskin, *19*; trencher, 170
Cloak, women's, 39, *42*, 325
Clogs, 31, *348*, 349
Clothes, bequeathed by will, 157, 295; old, given to servants, 156, 173, 195; provided by employer, 27, 123, 137, 159, 162, 176, 178, 195, 198, 219, 220, 256
Coachman—
  Hackney, *223*, 224
  Mail, *see* Postal services
  Private, 173, 188, 189
  Stage, *see* Stage coach men
Coal backer, 73; basket men, 76, 77; carman, 76, 77; carrier, 72–76; heaver, 74, *75*, 77; miner, *see* Miners; porter, 73, *74*; seller, 72, *73*; whipper, 75
Coat, 30. *See also* Morning coat, Frockcoat
  Blue, butcher's, 118, 119, 120
  Bow St. Patrole, 252
  Cook's, *132*, 133, Pl. 21
  Cut-a-way, 185, 215, 221, 243
  Doctor's white, 309, 313, *314*
  Duffel, 178
  Dust, 229, 230
  Fireman's, 262, 264, 266, 272
  Footman's, 185
  Leather, 230
  Livery, 168, 173
  "Loose", 29, *30*
  Policeman's, 255
  Railwayman's, 217
  Sackcloth, 224
  Sailor's, 56, 59
  Tail, 243, *306*
  Waterproof, 216, 231
  White, 336
Coatee, 185, 191, 193
Cobbler, shoemaker, *329*, *343*, *348*, 375, *376* Pl. 28
Cockade, 185, 189, 243, 380, Pl. 26
Coif, Men's, *17*, 114, *297*, *304*
  Women's, 43, 202, Pl. 28, Pl. 30
Collar, Men's, 61, 155, 172, 193, 218, 272, 308, 312
  Women's, 43, 65
Collier, *see* Miners
Cook, Female, *190*, 197, 198, *200*, *211*, *212*
  Male, 123–126, 129, 130–3, 134, Pl. 20, Pl. 21

Cooper, 138, 139
Copotain, 77, *234*
Corduroy, 35, 98, 218, 248, 250, 281
Corsets, 158. *See also* Stays
Costermonger, 149, *150*, *153*
Cote, 16, 17, 19, 22, 81, 232, Pl. 2
　white, 122
Cote-hardie, 122, *296*
Cotton, 332
Courtepye, Curstbye, 21
Covent Garden
　Basket woman, 151, *152*, *368*
Coverchief, *see* Veil
Cravat, 118, 133, 268, 315
Crest, family, *165*, 168, 183
Crinoline, *see* Petticoat
"Crocus", 316, Pl. 53
Cuffs, 321, 337

Dairywoman, *see* Landworkers, female
Dentist, 310, *311*
Doctor, *see* Physician
Dogswayne, 55
Domestic servants, 156–214
Doorman, 189, Pl. 27
Doublet, 22, 67, 114, *234*, 251, 282, *289*, *296*,
　301, Pl. 3, Pl. 4, Pl. 5
Dowlas, 43, 331
Dragsman, *see* Stagecoach driver
Drawers (tapsters), 169
　(undergarments), 69, 177
Drayman, 139–42, *140–3*, 386, Pl. 22
"Duckhunter", 193
Dungarees, 216, 335
Dustcoat, *see* Coat
Dustman, 277, *278*, 279, Pl. 47, Pl. 48

Elastic, 387
Embroidery—
　Aprons, 41, 198, 332
　Patriotic, 373
　Police uniform, 255
　Post office uniform, 245
　Railway uniforms, 217, 221
　Sailors' jerseys, 63, Pl. 12
　Sailors' slops, 58
　Smocks, 34, Pl. 7
　Tunic, 81
Escerelle, 358

Factory hands, *see* Industrial workers
Falconer, 168, *341*
Farmer, *see* Landworkers, male

Farrier, 103
Firemen, 261–76, Plates 43–46
Fire Brigades, 261–76
　Alfreton, 273
　Blackburn, 272
　Bristol Crown Fire Office, *265*
　Chelmsford, Pl. 46
　Edinburgh Fire Engine Establishment, 267,
　　Pl. 44
　Essex & Suffolk Fire Office, 271
　Friendly Society, 261
　Hand-in-Hand, 261, 267
　Hope Insurance Co., 267, *268*
　Kent Fire Insurance Co., 266
　London Assurance Co., 263
　London Auxiliary, 272
　London Fire Engine Establishment, 269, *270*
　Metropolitan (London), 270, *271*, Pl. 45
　Phoenix Fire Office, 266
　Royal Exchange Assurance Co., 263, 265,
　　268, Pl. 44
　Royal Society for Protection of Life from
　　Fire, 269
　Sheffield, 271
　Sun Fire Office, *264*, 266, Pl. 43
　Uxbridge Volunteer, 272, *273*
　Weston-Super-Mare, 271
Fishermen, *54*, *55*, *57*, *60*, 61, 351, Pl. 11,
　Pl. 12, Pl. 13
Fisherwoman, 64–*65*, Pl. 13, Pl. 56
Flannel, 48, 70, 98, 178
"Flash" (bow behind neck), *182*, *184*
Freemason, 91, *374*, Pl. 48
Fret, 101
Frock, man's, 173, 178, 223
Frock, Smock-frock, *see* Smock
Frockcoat, 63, 152, 215, 217, 219, 221, 226–8,
　237, 243, 294
　Butcher's, 120, *122*
　Doctor's, 307, *308*, 312
　Fireman's, 267, 268
Fustian, 167; coat, 99, 193; doublet, 22;
　jacket, 75, 188; trousers, 35

Gaberdine, gabardine, 171, 302, *303*
Gaiters, 30, 34, 51, 189, 216, 225, 347, Pl. 8
Gamash, 346
Gansey, ganzey, *see* Guernsey
Garboldi, Garibaldi, 71
Gardeners, 25, *36–38*, *338*, *391*, Pl. 2, Pl. 5
Garnache, 17 *footnote*, *18*, Pl. 2
Garter, *19*, *20*, 42, 137, 266, 267, 387
Gauntlet, *see* Glove

Gelder, *383*
Gipon, 158, *310*
Gloves, 18, 41, 51, 100, 226, 259, 325, 339–43,
    363
  Berlin, 185
  Black, 260
  Buckskin, 248
  Dogskin, 249
  Gauntlet, 55, 168, 199, 341, Pl. 3
  Rubber, 313, 342
  White, 161, 180, 185, 191, 240, 257, 260
Galoshes, 351
Gown, Man's—
  Livery, 295, *371*
  Sailor's, 52, 55
  Servant's, 164, 167, Pl. 24
  Shepherd's, Pl. 4
  University, 379
  Watchman's, 251
Gown, Women's, 39, 42, 43, *44*, 47, 105, Pl.
    10
  Polonese, polonaise, 49, 205
  Two-piece, 47, 150
Gravedigger, Pl. 60
Greatcoat, 188, 216, 222–5, 253. *See also*
    Overcoat
Guernsey, 63, 75. *See also* Jersey

Habit, Monk's, 67, 299
  Nun's, 318
Hairdresser, *see* Barber
Handkerchief, 47, 48, 51, 58
Hair, powdered, 184, 292
Hair-net, 39, 40, 101
Hand-leather, 343
Hat, Men's, 16, 18, 21, 94, 338, 363, 377, 378,
    385, Pl. 2, Pl. 5
  Beaver, 174, 240, 250
  Boater, *see* Straw
  Billy cock, 35, 100
  Bollinger, 225
  Bowler, 63, 100, 119, 121, 226, 229, 281
  Bullycock, 31, 35, Pl. 7
  Cocked, 174, 188, 223
  Fantail, 73, 74, 75, 277–9, 339, Pl. 47
  Feathered, 26, *382*
  Felt, 35, 308
  Flat, 215
  Footman's, 58, 184
  Glazed, 215, 243, 260
  Homburg, 229
  Jew's, 81
  Laced, 58, 184, 378

Hat, Men's (contd.)
  Leather, 257, 260
  Master blacksmith's, 101, 102
  Miner's, 71
  Oilskin, 62, 72
  Padded for carrying, 145
  Police, 256
  Protective, 338, 339, Pl. 14
  Round, 60, 61, 223, 266, 286
  Sailor, 226, *227*, 271
  Slouch, 223, 224, 253, 279
  Shako, 245, *246*
  Straw, 18, 35, 119, 121, 228, 246, 374,
    Plates 3, 19, 61
  Sugarloaf, 27, 82, 83, 108
  Tall, 35, 256, 268
  Tarpaulin, 59, 60
  Thrum, 56
  Top, 37, 119, 141, 185, 217, 221, 225, 228,
    256, 267, 268, 278, 281, *308*, Pl. 21, Pl. 27,
    Pl. 36, Pl. 40
  Tricorne, 60, 108, 137, 140, 265
  Velvet, 130
  Wideawake, 100
Hat, Women's, 48, 64
  Bergère or Milkmaid, 48, 49, 150, 154, Pl. 10
  Carrying upon, 64, 145, 149, 151, *368*
  Straw, 46, 48, 151
  Top, Pl. 23
Hat, not worn by servants, 159, 160, 171, 379
Hatter, *88*, 334, *386*
Hawkers, 147–*148*, 151
  at Covent Garden, 151
Haybands, used as gaiters, 34, 225, Pl. 33
Headdress, Headgear, 38, 363–5
  Sea also Cap, Hat, etc.
Headkerchief, *see* Handkerchief
Head Pad, 366–8
Helmet, Cork, 272
  Brass, fireman's 219, 270–3, Pl. 45, Pl. 46
  Felt, 272
  Leather, fireman's, 265–9, 272, 275, Pl. 43,
    Pl. 44
  Policeman's, 256, 257, Pl. 41, Pl. 42
Herdsmen, 22, 28. *See also* Shepherd
Hessian, 331
Hip Pad, 370
Highlows, *see* Boots
Hodden Gray, 20
Holland, 326, 331
Hood, Men's, 15, 18, 54, 94, 302, 365, 371,
    372, Pl. 1, Pl. 2, Pl. 4
  Women's, 40, *41*, 45, *46*, 50, 203, 320

Hoop (petticoat), 203, 204, 210
Horn, 233, 234, 239. *See also* Post Horn
Hose, 14, 18, 52, 53, 387
  Footless, 18, *20*, 94, Pl. 3
  Slop, 56, 57, 60, Pl. 11
  Soled, 18, 93, Pl. 2, Pl. 3
  Stirrup, 18, *19*
  Trunk, 22–24, 164, *165*, 170, *301*
Hospitals—
  St. Bartholomew's, 318, *321*, Pl. 50
  King's College, 323
  Guy's, 322
  Great Ormond St., 323
  Middlesex, 320, 321
  Norfolk & Norwich, 323
  Putney Incurables, 323
  Royal Albert, 323
  Royal Free, Pl. 51, Pl. 52
  St. Thomas's, 325
  University College, 323
Hotel, *see* Inn
Howard Household Accts., 53, 163, 198, 232
Hygiene, 128, 309, 323, 333, Pl. 14

Industrial workers, boxmaker, *333*; button
    maker, *333*; dyer, *347*; factory hand, *335*;
    feltmonger, *330*; shoemaker, *see* Cobbler;
    soapboiler, *333*; umbrella maker, *362*
  See also Builders, Textile workers, etc.
Inn and Hotel Staff, chambermaid, *204*;
    chef, *see* Cook, male; housemaid, *213*;
    innkeeper's wife, *200*; ostler, *192*;
    waiter, *161*, *172*, 192–3
Insurance Companies' Fire Brigades, *see* Fire
    Brigades and Uniforms

Jack-boots, *see* Boots
Jack-of-all-trades, Pl. 62
Jacket, Men's, 22, *25*, 27, 95, 309, Pl. 32, Pl.
    47, Pl. 48. *See also* Coat
  Butler's, 180
  Chimney sweep's, 280
  Drill, 35, 313
  Fireman's, 267, 270
  Flannel, 98
  Footman's, 171
  Pea, 62, 216, 220
  Railwaymen's, 215–18
  Reinforced, 141
  Running footman's, 177
  Sailor's, 54, 55, 57, 59
  Sheepskin, 163
  Stable, 191

Striped, 193, 286, Pl. 56
  Waiter's, 193, 194
Jacket, Women's, 50, 208, 323, 327
Jacket-bodice, *see* Bodice
Jack Tar, 59
"Jaggers", 288
Jean, 120, 187
Jersey, 62, 63, 152, 260, Pl. 12
Jerkin, 22, *23*, 27, Pl. 5, Pl. 60
  Buff, 22, 166, 264
Joiner, 83, *84*
"Jump", 280

Kerchief, *45*, 150, 202. *See also* Neckerchief
Kersey, 13, 58, 216
"Kicksies", 153
"Kingsman", 153
Kirtle, 39, 43, 105, 134, 136, *196*, 198, *388*,
    Pl. 3, Pl. 28
Knee-pad, 345, Pl. 57
Knickerbockers, 248
Knitter, 109–10, Pl. 17
Knitting Pad, 110

Labourer, *see* Landworker
Lace (Braiding, etc.), 217, 269
Lamp, 286; cap, 71, 72; Davy, 71; electric,
    72; fireman's, 270. *See also* Lantern
Lamplighter, 285–*287*, Pl. 49
Landworkers, Female, 38–51
  Dairywoman, 49
  Gleaning, 39, *40*
  Haymaking, *45*, 47, Pl. 9, Pl. 10
  Labouring, 39, 43, 47, 51
  Reaping, 51
  Weeding, 41, *50*, 51
  See also Milkmaid, etc.
Landworkers, Male, 13–36
  Farmer, 14, 22
  Fruit gathering, *365*
  Harvesting, *40*
  Haymaking, *45*, Pl. 10
  Hedging, 30, Pl. 6
  Labouring, 14, 15, *17*, *20*, 21, 22, *25*, 27, 29,
    30, 35, Pl. 7
  Mowing, 361, *362*, Pl. 1, Pl. 4
  Ploughing, 17, *18*, *19*, 22, *23*, 28
  Pruning, *21*, 25
  Reaping, Pl. 3, Pl. 8
  Scaring birds, *372*
  Slinging stones, *355*
  Thatcher, 345, Pl. 57
  Threshing, *16*

Landworkers, Male (contd.)
  Turf cutting, *344*
  See also Carter, Gardener, Shepherd, etc.
Lantern, Lanthorn, 285; police, *258*; watchman's, 251
Leather—apron, *see* Apron, leather
  Doublet, 22
  Hat, 257
  Miner's clothes, 68
Leech gatherers, Pl. 59
Leg bandages, 14, 171, Pl. 1
Leggings, 34, 216, 222, 226, 229, 256, 276, 346, Pl. 26
Leg-shields, 117, 240, *330*, 337, 344, *345*, 346, *347*
Letter bag, letter case, 232, *233*, 234, 235, 238, 241
Licence, label, or ticket, 377, Pl. 33
  Bus and tram, 224, *228*, 229
  Cabman, 224, 225, 230
  Chimney sweep, 281, *282*
  Link boy, 285
  Porter, 236
  Post-boy, 237
  Thames waterman, 263
Liger, *see* Yark
Linkboy, 282–5, Pl. 48
Linsey-Woolsey, 204, 331
Liripipe, *18*, 21, *94*, *297*, 303, *371*, *372*
Livery, Domestic, 123, 162, 163, *165*, 168, 170, 171, 173, 175, 178, 181–8, 194, 391, Pl. 25, Pl. 26, Pl. 27
  Fireman's, 261, 265, 266
  Livery companies', 115, 289, 295, *297*, 298, 370–2
  Post, 235, 237
"Lowkers", *50*

Mac(k)intosh, 121, 220. *See also* Waterproof
Mail coach men, *see* Postal Services
Mandilion, 166
Mantle, 301, *309*, *310*, 318
Masons, 91–100, Pl. 16
Mechanic, 334
Mersea Patten (backster), 349, Pl. 58
Messenger, District, 287, *288*. *See also* Postal Services
Milk-maid, *31*, *41*, 44, *45*, *46*, 49, 50, *388*, Pl. 9
Milk sellers, 150, *154*, 155, Pl. 10, Pl. 23, Pl. 55
Milking hood, 50
Miller, 122, *333*
Miners, 67–72, *68*, *70*, *72*, Pl. 14, Pl. 15

Mittens, mitts, 18, 19, 57, 71, 339, *340*, Pl. 2, Pl. 6
Mob-cap, *see* Cap, women's
Moleskin, 78 (*see footnote*), 140
  Trousers, 35, 78
Morning-coat, 217, 226, 229, 309
Mud-board (backster), 349, Pl. 58
Mules, *280*

Nakedness, 52, 69, 389, Pl. 64
Napkin, 160, *161*, *162*, 168, *172*, 202
Navigator, 76, 79
Navvies, 76–79
Neckcloth, 133, Pl. 21
Neckerchief, 43, 48, 206, 208, 210, Pl. 28, Pl. 30
Necktie, *see* Tie, Cravat *and* Starcher
Negro, *see* Servants, Household, male
Nether stocks, 24, 112
Nightcap, 58, 76, 79, 113, 116, 126, *128*, 131, 254, 312, Pl. 40
Nightgown, 197
Nightrail, 320
Nurses, 318–*324*
  Florence Nightingale, 323–5, Pl. 54
  Hospital, 318–23, *324*, Pl. 50, Pl. 51, Pl. 52
  Private, *324*–7

Oilskin, 62, 72, 216, 256, 331, 337, 339, Pl. 56
Omnibus companies—
  London General, 229, 230
  Metropolitan Railway, 228, Pl. 35
  Shillibeer's, 225
  Wilson's, 227
Omnibus crews, conductor (cad), 224, 226, *228*, 228, *230*, Pl. 34, Pl. 35; driver, 219, 225–30, Pl. 35; inspector, 230
Overall, 51, 119, 131, 155, 192, 213, 216, 272, 294, 334, Pl. 27
  Bib-and-brace, *62*, 335
Overcoat, Benjamin, 188
  Bus Inspector's, 231
  Coachman's, 188
  Footman's, 185, *187*
  Policeman's, 256, Pl. 41
  Tram driver's, 229
  See also Greatcoat
Oversleeves, *see* Sleeves, protective
Overskirt, 46, *50*, 64, 149, 150, Pl. 10
Over-stockings, *23*

Palm, thatcher's, 343
Paltock, 159

Panetaria, 195
Panter, *see* Servants, Butler
Paper-cap, 86–90, 138
Pattens, 43, *44*
Pauline-apparel, *274*, 275
Paviour, pavier, 77, *78*
Pea jacket, *see* Jacket
Petticoat, 43, 46, 47, 48, 151, 153, 205, 327,
 Pl. 9
 Crinoline, 210, *211*, 389, Pl. 34
 Hoop, 203, 204, 210
 Sailor's and Fisherman's, 56, 60, 61
 Scotch fishergirl's, *65*, 66
Petticoat breeches, 177, 304, Pl. 24
Physician, *297*, 299, *300–6*, 307, *308*, 309,
 Pl. 50, Pl. 51
Pig-tail, 58
Pilcher, 70
Pileus, *300*, 302
Pinafore, 71, 111, 213
 Waterseller's, 145
Pinafore-topped dress, 51
Pinner, *see* Aprons, men's
 Cap, Pl. 30
Piping, 237, 243
Pitsea, *see* Yark
Ploughman, *see* Landworkers
Ploughman's beaters, 345
Pocket, 353–4
 Barber's, 292, 293
 Butcher's, 116, 121
 Carmen's, 76
 Coachman's, 188
 Drayman's, 142
 Footman's, 188
 Market woman's, 353, *354*
 Mason's, 99
 Painter's, 354
 Poacher's, 353
 Policeman's, 260
Police, 254–60
 Constable, *255*, 256, 257, *258*, *259*, Pl. 40,
 Pl. 42
 Fireman, 272
 Sergeant, 256, 257, Pl. 41, Pl. 42
 See also under Railwaymen
Police Forces—
 Birmingham, 257
 Blackburn, 272
 City of London, 257
 Colchester, 257
 Manchester, 257, Pl. 41, Pl. 42
 Metropolitan, 254, 256, 257, Pl. 41

Provincial, 257, Pl. 40
 River, 260
 Sheffield, 271, 272
Porter—
 Fire, 263, *264*, *265*
 Fish, 152
 Meat, 121
 Railway, 216–*220*
 Ticket, 236, *369*
Porter's knot, 366–8, *369*
Post bag, *see* Letter bag
Postal Services, 232–48
 Bellman, 241, *242*, 244
 Driver, mail, 240, Pl. 36
 Guard, mail, 239, 240, *241*
 Letter carrier, 232, *233*, *234*, 243, *244*, Pl. 37
 Messenger, 232
 Post-boy, *233–235*, *237–239*, Pl. 38, Pl. 58
 Postilion, 240
 Postman, *242*, *245–7*, *Frontispiece*, Pl. 37
 Postwoman, 246
 Telegraph boy, 247, Pl. 38
Post horn, 226, 238
Postilion, *see* Servants *and* Postal services, *and*
 Stage coach men
Pouch, *26*, *341*, *358*, 360, *361*
Prince Lionel—
 Household Accts., 195
Protective clothing, 328–52
 Footwear, 347–52
 Padding, 145, 366–70
Publicity, 227, 261. *See also* Advertisement
Pumps, 176, 182
Purse, 41, 65
Puttees, 248

Quack doctors, 314–*316*, *381*, Pl. 53. *See also*
 "Crocus"

Railway Companies—
 London & Southampton, 221, 222
 Gt. Western, 215, 217, 218, 221, 222
 North Eastern, 219, 220, 222
 London & North Western, 216, 217, 221,
 Pl. 32
 London & South Western, 217, 220
 South Eastern, 218
 Sheffield, Ashton-u-Lyne & Manchester,
 215, 217
 Stockton & Darlington, 215
Railwaymen—
 Engine driver, 215, 216, Pl. 32
 Firemen, 215

Railwaymen (contd.)
    Guard, *216–18*, Pl. 32
    Policemen, 220–2
    Porter, 216, 218, *219*, 220
    Station Master, 217, 220
    Ticket Collector, 217
Rat catcher, *342*, *361*, *384*, *385*
Rattle, 251, 252, 257, 270, 277, Pl. 40
"Roberts" hood, 275
"Robin Redbreast", 252, 257
Rocket, Rocklo, 237
Roquelaure, *see* Rocket
Roudge, 55
Rubber, 62; aprons, 332; boots, 276, 351;
    gloves, 313, 342
Ruff, 26, 43, 56, *234*, 303, Pl. 5
Rug, 226, 228, 231
Rugge, 55
Rump, *see* Bustle
Russet, 13, 22, 42–44, 138

Sabots, 349
Sackcloth, 20. *See also* Aprons, Women's
Sailor, 52–63, *53–55*, *57*, *59–62*, Pl. 11, Pl. 12
Sandal, 209
Sash, 177, 382, *383*, *384*
Satchel, Money, 227, 229
Scarf, 325
Seaman, *see* Sailor
Serge, 331
Servants, Household, Female, 195–214
    Chambermaid, 196, 199, *204*
    Charwoman, 214
    Cook, *see* Cook, female
    "General", 200, *206*, *210*
    Housekeeper, 195–7, *198*
    Housemaid, 202, *207*, *209*, *213*
    Ladies' maids, 195–7, *199*, Pl. 29
    Maid, maidservant, 157–8, *195–201*, *203*,
        Pl. 28, Pl. 29, Pl. 30
    "Nanny", *212*
    Office cleaner, *205*, 206
    Panetaria, 195
    Parlour Maid, *208*, 210, *211*, Pl. 30, 31
    Waiting-woman, 195, 196
Servants, Household, Male, 156–94, 389
    Bailiff, 168
    Butler, 161, *169*, 179, *180*, *181*
    Carver, *164*
    Chamberlain, *158*
    Chauffeur, 189, Pl. 26
    Coachman, 173, 188–9
    Cook. *see* Cook, male

Servants, Household, Male (contd.)
    Cup-bearer, *162*
    Falconer, 168, *341*
    Footman, 162, *166*, 174, 179, *181*, 182–*187*,
        190, 208
    Groom, Indoor, 162
        Outdoor, 162, 164, *165*, 188, *191*, 192,
        Pl. 27
    Livery, *see* Livery, domestic
    Marshall, 158, 160, Pl. 24
    Negro, 177, Pl. 24, Pl. 25
    Ostler, 191, *192*
    Page, 159, *166*, 170, *190*, 391, Pl. 25, Pl. 26,
        Pl. 30
    Postilion, 164, 175, 188
    Running Footman, 176, Pl. 24
    Steward, 168, 170
    Tiger, 189, Pl. 26
    Valet, 157, 172, 178, *179*
    "Work", "Undress" and "Pantry" clothes,
        171, 176, 180, 187
Shagg, 58
Shako, *see* Hat
Shawl, 149
Shepherd, *15*, *21*, *23*, *26*, *30*, *32*, *356*, *359*,
    360, Plates 1, 2, 3, 4, 8
Shepherdess, 40, *42*
Shift, 39, 149, Pl. 23
Shirts, 22, 58, *72*, 77, *78*, *84*, *85*, 100, 117, 126,
    128, 170, 215, 307, Pl. 10, Pl. 15, Pl. 16
Shoes, 56, 205, 348, Pl. 3; ankle-strap, 81, 94;
    double-soled, 57; hob-nailed, 19, 30,
    267, 348; piked, 95; round toed, 266.
    See also Clogs
Shoe-black, 374, 382, Pl. 61, Pl. 63
Shoe-maker, *see* Cobbler
Shopkeeper, 334
Shoulder knot, 174, *175*, 182, 188, 272, Pl. 24,
    Pl. 25
Shoulder-pad, Shoulder piece, 369, 370
Shrimp girl, *64*
Skirt, 38, 43, *44*, 45, 109, 150, 355, *388*, Pl. 10
    pinned up, 47, 149, *151*, *206*
    short, 41, 51, *65*, *66*, 109, 208, 210, *354*,
    Pl. 23, Pl. 59
Slaughtermen, 117
Sleeves, bagpipe, *21*, *42*, Pl. 4; hanging, 168,
    171, 302; miscellaneous, 39, *198*, 389
Sleeves, Protective, 48, *50*, 77, 111, 116, 117,
    119, 121, *126*, 213, 311, 312, 318, 336–8,
    Pl. 56
    Stocking-, 111, 337
Slippers, 42

Slop-frock, *see* Smock

Slop, slop-hose, 56, 57, 60, Pl. 11

Sloppy, 35

Smith, *100–5*, Pl. 17, Pl. 58; coppersmith, 103, *104*; woman, *101*, 103. *See also* Farrier

Smock, Men's (smock-frock, slop-frock, frock), 17, 29, *31–34*, 51, 74, 121–3, 139, 148, 176, 278, 281, 335, 375, Pl. 6, Pl. 7, Pl. 8, Pl. 27, Pl. 47

Smock, Women's undergarment, 39, 141, *202*

Smoke-mask, *274*, *275*

Sou'wester, 55, 62

Soyer, Alexis, 130, *131*

Spatterdash, 346

Spats, 73, *117*, 277, 345, 347, Pl. 47

Spinner, spinning, *106–10*, *388*

Splasher (backster), 349, Pl. 58

Stage coach men—driver, 248, 249; postilion (post-boy), 249, 250, Pl. 38

Stamin, stammel, 106, 331

"Starcher", 192, Pl. 27

Startups, Stertops, *see* Boots

Status symbols, 378, 380, 390

Stays, 47, 48, 149, Pl. 23

Steel, Butcher's, 116, Pl. 19

Stiffening—for bodice, 202; for cook's cap, 129; for skirt, 203, 204; starch, 204, 213

Stock, 258, 268

Stockings, *see also* Hose
 Cloth, 14, 42
 Knitted, 56, 110, 204
 Roll-up, 265, 267, 315
 Striped, 286
 Used as mittens, 71

Stonebreaker, Flint-knapper, 77, 345, Pl. 15

Straights, 349

Street Vendors, 126, *127*, *129*, 143–55, *354*, *357*, *358*, *363*, *364*, *366*, 381, *382*, *385*. *See also* Costermonger, Hawker, etc.

Stripe, on trousers—postman's, 245; railwayman's, 217

Sumptuary Laws, 156, 162, 167, 170, 202, 380

Supertunic, Men's, 16, *18*, 94, 301, Pl. 2

Supertunic, Women's, 39, 318

Surcote, men's, 16, 94; women's, 39, *41*

Surgeon, *297*, 301, *309–314*, Pl. 51, Pl. 52

Suspenders (braces), 63, 111; for hose, 387

Sweat-rag, 100, 133

Sweep (chimney-sweep), *279–283*

Swineherd, 28

Sword, 171, 174, 183, 258, 260, 305

Tabard, 17, Pl. 2

Tail coat, *36*, 37, *306*

Tailors, 111–13, *112*, Pl. 18

Tam-o'-Shanter, *see* Cap

Tarpaulin, 56, 59, 60, 62, 270

Textile workers, *89*, 105–11, Pl. 18

Thigh pads, 345, Pl. 57

Ticken, ticking, 58

Ticket, *see* Licence

Ticket porter, 236, *369*

Ticket punch, 227, 229

Tie, 98, 218, 220, 226, 230, 272, 308
 Bow, 193
 Mailcoach, 240

"Tights", 21, 164

Tinker, *151*

Tippet, 21, 372

Top-hat, Topper, *see* Hat

Toque, 129, *133*

Towel, 145, 161

Tram crews, 229; conductor, 227, 229, Pl. 35; driver, 228, 229, Pl. 35; inspector, 229

Tramways, Croydon, 228; Ipswich, 229; L.C.C., 229; Train's, 227

Trouncer, 139, Pl. 22

"Trouser", 71

Trousers, trouser-like garments, 16
 Bell-bottom, 61, 153
 Corduroy, 35, 98, 218, 281
 Cotton, 37, 133
 District messenger's, 287
 Doctor's, 307
 Draymen's, 142
 Dustman's, 279
 Fireman's, 267, 268
 Gun-mouthed, 61
 Landworker's, 28, 34, 35, 37
 Linen, 128
 Ostler's, 192
 Policeman's, 256, 260
 Railwayman's, 215, 216, 217, 218, 221, Pl. 32
 Sailor's, 58, *59*, 59, *62*, Pl. 11
 Worn by servants, 172
 Worn by women, 51, 70

Trunk hose, *see* Hose

Tunic—Men's, 16, 17, *18*, 52, 80, *81*, 92, 101, 114, 134, 135, 163, 232, Pl. 1, Pl. 2
 District messenger's, 287
 Fireman's, 272, Pl. 45, Pl. 46
 Police, 256, Pl. 41, Pl. 42
 Woman's, 318

Turnspit, Pl. 20

Umbrella, 228, 246, Pl. 35
Underskirt, under-petticoat, 46, 149, Plates 9, 10, 30
Underwear, Men's, 15, 52, 56, 177
  Women's, 39, 149, 202, Pl. 23
Uniform—
  Bow St. Patrole, 252, 254, 257
  Fireman's, 263, 269, 270, 271, 272, 273, Pls. 43–46
  Fireman's, Table of Insurance Cos., 269
  Letter Carrier's, 243, *244*
  Mailcoach, 240
  Nurse's, 319–26, Pl. 50, Pl. 52
  Omnibus Crew's, 227, 228, Pl. 35
  Police, 255, 257, Pls. 40, 41, 42
  Postman's, 243–6, Pl. 37
  Railwaymen's, 215–22, Pl. 32
  Royal Navy, 56, 63
  Telegraph Boy's, 247, Pl. 38
  Tram, 229, Pl. 35
  Windsor, 189, Pl. 27
Upper stocks, 24, 112
Upperall, 123

Veil, 39, *42*, 105, *107*, 232, *233*, 318, Pl. 28
Velveteen, 74, 78, 218
Venetians, *see* Breeches
Veterinarian, *359*
Vintner, 135

Waggoner, *see* Carter
Waggoner's frock, 32. *See also* Smock
Waistcoat, 30
  Bow St. Patrole, 252
  Butler's, 179, 180
  Coster's, 152
  Fireman's, 266
  Footman's, 185
  Navvies', 78–79
  Shoulder, 339, 370
  Striped, 185, 187, 193
  Taxi Driver's, 230

Waistcoat, sleeved, 97, 117, 217, 218, 225, 281, Pl. 22
Waiter, *160, 161,* 163, *172,* 192–3
Wallet, 358
Washable garments, 185, 193, *313,* 321, 323, 334, 336
Washing-dress, 210
Washing frock, 176
Watchman, 251–4, *253,* Pl. 39, Pl. 40
  Bellman, 251, 252
Water-seller, -carrier, *145–7*
Waterman, 224, 225, Pl. 33
  Thames, *262, 263,* 267
Waterproof('ing), 62, 219, 276, 350, 351
  Cape, 256
  Coats, 216, 231, 270
  Leggings, 216
  Oilskin, 62, 72, 216, 256, 331, 337
  Oversleeves, 337
  Tunic, 272
  Trousers, 270
  See also Mackintosh
Weaver, weaving, *107, 108,* 111
Well-digger, 350, Pl. 64
Wheelwright, *85, 89*
Whistle, 229, 257, 270, 365
Whitbread, Messrs., 139
  Brewery Employees, 139, 140
Wig, 31, 102, 170, 174, 178, 183, 184, 188, 290, 292, 305, 306, 307
  Styles of, 18th cent., 248, 249, *291, 292, 298,* 305, 315, 316, 318
Wimple, 39, 40, *42*
Wine making, *134, 135*
Wine merchant, *91,* 135
Wings, 267–8, 270, 273
Woodlander, Sussex, 346
Wrapper, 323
"Wrap-rascal", 174

"Yard of Cardboard", 71
Yark or York, 35, 74, *79,* 100, 365, Pl. 6, Pl. 8